Praise for *Patron Sai*

"For those who have been tempted to think that Christian history has little to teach the contemporary church, *Patron Saints for Postmoderns* may come as a delightful and unexpected surprise. In his beautifully crafted and well-researched volume, Chris Armstrong provides his readers with a winsome and convincing argument for the continued relevance of the past. *Patron Saints for Postmoderns* is both a treasure trove of valuable insight and a genuine joy to read."

GARTH M. ROSELL, Gordon-Conwell Theological Seminary

"Taken together these 'patron saints' become a most valuable 'cloud of witnesses' for the many and varied circumstances of Christian believers in our own day. Careful reading of this well-crafted book will pay rich rewards."

MARK A. NOLL, University of Notre Dame

"The church in America has no lack of novelty. Bloated with self-referential congratulations, our American Christendom needs a hearty dose of wisdom. In *Patron Saints for Postmoderns,* professor Chris Armstrong tells the stories of ten flawed yet wise historical figures who incarnated the gospel afresh at a pivotal time in the life of the church, each offering a glimpse of how we might critically bring flesh to the gospel in our own pivotal era."

MARK VAN STEENWYK, founder of Missio Dei and general editor of www.Jesus Manifesto.com

"Lives have consequences, and Armstrong reminds us just how consequential our lives are. In ten crisply drawn portraits of saints whose lives resonate with our times, he challenges us to take our freedom with eternal seriousness."

DAVID NEFF, editor-in-chief, *Christianity Today*

"Saints can be off-putting and unapproachable figures, trapped in pious pictures and stained-glass windows. The pleasure of Christopher Armstrong's attractively written book is in seeing the very human, quirky side of some of the greatest heroes and heroines of the Christian story."

PHILIP JENKINS, author of *The Lost History of Christianity*

There is properly no history, only biography.

—Ralph Waldo Emerson

Biography is the most universally pleasant
and profitable of all reading.

—Thomas Carlyle

Remember your leaders, who spoke the word of God to you.
Consider the outcome of their way of life and imitate their faith.
Jesus Christ is the same yesterday and today and forever.

—Hebrews 13:7-8

We do not want you to become lazy, but to imitate those
who through faith and patience inherit what has been promised.

—Hebrews 6:12

Patron Saints
for Postmoderns

FROM THE PAST
WHO SPEAK TO
OUR FUTURE

Chris R. Armstrong

IVP Books

An imprint of InterVarsity Press
Downers Grove, Illinois

InterVarsity Press
P.O. Box 1400, Downers Grove, IL 60515-1426
World Wide Web: www.ivpress.com
E-mail: email@ivpress.com

InterVarsity Press® is the book-publishing division of InterVarsity Christian Fellowship/USA®, a movement of students and faculty active on campus at hundreds of universities, colleges and schools of nursing in the United States of America, and a member movement of the International Fellowship of Evangelical Students. For information about local and regional activities, write Public Relations Dept., InterVarsity Christian Fellowship/USA, 6400 Schroeder Rd., P.O. Box 7895, Madison, WI 53707-7895, or visit the IVCF website at <www.intervarsity.org>.

All Scripture quotations, unless otherwise indicated, are taken from the Holy Bible, New International Version®. NIV®. Copyright ©1973, 1978, 1984 by International Bible Society. Used by permission of Zondervan Publishing House. All rights reserved.

Design: Cindy Kiple

Images: Dante Alighieri: Wikimedia Commons

Antony of Egypt: Master of the Osservanza at Louvre, Paris, France. Gérard Blot, Réunion des Musées Nationaux/Art Resource, NY

John Amos Comenius: John Amos Comenius/Wikipedia

Gregory the Great: Saint Gregory at Pushkin Museum of Fine Arts, Moscow, Russia. Alinari/Art Resource, NY

The Blinding of Tobit (for Margery Kempe): (detail) The British Library

John Newton: John Newton by W. Harvey; engraved by H. Robinson at Miriam and Ira D. Wallach Division. New York Public Library/Art Resource, NY

Dorothy L. Sayers: Used by permission of The Marion E. Wade Center, Wheaton College, Wheaton, IL

Charles Sheldon: Kansas State Historical Society

Charles Simeon: Charles Simeon by William Finden, after Sir William Beechey stipple engraving, published 1847 (1808), National Portrait Gallery, London

Amanda Berry Smith: Courtesy of William Hull

ISBN 978-0-8308-3719-9

Printed in the United States of America ∞

Library of Congress Cataloging-in-Publication Data

Armstrong, Chris R.
  Patron saints for postmoderns: ten from the past who speak to our
  future/Chris R. Armstrong.
      p. cm.
  Includes bibliographical references and index.
  ISBN 978-0-8308-3719-9 (pbk.: alk. paper)
  1. Christian biography. 2. Postmodernism—Religious
  aspects—Christianity. I. Title.
  BR1700.3.A76 2009
  270.092'2—dc22
  [B]
                                                      2009021526

P   22   21   20   19   18   17   16   15   14   13   12   11   10   9   8   7   6   5   4   3   2   1

Y   28   27   26   25   24   23   22   21   20   19   18   17   16   15   14   13   12   11   10   09

Contents

Introduction

I know that *saint* is a red-flag word for many readers—especially Protestants (and I am one of those). We might say: "We don't 'do' saints. They distract us from Jesus!" And in some historical cases, this seems to have been true. For example, after Saint Francis of Assisi (1182–1226) died, the head of his order feared that people would want so much to be close to this saint and revere him that they would steal his body. So he buried Francis's coffin beneath the main altar in the Basilica of Saint Francis in Assisi—under a slab of granite, gravel, ten welded bands of iron, a 190-pound grill and finally a 200-pound rock. (The plan, by the way, worked: the coffin wasn't discovered until the nineteenth century.) Protestants have tended to see such unabashed reverence as weak and dangerous—even idolatrous. It can seem like putting another mediator between ourselves and God, when we already have Christ.

Certainly, there is a danger of raising individual people to a level approaching that of "incarnations" of God. But however excessive we may feel the devotion to great Christian leaders has sometimes been in the past, we can also sense that we are missing something. Historically, Christians have valued the saints as exemplars of a life well lived in Christ. They have sought in their saints models for living—not living above circumstances or without sin, but living in the midst of challenges and failures, "warts and all." Maybe we need to share earlier Christians' gratefulness for the great gift God gives us in leaders who have lived challenging lives. As a Pentecostal preacher-friend of mine used to say, we sometimes just need to see "Jesus with skin on."

If Roman Catholic and Orthodox believers have seemed at times to court a kind of idolatry of the saints, they have also been able to draw strength from a vibrant, living appropriation of the witness of prominent people in the history of the church. To many today, Augustine, Francis, Thomas Aquinas and Ignatius Loyola live on! One Franciscan friar has said, "I read about Christian values in the Gospels, but in Francis I see someone living them out. That example both supports and inspires me. I want my life to be like his: totally centered on Christ." I think this is a helpful way to think about the saints: we can be grateful for their witness, reverent to their memory and ready to imitate them in certain areas—and as we do those things, we can always remain totally centered on Christ. What the saints do is cast more light on how we are to live out that Christ-centering: we walk with Jesus, but in the steps of his saints.

Of course I am aware of the sense in which we are all saints (as the apostle Paul used the word). But I think there is value in keeping the traditional Christian definition of that term. We need not say that some people are "more saved" than the rest of us. The saints I'm talking about had their obvious flaws and struggles (that's just what often endears them to us), and they received salvation as we all do—through God's amazing grace. And we need not accept such theological innovations as the "treasury of merits" or prayer to the saints in order to benefit from them. But we can allow the lives of certain special people to pierce our complacency and hold up for us the possibility of a better way—not only for us individually, but for the whole church. That is what I mean when I use the word *saint* in this book. I hope you'll join me in opening yourself to this piercing (Gregory the Great would have called it "compunction"—a rich idea we should recapture) and this possibility.

This study has its own history. As a Christian, I haven't always been conscious of the cloud of witnesses and their exemplary power for the church. I haven't always been grateful to the dead. Rediscovering my spiritual heritage has been a long journey. I remember the first glimmer. One day, as a church-going but unconverted teenager, I was browsing through a book containing an informal televised dialogue between two close friends—both of them poets and cultural critics. These were Archibald MacLeish and Mark Van Doren, two of the brilliant literary minds of mid-twentieth-century America. Between them, they had won four Pulitzer prizes. As a young man with pretensions to be a writer, I wanted very much to follow their conversation—though I confess, most of it was over my head. However, one off-hand comment really struck me. One of the two (I don't remember which one) remarked that when he was growing up, his parents and aunts and uncles would speak of Abraham, Isaac, Jacob, Joseph and the rest as vividly as if they were still with them at that day. To him, these Old Testament figures came to seem as real and present as any member of his family. This captivated me: what a wonderful way to grow up! What an inspiring thing—biblical characters seeming as real to you as your own family!

At the age of twenty-two, after years of resistance, I turned my life over to Christ. I began going to one of those modern charismatic churches in a giant auditorium decorated like a suburban living room— seafoam-green carpeting, rubber plants. I loved that church. It was so spiritually alive. On Sunday mornings I would walk in and feel the palpable presence of the living God. At Saturday night prayer meetings I was mentored by wise "parents in the Lord." On Monday nights I participated in the music ministry of a dynamic youth group.

Yet through the years, though this wonderful church formed me in the "joy of the Lord" and led me to expect the Holy Spirit to do amazing things in the lives of people today, I began to feel like we were missing something. Our church seemed somehow precarious. We stood in the midst of a threatening world that did not share our faith, on a foundation made up of the words of our favorite Bible passages and the sermons of our pastors and a few approved evangelists. There was no sense at all of the whole mystical, historical massiveness of the church. No sense that Christ had created and then defended and nurtured this church over two thousand years. No sense that our foundation actually stretched down and back through time to rest on such giants in the faith as John Wesley, Martin Luther, Bernard of Clairvaux and Ignatius of Antioch. I didn't have a clue yet who any of those historical figures were. I felt like the church, though powerful in some ways, was shallow and insecure in others, and that the cure was to reconnect with people who had gone before us. We needed to know whose shoulders we were standing on.

By ten years later, in 1994, this sense absorbed me so much that my wife, Sharon, and I made a family decision: I would shut down my profitable freelance business in corporate communications, and we would begin the arduous journey of graduate study. Along the way, in the midst of lectures, exams and late-night study sessions, I came across the people you're going to meet in this book, and I began to see that they had already tangled with some of the same questions and frustrations that I had. And the ways they responded to these questions challenged me. They had been "wrestling prophets" like Jacob, contending with God. They had demanded to know who he was and how they were to live in a way pleasing to him in the midst of a confusing and sinful world that doesn't recognize him. They had spoken and taught and especially lived prophetically, as goads and thorns and object lessons to the church in their own times and places. Then, having discharged their compelling, inescapable duty, they had gone to meet their Lord face to face.

Of course even then, none of these people really had the decency to stop disturbing the peace of the church. Their uncomfortable voices continue to ring out today from the cloud of witnesses—and we are wise to listen to them. "Ask the former generations and find out what their fathers learned," said the friends of Job (and for once, they were right!), "for we were born only yesterday and know nothing, and our days on earth are but a shadow. Will they not instruct you and tell you? Will they not bring forth words from their understanding?" (Job 8:8-10).

Do the "former generations" of wrestling prophets carry for us the canonical authority of the apostles? No. So why listen to them? Because as Christians, we are part of a religion that is irreducibly historical. A nineteenth-century historian, Adolph Harnack, insisted that the church shed itself of nineteen centuries of mistaken doctrines and embarrassing practices and return to the true, pure essence of Christianity: Jesus' message of love. American Protestant liberals in the nineteenth and twentieth centuries—people such as Henry Ward Beecher, Harry Emerson Fosdick and even chapter nine's Charles M. Sheldon (Mr. "What would Jesus do?")—followed Harnack in this assumption, teaching that Christianity's essence lay in "the Fatherhood of God and the brotherhood of man." They were wrong. There is no essence of Christianity that is not clothed in history.

The Old and New Testaments are full from one end to the other of historical accounts of God interacting with people. The New Testament's central, astounding doctrine is the incarnation: that God took on flesh and became a first-century Jewish carpenter from Nazareth. And the incarnation is not just about the person of Christ, but about the church as well. Not only was Jesus incarnated once in history and culture, but he has continued to be incarnated in a hundred cultures ever since— through his body, the church. And when we become part of the church, we join the historical brother- and sisterhood that operates by what G. K. Chesterton called a "democracy of the dead." In this polity, those long buried still have voices. Those historical voices should never trump the words of our Scriptures, but (and here's a secret the Reformers knew, though we've often forgotten it) we need those voices to help us understand those very Scriptures. And when we've gone astray, those voices always call out to us—to bring us back again to the basics, to shake us up, to inspire us and to change us.

The Protestant Heritage of Saints

I have suggested that careful attention to the saints is a Roman Catholic strength. But it is part of the Protestant heritage too. Despite their objections to saint veneration carried to extremes, Luther and Calvin themselves respected the church fathers and made frequent references to them in their writings. And this respect for tradition soon bloomed and grew as a seventeenth-century group of Luther's heirs called the Pietists developed church history into a theological discipline in its own right.

If you could get into a time machine and travel to seventeenth-century Germany, you would find folks writing long confessional documents that protected what they viewed as a pure, biblical faith, but that also erected barriers between their churches and other folks' churches. In the seminaries, you would find students and professors arguing heatedly over doctrine as if every tiny point of belief was worth dying for. (In fact, this might be so—a teacher of mine once remarked that the debates about orthodoxy became so heated that some professors packed pistols in their classes.)

Into this mess came Philip Jakob Spener. This pious Lutheran minister and scholar was appalled by the division and nastiness going on in the church. He saw too much emphasis being placed on doctrinal precision and not enough on Christlikeness. He called the theological thought of these would-be guardians of orthodoxy *theologia spinosa*—"prickly theology." He insisted that Christianity was not just the memorization of catechisms and forms so you could get your ideas right. Theology must be lived.

In Spener's Pietist movement, which is an important but often overlooked feeder stream to modern evangelical Protestantism, this emphasis on living orthodoxy manifested itself in many ways. Pietists met for small-group Bible study and discipleship. They worked to reform the seminaries. They kept spiritual diaries. They read spiritual and devotional works. They reached out across denominational barriers in a spirit of ecumenical brotherhood.

Most important for our purposes, the Pietists added to the curriculum of theological education the new discipline of church history. Not that histories of the church hadn't been written before, but these Pietists pioneered history and biography as vital theological disciplines. Why did they do this? Quite simply, they discovered that once you got out of the books and debates and into the stories of real people, it gave you a new angle on theology. It knocked some of the sharp edges off your theories and precious principles (which can be a very good thing: Dorothy L. Sayers once said, "The first thing a principle does is kill somebody"). It helped you see into the common passions and needs of the human heart. It gave you, in short, examples of what theology looked like when it was lived.

You see, a century before the Pietists, Martin Luther had seen the excesses of the people's veneration for saints (including some who were of questionable historicity) and had removed them from the church calendar. This was an important correction. But the martyrs Perpetua and Felicitas, the monks St. Bernard of Clairvaux and St. Francis of Assisi, and the hundreds of other recognized saints had provided transformative models for rank-and-file Christians for over a thousand years. And now these were gone.

Had early and medieval believers seen these saints as super-Christians who lived their lives laughing at temptation and drop-kicking demons? No, they had known that these were ordinary, struggling human beings used by God in extraordinary ways. But that's what had made them such powerful examples. This seems counterintuitive, but people could look at the saints and see people who had flaws, made mistakes, got cranky and had bad days; yet by God's grace these people did remarkable things. So hearing their stories, an ordinary Christian would know that no matter who you were, no matter how many flaws and faults you saw in yourself, you too could be changed by grace and used in great ways in the kingdom. What a relief! The kind of life you were currently living was not the only kind—there was this luminous possibility for you, beyond "life as usual."

This book assumes that we should follow the Pietists in this tradition of being transformed by the great cloud of witnesses who have gone before us. But it would be fair to ask, why the ten particular "witnesses" of this book? Though each of the ten folks in this book shows us exemplary, transformative ideas, practices and character traits, most are not "traditional saints." Why, then, were they chosen? One easy answer is that I want to show the depth of resources in Christian history: we can learn from so many more people than just the usual Protestant heroes, such as Billy Graham, Adoniram Judson, John Wesley and others, and even such usual giants of our earlier history as Augustine, Francis and Ignatius Loyola.

But more deeply, the people who fascinate me—the ones I think we most need to hear from today—are not the geniuses, the originators of systems of Christian thought. Rather, they are the hard-nosed doers—the incarnators of the gospel. These are the people who became human object-lessons, living out a culturally powerful "translation" of the Christ-message. Jesus said to the skeptical leaders of his day: "If anyone chooses to do God's will, he will find out whether my teaching comes from God or whether I speak on my own" (Jn 7:17). The "saints" of this book did just that; they chose to do God's will as it applied to their own settings. And the results of that choice showed many, including us, "whether Jesus' teaching comes from God." Theirs was the powerful apologetic of the life lived for God.

One seeming exception in this book actually proves my "rule of the incarnators": I have chosen a number of folks who are known for their ability to tell stories. Dante Alighieri, John Comenius, Charles Sheldon and Dorothy Sayers wrote imaginative narratives to speak theologically to the church (and John Newton, popular hymns with the same burden of putting practical theology in an imaginative key).

But these folks are in fact not exceptions to the practical, incarnational theme of this book. The act of creating culture is also a kind of incarnation. Stories emerge in a particular time and place, aiming to transform people in the midst of that cultural setting. Writing is doing. Moreover, the very nature of written imaginative narrative is incarnational. Instead of speaking the abstract language of theological systems (a crucial language in its place), it clothes those ideas in characters, places and events. It dwells in the human as it communicates the divine. J. R. R. Tolkien once said to W. H. Auden that he had created each of the characters in his *Lord of the Rings* to embody "in the garments of time and place, universal truth and everlasting life." This is exactly what Dante, Comenius, Sheldon, Sayers and Newton sought to do in their imaginative writings.

A Three-Stranded Cord

As this group of ten saints has gelled for me, it has seemed that, together, they powerfully portray three important themes. These form a three-stranded cord on which the biographical pearls of this book have been threaded.

First, these patron saints translated the gospel for their own times. The church in every age gets stuck in ruts. Even though the social, cultural situation outside its doors moves in a new direction, the church continues to say and do the same old things, things that no longer draw people upward to God. They are living out an old translation of the gospel when a new one, which addresses the new needs and questions of their times, is needed. This is when wrestling prophets, who feel the tension between church and world acutely and grieve over it, step in to proclaim and model the need for change. By incarnating the gospel in a way that makes sense for their day, these special leaders get their shoulders behind the church and jar it forward so that it can more effectively heal a hurting world.

Our ten figures played this prophetic, incarnational role in two distinctive and complementary ways. To begin with, they recaptured "basics"—the food and drink Christians need in order to survive. The church gets into a rut by losing touch not only with the surrounding culture but, even more seriously, with its own mission. Sunk into a slough of irrelevancy, it gets away from practices basic to the Christian life: deeply engaged Bible reading, intimate prayer and devotion, practical Christian love to those who are broken and hurting, discernment of spirits, devotional attention to Christ in his humanity as well as his divinity, and so forth. It is wrestling prophets like the ones in this book who call the church back to these old practices, insist on them and make them winsome for their brethren who have forgotten them.

Sometimes in order to recapture these basic elements of the faith, the saints had to fight to rid the church of some bad stuff. Gregory the Great fought corrupt church leadership. Dante Alighieri fought factionalism. John Newton and Charles Simeon fought entrenched churchly complacency. Smith fought racism. Sayers fought religious sentimentalism. But the goal has never been critique for the sake of critique. Each of these saints wanted to clear away the trash in order to set the banquet table.

In order to translate the gospel for their own times, the people in this book also crossed and broke down barriers. Part of the rut that mires the church when it loses touch with its world and its mission is this: It forgets that God is no respecter of persons, and that it is not his will that any should perish. It sets up barriers between itself and the world, and between different kinds of people within the church. But this is exactly the opposite of what the church has been doing since the beginning. Ever since the first, apostolic decades of explosive growth, courageous Christian leaders have been crossing barriers in both the world and the church (and ecclesial barriers, as every reformer discovers to his or her dismay, are often even harder to cross than societal ones) to bring the gospel to bear on every man, woman and child.

The gospel translation done by the people profiled in this book required them to go outside of their comfortable circles, often (as with Amanda Smith) while struggling with rejection and abuse from those who didn't look like them. Each faced a unique cultural moment, both in the wider society and within his or her church setting. And the "translation" each one created and lived usually challenged the churchly status quo as well as the wider culture. Most met resistance both from within the church and from the world outside. And all created a translation that was imperfect, overemphasizing some things and remaining blind to others (any honest, critical account of the saints must admit their stumbles and learn from their mistakes too).

Second, as well as translating the gospel for their own setting, each of the people in this book ministered both out of the brokenness that we all share as sinful human beings and out of a literal or figurative experience of homelessness. The theme of brokenness is easy to see. Every one of us is a broken vessel. Some of these figures are more obviously broken than others, and their awareness of that brokenness became a part of how they incarnated the gospel. By looking clear-eyed at their hurts and flaws, we can not only gain a deeper sympathy for them, but also gain even more from their lives and teachings. In the stories of these people, a sense of their own failures and neediness comes out clearly. We may ask as we read, How did each of these people reckon with that sense in themselves? How do we?

Each of these figures also lived in some sense out of a feeling of homelessness that pointed them back to their true home. This was either because they themselves were marginalized or separated from the mainstream, or because their home cultures were under threat of collapse by war or other crisis. What happens to a person marginalized and alienated from his or her own church, state or family—whether by social upheaval, a challenged social position, personal persecution or outright exile—is that they face questions of identity and power in a particularly sharp and personal form. What anchors our identity as Christians? What kinds of power should we or can we exercise in a world with its own power structures? These writers struggle deeply with such questions, and they are able, out of that struggling, to tell their audiences something about how we forge and keep a Christian identity as we live within those relationships of power.

From another perspective, prophetic writing comes most often from those who are in some way "on the margins," whose views, like those of Jesus in the Beatitudes, challenge the status quo of church and world. Prophecy emerges from lives driven by the question of G. K. Chesterton's book *What's Wrong with the World?* And in the modern (and if you like, postmodern—which is to say hypermodern) world, we are all exiles, torn from the old sources of identity. For thousands of years until the Enlightenment, people worldwide found their identity in traditions—the embodied wisdom handed down from generation to generation. In the modern period, all traditions have been radically questioned, challenged and deconstructed by the rapacious power of individual reason. Having sawed off the limb on which we have sat for millennia, we moderns (and postmoderns) lie isolated, bruised and disoriented on the unforgiving earth, prey to the peculiarly modern condition of anomie, that is, rootlessness and without a moral compass.

We are thus peculiarly situated to hear and benefit from the prophecies of the marginal because we have ourselves become marginal. Not
only don't we know what is wrong with the world; we don't know what
we're doing in it, or how we can fit in it and live in it. This idea leads us
to our third theme: the use of story.

One helpful way people have responded when their identities have
come into question is to "narrate themselves back into" their lost traditions through story. When we tell our stories, which are also God's
stories—if we believe what Genesis tells us about humans bearing his
image—we narrate ourselves into one or another kind of life. Some of
the saints in this book had stories written about them that did this,
and some wrote stories that did it. For example, the story of the life of
Antony of Egypt (this book's first figure) became for generations
of Christians "a sharp image of what a life committed to God demands
and promises." Augustine of Hippo was converted by hearing about it.
Monastic orders renewed themselves by holding themselves up to its
mirror. It became the fountainhead and pattern of all subsequent
saints' lives. That is the power of story—and we will discover it from
the perspective of the storyteller as we encounter the legacies of Dante,
John Comenius, John Newton, Charles Sheldon and Dorothy Sayers.
Reading or hearing a story can become for us the source of divine
transformation as we see our Christian identity incarnated in the lives
of others.

In the modern period we have lost our sense of the power of story.
Story has become something we read to entertain ourselves. It is a fun
thing, but a marginal thing, ghettoized to the realm of "entertainment."
I hope as we enter the lives of these ten patron saints, we will get a sense
of the power of story again, both in hearing their stories and in entering
the stories that some of them wrote.

How to Read This Book

I don't think we should go to the stories of such Christian leaders as these
looking for simplistic "fixes" to apply to our ministries today. The Christian life and Christian ministry are not, in any case, about learning a set

of cookie-cutter principles and then going out and applying them. They are about something much more difficult but also much more rewarding. They are about a transforming relationship with a living God.

In other words, when we come into contact with historical people who are our own brothers and sisters in the faith and who gave their lives entirely to that relationship with God in Christ, it doesn't just teach us a few good ideas. When we live vicariously through these people's challenges and their responses in the Lord, it touches our hearts. And it transforms us, if we're willing. Maybe sometimes if we're unwilling too. When we are drawn in to the personality and world of each of these saints, then we can become captivated and engage personally with the issues and methods represented in their stories. I'm not talking about picking through their lives for "methods" and cutting and pasting them in our own very different settings. Rather, I mean that we can absorb something of their spirit, the mode in which they translated the gospel for their time and the character traits that allowed them to do so, and this can speak to us about how to live the gospel in our own unique situations.

More than this, we can even begin to get the sense that these patron saints are truly present with us, urging us on. As I had first seen as a teenager reading MacLeish and Van Doren's reminiscences, the support we can gain from getting to know these saints is like the support of a close-knit family. It's a source of strength like no other. It's the knowledge that we are a part of the whole communion of saints—through time and space, and across cultures and confessions. In the end, I do believe we can learn a thing or two from these people about the how-to of living out the gospel and translating it for the lost world around us. But even more importantly, as we take the next few steps deeper into the fog of the future, we can find in these folks' stories a new resolve and a prophetic stance toward the church and world as we find them.

Finally, each of these stories reminds us that it is ultimately Christ—through the power of his Spirit and through his *whole* body, stretching across time as well as space—who builds the church so the gates of hell will not stand against it.

1

Antony of Egypt

PURSUING HOLINESS

AND LIVING POWERFULLY

Several decades after the legalization of Christianity, in the year 356, the first man to venture out into the desert as a monk reached the astonishing age of 105. Content that he had run his race well, he "lifted his feet, and as if seeing friends who had come to him and being cheered by them, he died and was taken to the fathers." That's how bishop Athanasius of Alexandria (298–373) described his friend Antony of Egypt's (251–356) death in his *Life of Antony*. Then he concluded with these significant words: "Even his death has become something imitable!"

Just before that good death, Antony had left one of his two sheepskin cloaks to his friend the bishop. And Athanasius, who rejoiced to have known this extraordinary hermit, wanted everyone to know just how exceptional this leather-skinned, bright-eyed spiritual hero of the late-ancient and medieval world was. Even the condition of the hermit's body at the end of his life, Athanasius exclaimed, proved his sanctity. Antony had

> never succumbed, due to old age, to extravagance in food, nor did he change his mode of dress because of frailty of the body, nor even bathe his feet with water, and yet in every way he remained free of injury. For he possessed eyes undimmed and sound, and he saw clearly. He lost none of his teeth—they simply had been worn to the gums because of the old man's great age. He also retained health in his feet and hands, and generally he seemed brighter and of more energetic strength than those who make use of baths and a variety of foods and clothing.

Antony's physical preservation and good health, Athanasius believed, reflected an inner wholeness—"salvation" in the fullest sense. And because Antony had reached this full salvation—and then had reached out to others to help them reach it—Athanasius insisted Antony's life, like his death, was *imitable:*

> Therefore, read these things now to the other brothers so that they may learn what the life of the monks ought to be, and so they may believe that our Lord and Savior Jesus Christ glorifies those who glorify him. . . . He makes them known and celebrated everywhere, both because of their own virtue and because of their assistance to others. And if the need arises, read this to the pagans as well, so they may understand by this means that our Lord Jesus Christ is God and Son of God.

Buying into the Disciplined Life

The son of a prosperous farmer, possibly illiterate in Greek, and certainly not given to philosophic study as were some later desert monastics (such as Evagrius Pontus), Antony launched into his life of desert spirituality as a young man. He took to heart the words "Sell all you have, give to the poor, and come, follow me" heard at church one day and sold his birthright (he had recently lost his father)—two hundred acres of lush, fertile Nile Valley land. Then he began to live as a solitary, at first just at the edge of his small town.

This sort of local eremitism—solitary living arrangements within the context of the larger community—was already known and practiced in Egypt during Antony's youth, and it fascinated the young man. He apprenticed himself to a local holy man, absorbing from his elder everything he could learn about the ascetic life.

Asceticism—in the Greek, *askesis*—meant "training." Before the Christian monks picked up the term, it referred to the cultivation of soul and body (stripping down and doing a few leg-lifts while reciting poetry) the Greeks had always been so keen to practice in their gymnasiums. Certainly, as anyone who has done physical training today knows, there were certain disciplines involved in this training. And as the Christian monks began to practice it, *askesis* never entailed merely giving up things, like food or sex. Rather, it was a mode of exercising and building up the heart in godliness.

We may think we know what these monks were about. They were afraid of their own sexuality, so they retreated to the desert to fight "demons," which were actually vivid manifestations of their own libido, right? We will soon see what sorts of temptations those demons *actually* presented to their would-be victims. Sure, fornication was among them. But what did fornication actually mean?

The Old Testament prophets had known that fornication stood for anything that dragged the heart away from God—any flirtation with any idolatrous replacement for their Lord. In fact, for the first monks of Egypt, fornication stood for *not* being a monk, for going home and being caught up in the care and support of a family in the Nile Valley. In ancient dream theory, if a man dreams of a woman, he is dreaming of his business—how he *supports* the woman. That was the deepest fear of the monk; not that he would merely indulge himself sexually in an illicit one-night stand, but that the entire direction of his life and affections would shift from his beloved God to the distracting entanglements of "regular life."

It has been popular to reinterpret these demons as facets of the monks' own psyches. However, a space may be opening up in our postmodern world for a more accepting stance toward the supernatural. A model is emerging, based on theologies from Christians in the Global South for whom demons and particular providences are just a matter of course. These new Christians simply assume that malevolent spirits exist and interfere in our lives, and that any God worth his salt will intervene powerfully to protect us. For them, as for Antony, and for Jesus and the disciples, the healing miracles and spiritual warfare that surround powerful ministries are an expectable result of dealing with a living God.

To the Desert and Back Again

Finding it hard to undertake this sort of spiritual discipline amidst the distractions of town life, this intense young man went out into the desert. This *real* desert was not for the faint of heart. It was the scorching expanse of sand that covered the vast majority of Egypt outside the thin strip made green by the Nile's seasonal flooding. It was said that nothing could live in those parts except demons. This suited Antony. Like many Eastern Christians who followed him, he had a keen sense of the spiritual battle that surrounds all of us.

First he sealed himself in a tomb not far from town, depending on some villagers who brought him food. Then he moved farther out to a ruined Roman fortress on a mountain by the Nile, which became his home for twenty years. There he indeed encountered demons, who took on the forms of wild beasts, sent by the devil into his cell to intimidate him. But Antony mocked them, reminding them that Christ had robbed them of any authority and cast them down. Not being able to withstand his scornful ridicule, they disappeared.

In 305, the second year of the last great persecution of the church, after twenty years shut away in his ruined fort, Antony enlisted some villagers to help him break down the fort's door. From his decades-long solitude, he emerged and stood before the people cheerful and in glowing health, in full possession of his senses, having attained the Greek ideal of *apatheia* or emotional equilibrium.

Learning of the persecution, Antony returned to the city and ministered to those under sentence of death. As Athanasius recounted this, "He rendered service to the confessors both in the mines and in the prisons. In the law court, he showed great enthusiasm, stirring to readiness those who were called forth as contestants, and receiving them as they underwent martyrdom and remaining in their company until they were perfected." Confessors and those en route to martyrdom shared a common spirit with monks like Antony: the willingness to give up all in the service of Christ. This shared spirit helps to explain the continued appreciation for monks as "Christian heroes" after the era of persecution ended with Constantine's legalization of Christianity shortly after Antony's death.

The judge ordered him out as a disturbance, but Antony "washed his upper garment" and returned to court the next day "in a prominent place in front, and to be clearly visible to the prefect." Amazingly, this obvious solidarity with his condemned Christian brothers and sisters did not lead to Antony's death. Editorialized Athanasius, "The Lord was protecting him to benefit us and others, so that he might be a teacher to many in the discipline that he had learned from the Scriptures. For *simply by seeing his conduct, many aspired to become imitators of his way of life.*" (Here again is that ubiquitous theme of imitation.)

The Desert Became a City

In this way Antony himself sought, but was denied, martyrdom. And once he returned to the desert, a stream of people increasingly sought him out. Some of these came, perhaps, to escape the threat of death under which Christians in the cities lived. Others came to prepare themselves for martyrdom—a serious and ritualized preparation involving contemplation and prayer, through which one hoped to discern whether one had been given "the gift of martyrdom." Still others simply came to see what all the fuss was about. As the visitors streamed in and many stayed, "the desert became a city," and Antony's fame spread far and wide as he dispensed healing miracles and words of wisdom to the gathering crowd of imitators and devotees.

There seems to be a paradox here. The root of the term "monastic" is *monos,* meaning "sole." The monastic life was a solitary life, in which the monk is dependent on God alone. Those who lived that life had decided, when they left their towns in the heavily communal, interdependent Nile Valley and went out to the desert, that they *wouldn't* depend on the ancient network of mutual support.

How and why, then, did this "city" of monks grow up in the desert? How and why did they excel in hospitality? For they certainly did.

One way to think of this is that to live as a monk does not mean that you push others away. Monks renounced the world, but they did not reject or hate other people. The monks had decided to depend only on God. This is the meaning behind two of the temptations the devil threw in Antony's way when he first went out into the desert: an illusory vision of a silver plate by the side of the road and then a real pile of gold. These things looked like free gifts. But for Antony, they represented the temptation to depend again on the currency of society.

For the monks, however, to stop depending on society did not mean to stop serving others. At the most basic, economic level, most monks eked out a living by simple handiwork—usually weaving rush mats or making pottery. A caravan would occasionally penetrate even to the hermits' most remote hideaways, bringing food in exchange for these handmade objects. In these ways, the monks still lived in interdependence with others. As we will see, this was not the only mode of their interdependence.

The rush mats illustrate another truth about the monastic life—it was a life of *praxis* rather than *theoria*. The monks did engage in inward contemplation, but everything, especially their reading of Scripture, was aimed at outward practice. So, for example, many of the wise words collected in the *Apophthegmata Patrum (Sayings of the Desert Fathers)* are words of relational and practical advice, born out of long experience and delivered in brotherly affection.

Finally, in his sixties, in the year 313, Antony again grew restless for solitude and sought a deeper, more private corner of the desert in which to pursue God. Moved by the Spirit, he went with a caravan of Arabs several days' journey into the desert toward the Red Sea to an isolated oasis at a mountain's foot. In fact, however, Antony's last attempt at solitude failed. Even at this remote retreat in the Eastern Desert, he found himself needing to maintain an herb garden to feed the many seekers who traveled through the arid desert to receive spiritual food from his lips. There at his "inner mountain," where today stands the monastery of Saint Anthony the Great, Antony lived out the rest of his 105 years.

When Antony had been a while in the inner mountain, the monks he had left behind traveled to see the holy man and importuned him to return with them for a while to the monastic city in the desert that they had made—the hive of cells, the network of monks. He returned with them, and he taught them to have faith, guard against lewd thoughts, flee vanity, pray and sing holy songs constantly, and keep in mind the deeds of the saints. Then, "he especially urged them to practice constantly the word of the Apostle, *Do not let the sun go down on your anger.*"

Fleeing the Wrath—Then Conquering It

I have said that for these monks, sex represented social entanglement. But engagement with the world could take on more sinister aspects. For Antony and the other desert fathers, sexual sin was bush-league stuff—the tip of the temptation iceberg. What worried them even more deeply was another sort of emotional/social snare: anger.

In fact, the ancient world focused on anger as a severe social threat. Many tracts and passages of ancient writing deal with this subject. And the Egyptian monks came from the Nile villages where anger loomed. These were tight communities, both deeply interdependent and precariously dependent on the periodic flooding of the Nile. And they dwelt, too, under a flood of litigation. Plausibly, one motive of those who retreated to the desert was simply to get away from all this nastiness. And since anger lives not outside but inside us, they found themselves continuing to struggle even as they disciplined themselves toward holiness.

Though anger seems to have been Antony's greatest concern, he linked it to other potential transgressions of community. Daily, Antony said, each one should

> recount to himself his actions of the day and night, and if he
> sinned, let him stop. But if he has not sinned, let him avoid boast-

ing; rather, let him persist in the good, and not become careless, nor condemnatory of a neighbor . . . For frequently we are unaware of the things we do . . . Therefore, yielding the judgment to [the Lord], let us treat each other with compassion, and let us bear one another's burdens.

This relational language is so clearly aimed at those living in communal interdependence.

Even the secular Greeks recognized these holy men's wisdom in the area of social harmony. As I've mentioned, as an old man Antony was called down from the inner mountain for "judge duty." Athanasius records the event: "He was disconsolate at being annoyed by so many visitors and drawn to the outer mountain. For even all the judges requested that he descend from the mountain, for it was impossible for them to come there because of the litigants who followed them." At first, Antony turned down the judges, but "they persisted and even sent those who were in soldiers' custody, so that he might be moved to come down for their sake."

The ploy worked. Antony was indeed moved, and he set out for the outer mountain with its thriving monastic community. Reports Athanasius: "His arrival worked to the advantage and benefaction of many. He aided the judges, advising them to value justice over everything else, and to fear God, and to realize that by the judgment with which they judged, they themselves would be judged."

In other words, by moving *outside* of society in order to meet God and practice holiness, Antony had attained to such sanctity that his presence in the very midst of society's nexus of anger—the courtroom— sanctified and corrected the broken relationships whose jagged edges cut each of the litigants there.

For a sense of the power of this ministry, consider the horror with which the nineteenth-century American lawyer-turned-evangelist Charles G. Finney, after his conversion, regarded any prospect of a return to legal practice: "I had many . . . invitations to conduct law suits," said the evangelist, "but I uniformly refused. *I did not dare to trust my-*

self in the excitement of a contested lawsuit; and furthermore, the business itself of conducting other people's controversies appeared odious and disgusting to me." As a young law clerk, Finney had wrestled with his own sense of personal sinfulness until he was almost bodily propelled out into the forests of New York's frontier. Only there, he found, could he clear his head of that "odious and disgusting" business and meet God in a powerful, saving way. In turn, the great evangelist helped to birth a new revivalism that during the ensuing century helped people escape repeatedly from the urban centers where "all is seared with trade; bleared, smeared with toil; And wears man's smudge and shares man's smell" to the wilderness settings of the holiness camp meeting.

The Wisdom Wrought by Solitude

Antony, by this same maneuver of leaving society in search of holiness, had paradoxically come to transcend the angry cesspit of that world and thus had become equipped to bring wisdom and sanctity back into it. There may be no more vivid example of the power of the marginal prophet—the person who, by the very virtue of his or her separation from the centers of culture, gains a special ability and authority to speak God's empowering word into that culture.

In Athanasius's account, the wisdom Antony gained by his solitude was a thoroughly relational wisdom. He describes the effects of Antony's presence in that litigious community of the outer mountain like this: "For who went to him grieving and did not return rejoicing? Who went in lamentation over his dead, and did not immediately put aside his sorrow? Who visited while angered and was not changed to affection? . . . What monk, coming to him in discouragement, did not become all the stronger?" This was a man, in other words, who was wise in the ways of the inner life. This hints to us what we will discover about the fruits of monastic life in the next chapter (where we will meet the pope who was a monk, Gregory the Great). Again and again, paradoxically, monastic (solitary) wisdom is psychological, relational wisdom—a wisdom that discerns the churning motives and emotions at work within us and the ways those inner facts affect our relationships with others. By escaping from the marketplace, the monks become equipped to minister to the communal problems of that marketplace.

A warning is in order, though. For those of us who are already tied to the marketplace and the culture by responsibilities to work and family, this impulse to escape into sanctified space may prove not only misplaced, but harmful. To continue the modern parallel of the American holiness movement that Finney helped to pioneer, that movement produced, years later, the stern warning of an article by the holiness Methodist pastor and evangelist Reverend Lucius C. Matlack, titled "Holiness in the Family." Matlack observed that it was easy for the sanctified, reveling in the communal worship of the saints, to enjoy the equanimity and peace of "the experience of holiness" that "removes the distance between God and the soul." There, in that sweet heaven on earth, "the presence of others, the melody of song, the power of united faith," produced an unparalleled joy. However, "when these scenes pass away" and the worshiper returns home, "too often professors of holiness seem to be 'off guard' . . . greatly to their damage and greatly to the scandal of their profession." The family, Matlack concluded, was "a severer school of training than is anywhere else to be found," and many holiness believers were flunking out of it—failing to manifest the sanctified love that had seemed to flow so naturally in the supportive community of the holiness worship service.

Nonetheless, we can't deny—even in a modern evangelical culture that seems to sometimes elevate the family to an almost idolatrous plane—the power of Antony and the model of "holy separation" he represents. Nor can we categorically proclaim that nobody in this enlightened age is called to such separation. In fact, a movement of largely young Protestants *has* arisen in our midst that is seeking to "re-monk" the American church—they call themselves the "new monastics." New monastic leaders such as Shane Claiborne and Jonathan Wilson-Hartgrove are moving into troubled urban neighborhoods, living in intentional community with other Christians and in solidarity with the poor. (Claiborne's Philadelphia community is called The Simple Way; Wilson-Hartgrove's Durham, North Carolina, community is Rutba

House.) Though new monastic communities do tend to make space for couples and families as well as celibate singles, their members have concluded that at least some Christians must engage in some form of separation—not only from the culture at large but also from what they view as the increasingly compromised church—to model a life of true devotion and obedience to Christ.

Hooking Pagan Fish

Perhaps, then, such monastic exemplars as Antony can influence other Christians in positive ways. What about the "pagans" to whom Athanasius declared that *The Life of Antony* should be read? Athanasius was serious enough about this goal that he used classical Greek models for the literary form of his biography of Antony. Is there any indication that this ploy worked and that the story of Antony influenced any non-Christians to conversion? Indeed there is. Even Athanasius couldn't have dreamed of the pagan "big fish" his book would hook a few decades after its writing.

Many of us know—or think we know—the story of the famous "garden conversion" of the father of Western theology, Augustine of Hippo (354–430). On that day, an African officer in the imperial guard named Pontician visited Augustine and his friend Alypius at the villa where he was staying. Pontician noticed a book on a nearby table and started to flip idly through its pages. As he realized these were the epistles of Paul, his tongue was loosed by an inner joy. He testified to his own conversion and then went on to praise the monastic life pioneered by Antony. Two of Pontician's fellow soldiers had read Athanasius's *Life of Antony* not long before. Touched by the monk's story, they had decided on the spot to join a monastery, and their fiancées soon also gave themselves to the life of virginity.

Augustine became agitated on hearing the story of these young men and women's Antony-inspired commitment to God. Alone with Alypius later on, Augustine turned to him with a wild and agonized expression. "What is the matter with us? Didn't you hear? Unlearned men take heaven by force, but we, heartless and learned—see how we wallow in flesh and blood! Are we ashamed to follow because others have gone before?" Alypius was so alarmed by Augustine's passionate outburst that he followed when his friend stormed out of the house and into the garden, perhaps worried that this brilliant and mercurial man would harm himself.

Sitting and weeping in the garden, Augustine heard a child's voice chanting, "Take up and read." He opened the little book of Paul's letters at random and immediately his eye fell on a passage in Romans that challenged him to put aside his lustful habits and "put on the Lord Jesus Christ." And at that moment, stricken, his last resistance to the gospel stripped away, Augustine gave his life over to Christ.

Today's Christians, especially Protestants, tend to remember the part of the story where Augustine picks up the Bible and reads that passage from Romans. But what *really* set Augustine's heart on fire, what drove him out to that garden in the first place, frantic with shame and grief, desperate to find peace in God? It was hearing from a man how two other men had been turned to Christ by encountering the life of this saintly monk, Antony of Egypt. In this series of events leading up to Augustine's conversion, Athanasius's desire that others imitate his reclusive friend was fulfilled bountifully, as was his belief in the missional power of Antony's life story. Consider the irony: a "separated life" may turn out to be a most powerful evangelistic technique!

The Bishop's Book and the Monk's Fame

To understand why just hearing about Antony would pierce Augustine to the heart, it will help to know both how *The Life of Antony* was written and how it spread.

During one of Athanasius's five exiles from his beloved Alexandrian church at the hands of Arian-sympathizing emperors, the diminutive firebrand fulfilled a long-time dream by traveling out to the desert to share the life of the hermits there. During what became a long ascetic sojourn, he conceived what historian Derwas Chitty calls "the first great manifesto of the monastic ideal." This was not some tidy, orderly rule, but rather the gripping biography of his dear friend Antony.

Athanasius clearly wanted to write a compelling account of his larger-than-life subject, and he also wanted his audience to understand the twin energies of the monastic life. This double dynamic, learned from the apostles and early martyrs, consisted on the one hand of athletic, near-heroic self-exertion and self-interrogation, and on the other of reliance on God's gracious help from heaven through Christ—a duality that would shape all future monastic movements. The importance of both these elements to the Christian life was the key theological point of the book.

Within a few decades of the *Life*'s writing in 357, not only the Greek-speaking Christians of the eastern Mediterranean, but also the Latins in Italy and Gaul, knew of Antony. By 400 he was already a figure of legendary proportions—perhaps the first real "Christian celebrity"—and monasticism was already in full swing. This was no wild fringe movement at the edges of society and outside the control of the church. As Athanasius put it, "The name of the monks carries public weight."

On the face of it, this seems an implausible claim. When I have asked my students in the past, "What is monasticism?" I get suspicious, negative answers: "The monks isolated themselves in an unhealthy way." "They didn't evangelize." "They weren't engaged with the surrounding culture." "They thought the body and material world were evil." "They were too busy in self-centered devotions to care for others."

If these things are supposedly true of monasticism even in its common, coenobitic form (*koinos bios* = the communal life), then what possible "public weight" could an anchoritic (solitary) monk carry? What sort of fruitful and famous ministry was this that retreated farther and farther into the desert in order to remain separated from the distractions of civilization?

Even the brief summary of Antony's story that we have heard should help us understand the impact of this man's life. By the time of his death, hundreds and probably thousands of people had trekked deep into the desert just to see "the man of God." Hundreds stayed to imitate his way of life, so that, in Athanasius's words, "the desert was made a city." Community leaders called Antony repeatedly back to civilization from his inner mountain to act as judge in difficult legal cases. The emperor Constantine and his two sons Constantius and Constans wrote to him seeking his advice. Strange as it may seem, Athanasius was almost guilty of understatement when he said of this solitary hermit, "It was as if he were a physician given to Egypt by God."

Busting Myths About Monasticism

In fact, Antony's life demonstrates the birth and power of monastic ideals very different from those assumed by my students:

- Unhealthily isolated? The whole goal of the monastic life was spiritual health, and in that realm the monks and nuns led and counseled everyone around them. The solitary life itself was the universally accepted conduit to a fuller experience of God, as it allowed a level of self-mortification not available to husband or wife, father or mother—in short, ordinary citizens engaged in the hurly-burly of civic life. And those who attained such a fuller experience of God, in turn, were recognized by the early church as possessing a spiritual power that was a valuable resource for the community at large. Antony's mere prayers on another Christian's behalf, recognizes scholar Peter Brown, could "open the gates of heaven" for them.

- Shirking gospel witness? Although monasticism did go through cycles of decline and abuse, for much of their history the mere living presence of the monks and nuns spurred countless souls to a dedicated Christian life—arguably the form of "evangelism" needed in a Western society where everyone was already assumed to be Christian. Antony himself met and bested pagan philosophers; however, the power of the monks lay not in argument, but example (they were, as Athanasius saw, "imitable"). As Protestant church historian Mark Noll says, "The rise of monasticism was, after Christ's commission to his disciples, the most important—and in many ways the most beneficial—institutional event in the history of Christianity. For over a millennium, in the centuries between the reign of Constantine and the Protestant Reformation, almost everything in the church that approached the highest, noblest, and truest ideals of the gospel was done either by those who had chosen the monastic way or by those who had been inspired in their Christian life by the monks."

- Disengaged from society? From Antony's time onward, monks were offered bishoprics, maintained pilgrimage sites, anchored councils, and wrote and preached to audiences far beyond their cloisters. Antony himself wrote to emperors, imploring them to be "men of concern, and to give attention to justice and to the poor." What monks learned in the desert, as Rowan Williams says, is "not some individual technique for communing with the divine but the business of becoming a means of reconciliation and healing for the neighbor." Monks fled to the desert, in other words, "not to escape neighbors but to grasp more fully what the neighbor is—the way to life for you, to the degree that you put yourself at their disposal in connecting them with God." By the high middle ages, Western society comprised three essential groups: those who worked (peasants, craftsmen and merchants), those who fought (knights and nobles) and those who prayed (ministers, monks and nuns). And even in the painful periods of monastic decadence, medieval people believed that "those who prayed" served society in essential ways.

- Anti-body and inward-focused? Both Antony and Benedict—the two seminal figures for monasticism in the West—counseled moderation in bodily asceticism, affirmed the goodness of God's creation, considered the work of the hands an essential part of their discipline and stressed hospitality as the highest virtue, so that the monasteries that grew up after them often became "social service centers" for the rest of the medieval world.

Image of a Committed Life

Clearly Bishop Athanasius's wish—that Antony's monastic way would become a focus of imitation for the church—came true. The Elisha-like symbolic act at the end of Antony's life, in which he had one of his two sheepskin cloaks given to his friend and biographer, reminds us that desert monasticism ran on the rails of master-disciple relationships.

Younger monks regularly sought out older monks, and the fruit of a few of these countless conversations has been collected in *The Sayings of the Desert Fathers*. Benedicta Ward (probably one of the greatest living expositors of the desert tradition) says this: "The essence of the spirituality of the desert is that it was not taught but caught; it was a whole way of life. . . . The Desert Fathers . . . did not have a systematic way; they had the hard work and experience of a lifetime of striving to re-direct every aspect of body, mind, and soul to God."

By the dawning of the Middle Ages at the opening of the seventh century, although only a dwindling few chose to imitate Antony's solitary form of spiritual life, thousands flocked to the communal form, pioneered by a man named Pachomius. Antony remained, however, the beloved father of all monks. Throughout the medieval period, each monastic revival looked back and held itself up to the glass of Antony's ancient Egyptian movement. In this way the life story of Antony has become for his heirs, says the late Dom Jean Leclercq, "a living text, a means of formation of a monastic life."

When we understand that monasticism is a thing you *do* rather than think about or learn, then it becomes clear why a biography, rather than a rule, is really the founding document of the movement. Says the modern English translator of the *Life,* Robert Gregg, "The testings and miracles of Antony fixed themselves in the consciousness of the Church and of Western culture as a sharp image of what a life committed to God demands and promises."

The story of this remarkable desert monk—a self-exiled figure whose very life challenged the church to go "back to basics"—is still worthy of that attention, and imitation, today.

Gregory the Great

DISCERNING HEARTS
AND FINDING BALANCE

What follows is the story of the first practicing monk to be elected to the papacy, Gregory I ("the Great"; ca. 540–604). Among other things, he is the greatest counterexample I know to the stereotype that all administrators are "empty suits" with nothing to teach us spiritually. In fact, it's not a stretch to say that as Augustine was the father of medieval theology, Gregory was the father of medieval spirituality. Gregory's concepts of the active and contemplative lives, the sacramental quality of creation, the meaning of suffering, the psychology of spiritual desire, the delicate balances within the practice of pastoral care, and much else profoundly shaped the host of great medieval spiritual masters.

Many evangelicals today want to explore, understand and retrieve the spirituality of the Middle Ages. We perceive that our faith has often taken on the thought-structures of modernity, posing the gospel as a sort of counterscience, replete with propositions arrayed in iron-clad logical chains. And we hope that we can get behind this "modernized" faith to a more genuine, rooted Christianity by traveling the byways of medieval spirituality: monastic community; spiritual techniques such as labyrinths, candles and the slow meditative *lectio divina;* and the sacramentality of everyday things.

However, despite the wise guidance today of such authors as Richard Foster, Dallas Willard and Eugene Peterson, all of this remains superficial experientialism if we do not understand the thought-world that lies behind those practices. True spirituality always engages not just the heart's emotions, but also the mind's reasons—and contrary to much modern opinion, medieval spirituality rested on a solid foundation of ideas. If we want to know what those ideas were, in order to benefit from the spiritual riches of the Middle Ages, then we need to know Gregory the Great. And we need to know him both as a wise interpreter of such earlier teachers as Augustine and John Cassian and as one whose spirituality, as with Augustine's theology, emerged from a life of struggle, suffering and spiritual triumph.

A World Aflame

Gregory lived at a point of transition in Western history. The Western Roman Empire, after having endured steady incursion into its territory by surrounding tribes, was finally overrun some time in the late fifth century. In the midst of this turmoil, Gregory was born into a wealthy, established Roman family, whose estate loomed across from the Circus Maximus. Throughout his lifetime the territories of the former Western empire lived under severe, sustained duress from invading tribes. In 535 Justinian, the Eastern emperor, decided that he was going to win back the West from the "barbarians" and recreate the old Golden Age of the empire. Thus began almost two decades of ravaging wars across Italy, during which Rome fell repeatedly under siege. During Gregory's boyhood, Rome changed hands no fewer than four times. While pushing back the Goths and Ostrogoths, Justinian's soldiers also looted farms and wreaked general havoc. Finally in 554, peace returned to Italy, but it was not to last. In 568 the fierce Lombards crossed the Alps. During the remainder of the century they both limited the Eastern power and disrupted the church.

In the midst of this disruption, plague and famine devastated the population—reducing it from about 100,000 inhabitants at the beginning of the sixth century to a mere 30,000 by midcentury. The old administrative center of the imperial city, site of the dissolved senate and the abandoned senators' residences, declined into a depressing state of neglect. "Large areas of Rome became deserted, given over to wasteland, a few vines, and plots of cultivated crops." The once-glorious capital was rotting from the inside—its forum, temples, monuments and government buildings empty and crumbling, rats scrambling through its baths.

This chaotic world shaped the future Pope Gregory, not as a proving ground for his strengths, but rather as a school of weakness and brokenness. In particular, Gregory lived through a number of wrenching kinds of homelessness. It was these experiences, more than his high birth, wealth or outstanding education, that shaped him into the leader he became.

First, Gregory shared with all people of his time the most basic kind of homelessness—the uncertainty of physical life itself. Growing up, Gregory saw everything by which humans seek to secure their lives battered and torn, as by a hurricane. Plague, famine and warfare shook all that was solid—a constant reminder of Peter's words that we are all like the grass that withers and the flowers that fall. It is no wonder that the minds of his generation—arguably the first medieval generation—turned easily and constantly toward God.

Rebirth Amid a Dying Culture

The second level of Gregory's exilic experience was a cultural and intellectual one. Along with the physical devastations of plague, famine and war, Gregory lived through something just as profound and jarring: the death of the culture in which he had been nurtured as a child and young man. In the fragmented world of the decaying empire, the political structures of the old order and the rhetorical arts and sciences of classical thought—the anchors and verities of Gregory's youthful training—had lost their power and relevance.

It is hard to imagine the shock of this cultural holocaust. The Western Roman Empire had weathered many centuries. Augustine had lived only at the very beginning of the empire's collapse, and he was thus able to maintain a scholarly agnosticism about the ultimate fate of the world's kingdoms. But Gregory and his generation felt the world's end breathing down their necks. Throughout his life Gregory expected to see, at any moment, Jesus return on clouds of glory—and this colored his thought in every area.

One can guess that this cultural collapse had something to do with the turning point that came in the prime of Gregory's life. It started with a piece of worldly fortune that to most people would have been welcomed as God's gift.

Gregory's education had probably been quite good, focusing on grammar, rhetoric, law and letters. Both this education and his aristocratic background prepared him for public service, and in 573 he was appointed to the highest civil position in Rome, that of prefect. For at least a year he oversaw the city's police force, food supply and finances. But this honored position did not fit him well; he was troubled in his heart.

What was bothering Gregory? He had been raised in a pious family. His mother and two of her sisters are regarded as saints in the Roman Catholic Church, and his lineage also contained two popes, Felix III (483–492) and Agapetus I (535–536). For a time in his youth he had read and meditated on Scripture, seeking God's face and thirsting for his presence. But other interests had crowded in, and young Gregory had begun (as he later told it) to resist the rigors of a spiritual life. Now, for the busy prefect, such devotion seemed a remote possibility reserved for other people: monks, nuns. "While my mind obliged me to serve this present world in outward action," he wrote, "its cares began to threaten me so that I was in danger of being engulfed in it not only in outward action, but, what is more serious, in my mind."

Soon after he ended his brief term of office, Gregory made a decision that he described as a conversion. In a letter to his friend the Spanish bishop Leander, Gregory explained that, led astray by "long-standing habit" and a sense of civic duty, he had put off conversion for too long.

Now, however, he said, "I fled all this with anxiety. . . . Having left behind what belongs to the world . . . I escaped naked from the shipwreck of this life." What Gregory did, in fact, was take oaths of obedience, poverty and celibacy and become a monk.

Gregory moved quickly. He dissolved the extensive estates he had inherited from his father, converting them to six monastic houses in Sicily and a seventh in Rome, the famous St. Andrew, "from which so much of the seventh-century leadership of the church was destined to come." He abjured classical learning, giving himself wholly to biblical wisdom. He threw himself on the mercy of God, allowing himself to be remade as a new creature in a radically changed world. By entering the monastery's daily rounds of discipline, prayer and Bible reading, Gregory was launching upon what seemed the surest way to a holy life and joyous fellowship with God in Christ.

In this moment, Gregory became a man without a cultural home. He no longer belonged to the crumbling classical world culture that had belonged to his parents. And he could not yet see the world culture that would soon emerge: that of medieval Christendom. But this much he knew: within the peaceful, secure nest of the monastery, he could follow the ancient contemplative path to intimacy with God.

When Gregory entered the monastery, he no doubt expected to spend his life there, "working out his own salvation with fear and trembling as God worked within him." And for three years, a period he later remembered as the happiest in his life, he enjoyed that serene life. But this blessed respite from worldly care would be fleeting. Too soon he would experience his third and most painful homelessness—neither physical nor social, but spiritual.

It is hard for many modern Christians to appreciate what that monastery meant to Gregory. We may think of monasticism as an intense and rather gloomy life of self-denial. We have very little sense of why anyone would want to spend his or her life in such conditions. In particular, we struggle with the meaning of the contemplative life.

The story of Antony of Egypt—a man who followed gospel commands literally, selling all, fleeing the things of this world and seeking only

God—formed the blueprint for the contemplative life as it would be practiced throughout the medieval period. By Gregory's day the monastic vision based on Antony and his Egyptian "desert fathers"—now thoroughly communal rather than solitary—had grown into an empire-wide phenomenon. As they multiplied in number and spread out into the empire's hinterlands, the early medieval monks learned not only from Antony and the Gospels, but also from Plato and such Neoplatonists as Plotinus (205–270). These and other Greek philosophers had sought truth with their whole hearts—desiring above all to see God (the ultimate Form behind the appearances of the world) and yearning to undergo the necessary disciplines to do so. A Christianized version of this platonic, ascetic quest—known as "the way of contemplation"—reached and captivated Gregory by way of his two favorite authors, Augustine and John Cassian. For both these figures, the contemplative way involved "the soul's effort in entering into itself, gathering itself from dispersal among the material images of its daily occupation, and rising in inner ascent." This effortful contemplation demanded both self-discipline and discernment *(discretio)*.

But Gregory's vision of the monastic life was not harshly ascetic. While he agreed that serious effort was needed to separate oneself from the distractions of daily life, he spoke more often of the joys and graces of the contemplative life. In his *Commentary on I Kings,* he insisted that "to enjoy the light within is not the result of our effort but of God's loving kindness." On asceticism, Gregory followed Benedict's more moderate way, connecting the care and balance required in the monastic life with the virtues of the classical philosophers. Though modern Christians tend to suspect that the founders of monasticism believed that spiritual things are good and material things (including the body and its comforts) evil, this was not the creed of Benedict, nor of Gregory.

One thing is clear: for Gregory, the monastery would provide blessed relief from the never-ending details of administration, the lot of the leader. When he entered the monastery, he no doubt thought he had escaped the administrative grind once and for all. And for three blissfully happy years, it seemed as though he had.

Losing the Beloved Cloister

But it was not to be. Pope Benedict I recognized a masterful administrator when he saw one, and in 578 he called Gregory out of his happy seclusion to become one of the seven deacons of Rome, an office carrying heavy duties. Then the next year Pope Pelagius II sent the talented monk as *apocrisiarus* (residential ambassador) to Constantinople, the center of the beset empire, to seek military support from the Emperor Justinian. There Gregory would stay for seven years, making his petitions, but shunning the pomp and glory of the emperor's court. Instead he lived as monastic a life as he could with some of his brother monks who accompanied him from Rome, applying himself to learning.

It was likely during his Constantinople years that the barrier-busting Gregory was born. At the least, he must have gained a profound sense of the universality of the church. He observed, and at least once participated in, the Eastern controversies over Nestorianism and Monophysitism, so remote to Latin sensibilities. And he had ample opportunity to observe the customs of the Eastern Church, with their many divergences from Western practice. As pope, Gregory would later show an acute awareness that within the unity of the church there must be allowance for a diversity of regional practices—this was the hallmark of his famous mission to England. Long before he sent Augustine of Canterbury and his monks to England, here in the East he would have seen that the church was bigger than his little Italian church.

In 586, Gregory was at last recalled from his fruitless Eastern duty (the emperor never did pledge support to the beleaguered West). He reentered his beloved monastery, St. Andrew, where he again prayed, sang and studied Scripture with the brothers. But now he also labored as aide to Pope Pelagius II, his schedule increasingly filled with "worldly duties"—a taste of things to come.

Then during the bitter winter of 589–590, the Tiber River burst its banks, destroying property, farmland and lives, and carrying more plague and famine in its wake. In February 590 Pope Pelagius II died—and the people and church turned to Gregory, unanimously electing him pope.

Gregory was devastated. He knew if he accepted the office, this would mean the end of his beloved contemplative life. Some accounts say he went into hiding. He certainly wrote a letter to the emperor, begging to be let off. But when the emperor's response arrived six months later, it confirmed Gregory's election. He was horrified, but the people of Rome would not be denied their chosen leader. On September 3, 590, led by Roman ministers, a crowd grabbed Gregory bodily and thrust him into the Basilica of St. Peter. On that day, the Western Church gained one of its most outstanding leaders. And Gregory lost the desire of his heart: an uninterrupted life of study and contemplation.

Immediately, Gregory was swamped with business as never before. It absorbed his hours, filled his thoughts and troubled his heart. To a former bishop of Antioch he wrote: "I am being smashed by many waves of affairs and afflicted by the storms of a life of tumults, so that I may rightly say: *I am come into deep waters where the floods overflow me* [Ps. 69:2]." His separation from the contemplative life now seemed absolute and irreversible. He wrote: "My sad mind, labouring under the soreness of its engagements, remembers how it went with me formerly in the monastery, how all perishable things were beneath it, how it rose above all that was transitory, and, though still in the body, went out in contemplation beyond the bars of the flesh."

The worst danger of his new position, Gregory freely admitted, was that despite his desire for the cloister's peace, part of him loved the prominence and importance of the papacy. What great self-discipline, vigilance and penitence it would take to keep this pride from destroying his eternal soul!

Whatever the dangers to his soul, the new pope felt obliged to pour himself out in labor for his people, healing and calming whom he could among a populace battered by war, plague and famine. His heart still aching for the life of the monastery, the shepherd spent his life for his sheep. First, he immediately began to lead penitential processions through the seven districts of Rome, praying for relief from their material distress. Then he turned to relieving his people's distress with the resources of the church; with the senators and other civil administrators gone, the church was the people's last resort. In the end, he nearly drained the church treasury, selling off church lands to provide for the poor; under Gregory the church took a giant step toward its medieval status as the agency most responsible for the general welfare of society, though not synonymous with the state. In their time of crisis, the Romans looked to their bishop not just for spiritual aid but also for material help.

This new role of Rome's bishop came most starkly to the fore in Gregory's famous run-in with the Lombards. By the time he became pope, Rome had been beset for several years by this fierce Germanic tribe. They had crossed the Alps and borne down on the Eternal City, poised to raze it and subjugate its people. Conditions were bad enough in Rome that the city's wealthy senatorial class had fled with their goods, abdicating their leadership and leaving behind the laboring poor to fend for themselves. The emperor, distant in Constantinople, was distracted by a war with Persia, and in any case it took over a month for messages to travel to him from Rome.

So the newly elected pope was thrust immediately into such worldly activities as managing supply lines and troop movements. In July 592, he averted disaster by negotiating a difficult peace with a local Lombard duke. But the following year the worst occurred: the Lombard king himself, Agilulf, besieged Rome. In an act that was the stuff of legend, Gregory met Agilulf on the very steps of St. Peter to negotiate with him. And Romans came to owe their pope more than a spiritual allegiance. With diplomatic words and costly tribute, Gregory prevailed on the king to leave the city untouched.

Living the Spiritual Cycle

Through the agonizing necessity of entering the papacy and fulfilling it in a way that honored God, Gregory was forced to confront the defining issue of his life and ministry: the question of the relationship between the contemplative and the active life. The contemplative life was focused on the only things that finally mattered to one's soul: the spiritual things that last eternally. The active life was lived in the midst of the world's distractions. It was the "secular" life—the term comes from the Latin *saeculum,* meaning "this present generation." It demanded of layfolk, parish priests and popes alike daily attention to the actions and concerns of men and women living according to the passing but pressing concerns of their generation.

The cloister was considered a blessed, privileged place, free from the often false and misleading urgencies of life in the here and now. To many, including Gregory in his younger years, it seemed that the active and contemplative lives could not be reconciled. How could one concentrate on eternal things when dealing constantly with people whose needs were so . . . daily?

In the first five months of his papacy, Gregory did two things that brought him to some resolution. First, he rethought his own life vocation. And second, he wrote the book that would be "the most widely read single text in the history of pastoral care" for the next millennium: the *Rule of Pastoral Care.* In this process, working from clues in John Cassian and other authors, Gregory forged a remarkable synthesis between the active and contemplative lives.

The biblical story that came alive for him on this matter was that of Rachel and Leah. In that allegoric way of thinking that seems odd today but was standard then, Gregory saw Rachel as the contemplative life: beautiful but infertile, and at first completely unattainable. Instead, as Gregory wrote to the Empress Theoctista upon his elevation to the papacy, he had been "joined in the night . . . to the fertile Leah"—that is, the life of active ministry.

In the biblical story, "Jacob begins with Leah, attains Rachel, and returns to Leah." It was something like this that Gregory discovered while living in the eye of the Roman storm, as the church's spiritual leader. How could the "Leah life" and the "Rachel life" be joined? Gregory came to see that "activity precedes contemplation, but contemplation must be expressed in service to one's neighbor." At first he seems to have misunderstood Paul's "flesh-spirit" language to mean that the spirit was always higher and better than the flesh (understood in platonic terms as the worldly, the material). But then he saw that in order to become truly spiritual, one must move not only away from the distractions of the flesh to reach the spirit, but also back from the heights of the spiritual life to the carnal concerns of bodily life.

In other words, Gregory concluded that these two modes of life were not as mutually exclusive as he and the church had taught. Each strengthens the other in a never-ending cycle: the contemplative life equipping us for the active life, and the active life grounding us in acts of love to our neighbors, to keep us from floating off into spiritual pride and irrelevance. Now he saw those who lived the active life—marked at its best by such physical and spiritual ministries as feeding the hungry and caring for the sick, teaching the ignorant and humbling the proud— as *better equipped* to experience the contemplative life than those who absorbed all their hours in spiritual pursuits.

Pastors, insisted Gregory, must live a higher life, one that combines both action and contemplation. If we want to know why, we need only to look at the life of Jesus: he ate and drank with sinners by day, performing miracles of healing and feeding the multitudes. But throughout the night, he prayed on a mountain.

The lesson was clear: ministry and prayer are the two essential sides of a redemptive and productive ministry. By living an active life, full of works of neighbor-love, expressing the virtues of faith, hope and charity, growing in the fruit of the Spirit, one can quite naturally arrive at more intense and joyful contemplation.

Of course, the challenge is always, how do we achieve contemplation in the midst of busyness? Gregory recommended a number of specific practices to pursue as time allows: read and study Scripture; cultivate humility and other virtues, such as discernment; recognize your own sinfulness and God's holiness; and allow yourself to experience the resulting "fear of the Lord." And when your busyness allows it, withdraw from exterior distractions into interior contemplation.

In the end, this monastic value of contemplation was still Gregory's bottom line. Whenever possible, you must "turn away from the distractions of knowing about *things* to the serious, even frightening, task of reflection on the inner self." But never, of course, should you remove yourself from the life of active charity to others. That was Gregory's temptation as a newly elected pope, yearning for the old peace of the cloister. But through a papacy remarkable for its intensive activity (his over 800 extant letters deal with every imaginable sort of administrative matter), he came to disagree with his culture's elevation of the monastic life above all others. In the midst of the storms, he found the "Rachel-Leah life," continuously cycling between contemplation and action. And he saw that it was good.

This was nothing short of revolutionary. Sadly, in the centuries since his death, Antony's monastic legacy had increasingly come to be the possession of an elite few. There were two classes of Christian, with the monks in the higher class and even the celibate "secular" (parish) clergy—and most certainly the married hoi polloi—clearly in the lower spiritual class. By affirming the spiritual value of the active life, Gregory, from the very top of the church's hierarchy, was breaking down that distinction and founding a new form of "worldly asceticism," accessible to all—from the busy bishop in his office to the married woman in her daily duties. Gregory was quite simply saying that all of us, whether we find ourselves in a cloister or the priesthood or the workaday world, can at times enjoy blessed contemplation. And when we do, we must never stay there: our souls and our effectiveness both depend on serving others too.

A Spirituality of the Everyday

In the end, Gregory's synthesis might seem to us a sort of spiritual cliché: *Of course* we must serve others to grow in grace. *Of course* we must recharge our spiritual batteries to be effective leaders. But Gregory went beyond these simple ideas. He insisted that while pastors or laypeople are engaged in the active life, *everything in their experience and in the world becomes potentially an instrument of God's direct, special communication to them.* Chance meetings. Storms. Landscapes. Crafted objects. A thousand other things. God is always speaking to us if we but have ears to hear and eyes to see. Unlike Augustine, who believed that God both hid and revealed himself (thus keeping humans aware of how dependent they are on him), Gregory emphasized "God's involvement with creation and the sacramental presence of spiritual truths in the things of this world." In teaching this world-sacramentalism, Gregory launched another powerful force in the emergence of the new, sacred world of the medievals.

Of course, the possibility that God is speaking to us in our daily experiences in the world raises the question: how can we tell when it's God talking? Here Gregory insisted that Christians foster and practice *discretio* (discernment). In the ancient world, this virtue belonged almost exclusively to the monk, nun and priest. But Gregory believed any person could attain spiritual discernment.

One of the places Gregory felt the average person heard most clearly from God was in experiences of suffering. Surrounded by the miseries of war, plague and famine, Gregory himself suffered from ill-health for the whole of his pontificate. (A wise professor of mine once said that the great spiritual divide between people runs not between rich and poor, female and male, young or old, or the like, but between those who've enjoyed good health and those who've had serious physical ills. I think he was right. Perhaps nothing more radically impinges on a person's soul than chronic or incurable disease.) From his own experiences of suffering, along with deep exegetical engagement with the book of Job, he concluded that suffering was *not* an absolute evil, but rather a special case of God's personal communication to his people. Suffering forces us beyond our own resources to discern our dependence on God.

Despite Gregory's frankness about suffering and his pessimism about the fate of the world, we find in his writing "an underlying sense of the triumph of joy and peace." In the midst of all our trials, our longing for God "transforms the suffering we undergo, *and even the sins we continue to commit,* into stages of growth." He did not counsel his readers to inflict suffering on themselves, as did the extreme ascetics. Rather, he told them to humbly accept God's will and expect that he is faithful to complete the work he has begun in us.

Because even in times of sin and suffering, God is at work to discipline and form us for further service, the goal of the Christian life for

Gregory was not the complete protection from any possibility of sin—as it seems to have been for some monastics. Rather, by integrating the active life, with all its brokenness and distraction and suffering, into his understanding of the spiritual life, Gregory gave all Christians a chance to develop discernment, holy sorrow, stability of life and tranquility of soul. *All* Christians. This is an inclusive, open-ended spirituality. Because "no part of life remains untouched by the sacred, no part of life need necessarily be excluded from the Christian." Ordinary layfolk might even, by the grace of God, experience in their daily lives the stability and tranquility formerly thought to be available only to monastics.

The virtue of *compunctio* ("compunction") was perhaps the dearest of the virtues to Gregory. Often thought of as a kind of godly sorrow (2 Cor 7:10-11), the Latin word literally means "piercing." It is rooted in Acts 2:37, which tells how Peter's hearers at Pentecost were "pierced to the heart" (NASB). Cassian, Benedict and others had followed up this clue by closely associating compunction with conversion, but it was Gregory who made it a central value in Western spirituality.

Gregory's teaching on compunction emerged from his "deeply felt sense of the radical insufficiency of all terrestrial goods in relation to those of the heavenly world." Moving compunction beyond simple sorrow for sin, he expanded the term to refer to "the whole of the Christian's attitude toward present existence in relation to the underlying desire for the stability and joy of heaven." Compunction certainly involved tears, and sometimes it might involve a terrifying fear of God. But though those sorts of negative feelings might come chronologically first in our lives, they provided a doorway to a higher emotion: "the compunction of love"—or more simply, desire for God.

Augustine had experienced this God-directed desire, replacing his out-of-control sexual desires—"Our hearts are restless until they rest in [God]," he had said in his *Confessions.* Now Gregory deepened and elaborated Augustine's thought. Our desire for union with God operates in a kind of cycle, never to be fulfilled on this earth. Every time we come closer to God, our desire for him is amplified; in the very fulfillment of the desire, there is planted a deeper yearning to experience more of the beloved. We sense the beauty of God. We desire him. We experience him, yet immediately desire him more. In a later chapter, on Margery Kempe, we will see how powerful this Gregorian teaching about compunction would become for medieval Christians. This sort of influence led the great modern writer on monasticism and mysticism Jean Leclercq to call Gregory "The Doctor of Desire."

The Subtle Art of Leadership

Gregory's exemplary leadership in Rome's hour of crisis and his writing of the *Rule of Pastoral Care* both point to another cluster of virtues taught by the "monk pope"—this time aimed not at all Christians, but at Christian leaders. Bluntly put, the church hierarchy Gregory now came to know intimately was in serious need of reform. Wicked and hypocritical people sought positions of leadership out of motives of vanity and material gain. Bishops traded in church offices. Church officials "were not above usurping funds or land, and bishops sometimes turned greedy eyes toward the property of orphans and monks." Gregory campaigned against these abuses and returned ill-gotten gains wherever possible. He also shook up his own papal hierarchy, ousting lay attendants and even replacing "secular" clerics with monastics, on the principle that "only they who despised power could be trusted to exercise it wisely." (Here, however, we find one of the rare warts on Gregory's papal career. By inserting a cadre of monks into the hierarchy, he ironically caused more trouble than he solved, as uncontrolled bickering broke out between the clerical old-guard and the monastic interlopers.)

When in 593 the patriarch in Constantinople, John IV (582-595), took for himself the title "ecumenical patriarch," Gregory reacted strongly. This was not to protect the prerogative of Rome, but rather because he felt the patriarch had become smitten with his own authority and so had fallen into the sin of pride. He wrote to John and to the emperor and empress of the day, complaining of the "diabolical arrogance" involved in John's use of this title. To model the humility he found so lacking in the patriarch, Gregory began to start all of his own letters with the title "from the servant of the servants of God."

A theme that preoccupied Gregory during his papacy was the question of how to use power rightly. He wrote his *Rule of Pastoral Care* for bishops and pastors, and spoke much in it about both serving and ruling others well as a spiritual leader: "how one should come to government, the life of a pastor, how a ruler ought to teach and admonish his subordinates, and how, finally, a preacher ought to return to himself, lest his life or teaching make him proud." He believed this to be among the most difficult and subtle arts for a human to practice—to turn one's back on glory and keep oneself humble while holding high position.

Gregory's *Rule* is also profoundly sensitive to the diversity of personalities within every congregation. Part three of the book reminds the pastor that different folks require different strokes—or in the colorful imagery of his time, "gentle hissing that calms horses, excites young puppies." The preacher must thus adapt his message to the diversity of personalities and experiences in his congregation. Gregory then lists thirty-six pairs of "types" a pastor may expect to find in his church and offers sage advice on how to preach differently to each pole of each pair. These extend from the obvious—"men and women; the young and the old; the poor and the rich"—to the subtle—"those who grieve for their sins yet do not abandon them, and those who abandon their sins yet do not grieve for them; those who do evil secretly and good openly, and those who hide the good they do, yet allow themselves to be thought ill of because of some things they do in public."

Gregory insisted that the hardest things for a pastor to do were, first, to vary the measures of stern discipline and gentle compassion on a case-by-case basis, depending on the parishioner's temperament, and second, to perceive when a virtue was contorting itself into a corresponding vice. The pastor must be all things to all people, letting his counsel and reproof be guided by empathy and insight into each congregant's unique makeup and situation. Not surprisingly, as Gregory's "rule" seems to have been modeled at least to some degree on Benedict's famous monastic rule, this counsel of sympathy, moderation and discernment in spiritual leadership is very Benedictine in tone.

Throughout the medieval era the church, recognizing the value of Gregory's counsel, put his book into the hands of every bishop upon his consecration. The advisor of Charlemagne, Alcuin, wrote early in the ninth century to Eanbald, archbishop of York: "Wherever you go, let the *Pastoral Book* of St. Gregory go with you. Read it and re-read it often. . . . The book is a mirror of the bishop's life and a medicine for all the wounds inflicted by the devil's deception." For nearly a thousand years, this book of Gregory's was recognized as one of the church's great treasures.

Dancing with Celts . . . and Pagans

Gregory extended the Benedictine principles of sympathy and moderation as he counseled the monks whom he sent to establish the Roman church in England. In 597, Augustine of Canterbury (not to be confused with Augustine of Hippo) and his party landed in Kent, in the southeast of England. What happened next—the whole career of that English mission—is told in *The Ecclesiastical History of the English People* by the Venerable Bede. One of the most praiseworthy documents ever written by a pope is the letter Gregory sent to Augustine in response to the latter's questions, recorded in 1.27 of Bede's *History*. Augustine asked what he should do with the many cultural differences he found there among the scattered Celtic and Gaulish churches that predated his mission. "Since we hold the same faith," asked Augustine, "why do customs vary in different churches; why does the method of saying Mass differ in the Roman and Gaulish churches?"

Gregory replied: "You are familiar with the usage of the Roman Church, in which you were brought up. But if you have found customs . . . that may be more acceptable to God, I wish you to make a careful selection of them, and teach the Church of the English . . . whatever you have been able to learn with profit from the various Churches. For things should not be loved for the sake of places, but places for the sake of good things. Therefore select from each of the Churches whatever things are devout, religious, and right, and when you have bound them, as it were, into a sheaf, let the minds of the English grow accustomed to it." In other words, do not love a practice because it is Roman, but rather because it is *good*.

One specific area in which Gregory counseled Augustine was on the problem of what were considered incestuous marriages: that is, people who had married in-laws. Gregory told Augustine that these people were "not on that account to be deprived of communion, lest they seem to be punished for sins committed unknowingly before baptism." Gregory knew that an ecclesiastical authority couldn't go into a new area and blame people for things that appeared under current church law to be forbidden. One must go slowly. And many modern missionaries both Catholic and Protestant have taken a similar tack.

The even tougher question was how the church should spread the gospel among pagan groups. Gregory wrote a famous letter on this subject to Mellitus, an abbot who worked with Augustine of Canterbury on the British mission. He said,

> The temples of the idols among that people should on no account be destroyed . . . but the temples themselves are to be aspersed with holy water, altars set up in them, and relics deposited there. . . . They must be purified from the worship of demons and dedicated to the service of the true God . . . that the people . . . may abandon their error and, flocking more readily to their accustomed resorts, may come to know and adore the true God.

In other words, if the people are allowed to keep some of their accustomed ways, they will more readily come to desire the eternal things—the mountain is to be climbed slowly. From Gregory's time on, an influential stream of teaching has counseled missionaries not to impose their particular cultural version of the faith on others but rather to seek ways to accommodate the customs and work in the thought-categories of indigenous peoples. This is what missiologist Lamin Sanneh calls the principle of "translatability": while there is a core of beliefs without which it is impossible to be Christian, there are many more beliefs and practices that have been translated from culture to culture throughout Christian history—and these are simply different expressions of the same gospel.

All of this—the pastoral sensitivity of the *Rule of Pastoral Care* and the missionary sensitivity of the letters to Augustine and Mellitus— came from a single principle in Gregory. He saw the church as unified in Christ and his sacraments, yet diverse in customs, languages and individual personalities. He stated his principle: "In the church, because united in one faith, diversity of usages does no harm." Boundary crossing and empathy for those unlike oneself thus were for him cardinal virtues of pastor and missionary alike.

Gregory was one of the greatest examples in Christian history of a person "wise as a serpent and gentle as a dove." In his sensitivity to human failings and human differences, his insight into the psychology of Christian devotion, his critique and reform of Christian leadership, his openness to God's working through creation, and his compassion for the sheep of Christ's fold, Gregory was a gift and a treasure to the church. May more of us reclaim him and learn from him.

Dante Alighieri

LOVING THE UNIVERSE
AND SAVING OUR SOULS

Midway this way of life we're bound upon
I woke to find myself in a dark wood
Where the right road was wholly lost and gone.

When I first dove into Dante Alighieri's (1265–1321) *Divine Comedy*, in a monastery in North Carolina, these opening lines captivated me. I was nearing my own "midway point" (my fortieth birthday) and struggling with my own doubtful agendas, shameful sins and dull regrets. How refreshing to find a famous person confessing that he, too, had struggled.

Before long I was hooked, and I followed "Dante the pilgrim" (the poet himself, inserted as the protagonist in his own epic poem) down through hell, up the mountain of purgatory and out into the cosmic "spheres" that medievals believed circled the earth in concentric rings, to the very topmost heaven. There he—and I—beheld God who is both indescribable and yet somehow "marked with our image." There, with Dante, "my heart and will were wheeled by love, The Love that moves the sun and the other stars."

In other words, I found as I read breathlessly on in that monastery a story of salvation. Yes, this is Dante's own salvation, but also all of ours—for he pours into his tale not only his own experiences of making bad decisions, descending into despair and finding redemption, but also the imagined experiences of countless others. We see these people from the ultimate perspective: the final divine reckoning of their lives' choices.

Dante's tale is an allegory—but of a special kind. His drama is not acted out by "perambulating labels" in the manner of John Bunyan's tale, with its Greatheart, Vanity and the like. Rather, its players are historical people—though Dante can't resist throwing in a few characters of myth and legend—and the cast includes many of the most significant figures from Christian history up to Dante's day. As did Athanasius in his *Life of Antony*, Dante plies the medieval craft of biography-for-imitation (and-for-warning!). The people inhabiting this great "drama of the soul's choice" show us—simply by being who they are—how to live.

I have said that the *Comedy* is a story not only about our salvation, but about Dante's particular journey to redemption. In fact, it tells of three distinctive kinds of sin from which Dante himself needed to be redeemed. In telling of these three sins and their three redemptions, Dante was following the man who loomed over all of medieval theology: Augustine. As every medieval boy and girl knew, that great North African writer had taught that all sin comes from some disordered love. All created things are good (God said so), and it is good for us to desire them. But because of the Fall, we find ourselves habitually desiring good things in bad ways: we love too much, or too little, or at the wrong time, or in the wrong way—and most of all, we tend to love created things, including other people, with an *ultimate* love that rightly belongs to God alone. In the *Comedy*, Dante takes his readers through his own personal—but also somehow universal—journey of being released from three ways that his own loves had become disordered.

Dante Alighieri was born in 1265, some time in May or June, in the northern Italian administrative center of Florence. Though his family liked to think of themselves as part of the nobility, and his father owned a small amount of land, they were probably not of noble blood—and in any case they were certainly not among the powerful upper crust of the city. Dante's birth year also saw the death of the great "Dumb Ox," the theologian Thomas Aquinas—a person whose influence on Dante and his *Comedy* was immense. Dante's early education took place in Latin at a grammar school, where he was also exposed to French and Provencal poetry and some classical literature. When he was still a teen, his father died, and Dante took legal responsibility for the whole family. This would later thrust him into the public life of Florence—a circumstance with momentous results in his life.

Dante's Muse

The first and perhaps most important of the formative events in Dante's life was his encounter with the girl who would become his lifelong inspiration. It happened like this: At the age of nine, Dante was attending one of the parties that structured the social world of the Florentine upper classes. He was no doubt already being trained in the graces and gravitas so important to a middle-class family with aspirations to nobility. But none of his parents' coaching could have prepared him for what happened next. Suddenly, as if illuminated by a flash of lightning, a vision shone out amidst the throng—the most enchanting girl Dante had ever seen. Dressed in "noble crimson," she possessed a luminous physical beauty that awakened Dante's senses. But there was more than this. As if in a dream, he watched her as she conversed graciously with those around her. And he was overwhelmed by her *spiritual* beauty. Her presence seemed that of an angel, and it shook him to his core. He began to tremble. And from that moment, this girl a few months his junior, "little Beatrice, daughter of Folco Portinari," filled his waking thoughts and his dreams, becoming his muse, his inspiration—in his own words, "the glorious lady of my mind."

The infatuation grew over the years, and as a teenager, Dante began to write poetic homages to Beatrice. He hymned the elegance of her clothes; "her stride; her eyes; her silence; her smile; her aura." Above all, these poems described Beatrice as a young lady of exceptional, virtuous *grace,* who transformed all around her, so that they could speak only "whatever is true, . . . honorable, . . . right, . . . pure, . . . lovely," and of good repute" (Phil 4:8 NASB). In short, these poems hint—and the young poet makes this explicit in his autobiographical *Vita Nuova*—that Beatrice's presence in his life was far more than a youthful "crush." As love for a woman has done for many men, only in this case from an agonizingly unbridgeable distance (she far outranked him socially), Beatrice's luminous person set Dante on "the path of self-discovery"—emotionally, vocationally and spiritually. Her influence on the young poet convinced him in later years that God uses romantic love as a sort of mediating influence to lead humans to the Being who is Love himself. In fact, it is not too extreme to call Beatrice (and Dante said as much) a kind of Christ-figure in his life. In the culminating *Paradiso* of his divine trilogy, Dante says that it is through Beatrice he "first found entry to that faith which makes souls welcome unto God."

His Beatrice verses proved compelling and well-crafted enough to gain him the applause of literate Florentines. And after many years, when both were in their late teens, people began to guess who young Alighieri had in mind when he wrote them (revealing the name of your feminine muse was just not done among the day's Italian love-poets). Dante followed the convention of the time to throw the guessers and scandal-mongers off the scent: he feigned affection for another young woman, a "screen love." Unfortunately for poor Dante's battered heart, Beatrice caught wind of this subterfuge and, one day on a Florence street, turned away from the approaching Dante, refusing even to acknowledge his presence. He was crushed.

The rumored identity of Dante's romantic interest was no doubt material for scandal, or at least general amusement, because Beatrice's father, Folco, was patriarch of one of Florence's two richest and most powerful banking families (he endowed a Florentine hospital that is still in operation today). In other words, in that socially stratified time and place, there was no chance that Dante could marry Beatrice. Instead, she was soon married to a young man from the other most powerful banking family.

In 1290 Beatrice died at twenty-four, leaving Dante disconsolate for a long time. Finally, as he wallowed in the depths of his grief, Beatrice came to him in a vision:

> A miraculous vision appeared to me, in which I saw things which made me decide to write nothing more of this blessed one until such time as I could treat of her more worthily. And to achieve this I study as much as I can, as she truly knows. So that, if it pleases Him by whom all things live, that my life lasts a few years, I hope to write of her what has never been written of any woman.

The Danger of Love

It would be many years before Dante fulfilled this promise by producing one of the world's most unforgettable poems: the *Divine Comedy.* That epic begins with Beatrice sending a guide from beyond death, the Latin—and pagan!—poet Virgil, to rescue Dante from his midlife slide into sin and despondency and usher him into the three realms of the other world. His arduous journey turns Dante, step by step, from his darkness and sin and back to the joyous, shining presence of God. And at the poem's end, Dante joins Beatrice again in paradise itself.

Yet the *Comedy* was also written by an older and wiser Dante. If something in his all-encompassing and doomed love for Beatrice seems off-kilter to us, it is because this swooning passion also began to bother Dante himself. As a young man, he had written brilliantly and famously in the "courtly love" tradition. Yet in the *Comedy,* his alter ego discovers in hell the adulterous lovers Paolo and Francesca—who have been led into their sin by reading just such poetry as he himself had once written. Though Dante the poet portrays Dante the pilgrim as deeply sympathetic with the plight of these lovers, Dante the poet has clearly learned that love poetry, irresponsibly written and read, can endanger our eternal souls.

Then in the *Purgatorio* and *Paradiso,* Dante finally allows the intemperate love of his early years as a love poet to be transformed into something higher: in *Purgatorio* 32.11, when Dante the pilgrim sees Beatrice for the first time in ten years (the poem is set in 1300; Beatrice had died in 1290), Beatrice's companions cry out: "He should not look so hard!"—the Italian is *Troppo fisso!* meaning "Too fixed!" In *Paradiso* 10.55-60, when he does turn away from her to sing his gratitude to God, she smiles. And in *Paradiso* 18.21, as he gazes again at her, she admonishes: "Now turn around and listen well, not in my eyes alone is Paradise." All this amounts to "the complete reversal of the love affair of Paolo and Francesca," as "the lady turns to God and . . . her lover follows suit." The lesson here is Augustine's: romantic love can become disordered and lead to a kind of romantic idolatry, plunging the soul into hell. Dante said such love *can* prove redemptive (as did his love for Beatrice), but only if, in the end, our ultimate affection is weaned from our human beloved and turned toward God.

More went into this masterpiece than an obsession with an unattainable romantic object (if that were enough, then I suppose the world would be full of Dantes). Through his teen years and into young adulthood, Dante attained a wide and eclectic education in the schools of Florence and by self-study. In the schools, he pursued the usual course from the trivium of grammar, logic and rhetoric to the quadrivium of arithmetic, geometry, music and astronomy. He also became skilled in drawing and gained his first foundations in philosophy and ethics, subjects crucial to the *Comedia*.

Beyond his formal schooling, the young man grew intellectually under two mentors. The first was the learned Brunetto Latini, a prominent figure in Florentine politics, who had worked in Paris and other European centers as a notary and absorbed culture and learning. Back in Florence, he found himself in high demand by young men who wanted to broaden their intellectual horizons. The second was the famed poet Guido Cavalcanti. Dante's early verses impressed Guido enough to attract first his interest, and later his tutelage and friendship, which Dante repaid by immortalizing his mentor in the pages of the *Comedy*.

In 1285, while the true apple of his eye had still been alive but socially unattainable, Dante had married the young woman to whom he had been betrothed as a child, Gemma, of the noble Donati family. Though this was still an age of arranged marriages, the relationship seems to have been affectionate. The couple had four children together: three boys and a girl, Antonia, who would later spend the last years of her life in a convent, interestingly (and generously!) taking the conventual name of "Beatrice."

Restlessness and a New Lady

In 1289 Dante had fought in two of the endless skirmishes between Italian city-states. Once discharged, most men would have settled down to a quiet family life. Not the passionate Dante. His restlessness worsening after Beatrice's death, he plunged into a period of "gay parties [and] lavish banquets," even indulging in a public rhyming contest with Gemma's relative Forese Donati, "a sort of battle of insults in which literary virtuosity often degenerated into vulgarity." Though scholars find no evidence the young Florentine soldier-poet was ever unfaithful to his wife, his whirlwind public life gained him enough notoriety to draw a sharp reproof from his poetic mentor, Cavalcanti—written, of course, in the form of a sonnet:

> Much doth it grieve me that thy noble mind
> And virtue's plenitude are stripped from thee; . . .
>
> And now I care not, sith thy life is baseness
> To give the sign that thy speech pleaseth me,
> Nor come I to thee in guise visible . . .

In the midst of this whirl of partying and poetry, seeking solace for the loss of Beatrice, Dante found "another lady," of whom he was to write in his unfinished *Convivio (The Banquet)*. As he had the *Vita Nuova*, Dante formed *Convivio* as a series of poems accompanied by commentary. And though the lady of these poems at first seems to be a flesh-and-blood woman like Beatrice, several chapters into the proceedings Dante reveals the true identity of his new mistress: she was that same lady celebrated by the sixth-century Christian philosopher Boethius (ca. 480–524), whom Dante was reading closely during this period. The new passion of this passionate man was *philosophy.*

In Dante's time philosophy still meant, in the ancient tradition, the study of just about everything. It also entailed meditation on "the good life"—that is, questions of ethics and, ultimately, spiritual things. Though such Christian philosopher-theologians as Thomas Aquinas recognized that the revelation of Scripture and tradition was necessary to reach that final elusive goal of the philosopher—the ecstatic "beatific vision" of God that amounted to intimate union with him—they still believed reason could provide much that was valuable. And Dante's ambitious goal in his *Convivio* was to share with less fortunate souls the wealth of insight available in every department of philosophical study— knowledge he had gained through a period of intense study in the Franciscan and Dominican schools of his region.

In the *Convivio,* Dante describes how, while seeking solace for Beatrice's death, he had stumbled upon philosophy in the pages of Boethius's *Consolation of Philosophy* and a book by Cicero. Despite knowing Latin, he found it "hard at first to penetrate their meaning." But Dante was never one to give up easily; he dove into research with a will. Soon, just as "a man looking for silver accidentally hits on gold," he found in his books something far greater than mere comfort. Captivated by the "language of authors and sciences and books," Dante personified the world of knowledge as a noble, compassionate woman. And as Boethius did in his *Consolation,* Dante called this new love "Lady Philosophy"—a title that also echoed the ladies of courtly love and the beloved Lady Poverty of Francis of Assisi. This was no momentary infatuation, but a lifelong passion for learning that would rival his love for Beatrice. His "sense of truth" *(lo senso di vero)* drew him inexorably toward her, and like a love-besotted teenager, his longing for her consumed his thoughts: "O how many nights there were," he exulted, "when the eyes of others were closed in sleep and my own gazed fixedly at the dwelling of my beloved!" Frequenting religious schools and philosophical disputes in search of her, he launched into a period of intensive study that lasted some thirty months, well into the

1290s and beyond, even as his political involvements also intensified.

In short, Dante was experiencing an intellectual awakening—a broadening of horizons—from the private, intimate world of the love poets, to the public world of the ethicists and politicians, and beyond, to the very universe itself. Among other new vistas, Dante's study in this period opened up for him the teachings of Thomas Aquinas, the radical Franciscans (including the apocalyptic writer Joachim of Fiore) and a stream of political theology. Drinking in the world-embracing theology of Aquinas, Dante gained a near-mystical feeling for the order and unity of the objective universe: "Through the joy of sheer knowing, philosophy introduced him to an objective cosmos, grander than any dream—an immense, unfathomable order of parts in a whole." C. S. Lewis likely had Dante in mind when he said that in the Middle Ages people could "love the universe as a man can love his own city."

Desire and Dante's Besetting Sin

During this period of study, Dante came to see the universe as "'theomorphic,' or God-shaped. God is revealed, if we can but see it, wherever we might turn." This insight he claims to have received as Paul did—through direct revelation: "The glory of Him who moves all things penetrates the universe and shines in one part more and in another less. I was in the heaven that most receives His light." But if you find in this high view of creation echoes of Gregory the Great, then you see the continuity of the Middle Ages from one end to the other.

What is the payoff here? Just this: because God is revealed in creation, loving creation and desiring to seek out the truths of its rational beauty of order *is* loving God. Creation is the imprint of God's own beauty and order. The human soul itself has been imprinted with this beauty and order, and therefore it desires it and takes joy in it, in a divine way that knows no satisfaction short of union with God himself: "But your life . . . is breathed in directly by the supreme Good, who so enamors it of Himself that evermore it desires him."

If this seems reminiscent of the "argument from desire" used by C. S. Lewis in his apologetics (embedded in the title of his own short autobiography, *Surprised by Joy*), we should not be surprised. Dante echoes Augustine, and Lewis echoes both. Lewis and Dante also share with these older thinkers their favorite analogy for that spiritual desire: thirst—which of course comes from the Bible itself. Says Dante in *Purgatorio,* the desire for God as our source and creator is "the natural thirst which nothing slakes but that water the Samaritan woman asked for."

But this new passion, like his love for Beatrice, also had a darker side—a dimension of disorder from which Dante needed to be cleansed if he was to enter heaven and gaze on God's own face. Dante scholars agree that an odor rises from the pages of his *Convivio*—the smell of intellectual arrogance. The exact nature of the sin that led Dante off the narrow road and landed him in the "dark wood" of the *Comedia*'s introduction is unknown. But surely the besetting sin of the middle-aged man is pride—being unyieldingly full of ourselves, our ideas and agendas. Looking at the portraits of Dante Alighieri painted in or near his time, you can see something of this. His piercing eyes look down the Roman nose at you, and his jaw is set as solid as iron below. Here, even after the softening influence of his legendary love for Beatrice, the moral crisis of his middle years, and perhaps even the transporting joy of mystical experience, is a man both aware of his own talents and set in his ways.

Everything in the poet's turn-of-the-fourteenth-century Italian environment seemed designed to encourage this sin of pride: An economic boom-time birthing for the first time a new, powerful middle class of "self-made men." A political arena churned up by long-running feuds over matters of family honor that regularly burst the bonds of local strife into the sad and empty glories of war. A church lusting after secular power and selling its pastoral posts to the highest bidder. An intellectual world besotted with the glory of its scholastic systems. This was Dante's world.

It doesn't come as a surprise, then, that beyond the grandiose *Convivio* we find in the *Comedy* moments of almost unbelievable pride—as when he compares himself with the greatest poets the world has known. However, the overall impression he leaves in his epic poem is not one of pride.

Rather, he allows readers to see through his own pretensions—because by the time he is writing the *Comedy,* he has come to see his own intellectual pride as something requiring redemption. Certainly, he never denigrates learning and reason in the poem. Yet by the time his eponymous pilgrim has arrived in paradise, the poet will portray scholarly learning as a merely relative accomplishment, in that familiar gospel way of taking human wisdom down a peg or two. This echoes his insistence early in the *Comedia* that the souls in hell have lost "the good of the intellect"—that is, not that they have lost the ability to reason but that they have lost him without whom all human reasoning is as filthy rags, availing nothing. This intellectual pride, then, was Dante's second area of disordered love, and in the *Comedy* he shows us that he knew he must be redeemed from it too, as he must from the idolatry of young romance.

Life in the Danger Zone

The harsh events that matured Dante into the writer of the *Comedy* involved a third lesson that, like the other two, confronted him with another area of excessive love. This was his unconditional loyalties to Italy, Florence and his own political party. In 1295 these loyalties began to play a key role in his life as his attention turned to politics, serving in various civil offices over a number of years.

One Dante biographer has described the political world of Florence into which Dante now stepped as "a persistent danger zone." This continually expanding city, cluttered with houses, had grown so rapidly as to require three circles of walls (in cities, then as now, the wealthy removed themselves to the outer circle, building lavish villas on the outskirts of town). In that newly prospering urban center, everyone was on the make, jostling for power and prestige. The rising middle class chafed and strained against the old nobility.

Conflict arose not only from class difference, but also from clan strife. Families with new wealth fought with ancient and noble families; others prosecuted long-running battles as violent as any McCoy-Hatfield feud. A young man from one family would slight a young woman of another, plunging hundreds of people into decades of retaliation and counter-retaliation. Layers of tension piled up into the powder keg of violence that made the Italian word *vendetta* synonymous with vengeful party strife and provided the real-life models for Shakespeare's feuding Montagues and Capulets.

The most pervasive struggle embroiling two factions, the Guelfs and the Ghibellines, was driven not by pettiness but by a central question: to whom should Italians bow politically, the emperor or the pope? The Ghibellines argued that "God had chosen, after all, to submit himself in the person of Christ to Roman rule," and many Italians and indeed Europeans of the day thought of the Romans as chosen people—divinely ordained to bring law and order to the whole world. The Guelfs disagreed: "Wasn't the pope, after all, the Vicar of Christ? Didn't he bear 'the keys to the kingdom'? And to the degree that spiritual power was nobler and more exalted than earthly power, didn't it make sense to think of the pope as the superior of any earthly monarch?"

Exile and the Yearning to Return

In 1294 the weak Pope Celestine V abdicated to Boniface VIII, who set to work seizing power in Tuscany. With visions of theocracy dancing in his head, he enlisted the support of Corso Donati, leader of the Black Guelfs. This set the scene for events six years later, when in 1300 Dante, serving in Florence's highest leadership position of "prior," oversaw an exile of several violent leaders among both the Black and the White Guelfs, including his friend Guido Cavalcanti. Loyal to his White Guelf family and opposed to the papal alliance with the Blacks, Dante opposed Boniface's designs on Florence. When in 1301 Dante was sent to Rome to avert papal interference in Florence, Boniface VIII clearly recognized a potentially formidable enemy. While Boniface kept Dante back when the rest of the diplomatic party left, he made an alliance with the French king, Charles of Valois, who helped Corso Donati and the Black Guelfs take control of Florence. The Blacks chased out the Whites, including Dante, "destroyed their houses, and condemned by default those who had already left." In January 1302 a sentence against Dante was decreed—under cover of the charge of graft, that is, trading money for power. The charge is agreed to have been ludicrous as Dante was one of the least corruptible of the Italian politicos. The penalty was initially a huge fine, but when the poet-politician failed to return to Florence to clear his name, it was changed to public burning if he ever set foot in his beloved city again.

From that day, Dante underwent the experience of homelessness common to many in this book. He roamed northern Italy, staying twice for extended periods in Verona and once in Ravenna. He felt, as he wrote in the *Convivio,* "as a ship without sails and without rudder, driven to various harbors and shores by the parching wind which blows from pinching poverty." As the prophetic words of his own great poem put it, Dante was to spend the rest of his life knowing intimately "how salt the bread of strangers is, how hard / The up and down of someone else's stair."

Dante's exile, though bitter, proved fruitful. Its "bleak clarity" is woven through his writings. At first he dedicated himself to finding a way to return; however, after an unsuccessful coup attempt by a group of White Guelfs, and Ghibellines split along the factional lines, Dante reluctantly gave up hope for reinstatement. He "retreated from the grim squalid quarters where other Florentine expatriates spun endless, wicked conspiracies of revenge." In a real sense, the *Comedy* is his final attempt to heal divisions and bring unity (and not inconsequentially, himself) back to his beloved Florence.

Thus kept from his home city, "he must have longed during this time for an impossible restoration of his honor and his property, for the irrevocably lost security of a family life, for the conversations with his sweet friends along the banks of the river at the hour of dusk, and for a world of ordinary concerns." But out of his thirty-month baptism in Lady Philosophy's world of learning, he felt he had something to give the world that might improve it. And so he turned to writing.

Between 1304 and 1308 he worked on the *Convivio* (it was never finished). In 1305 he began an impassioned plea for the use of the Tuscan vernacular in public life, *De vulgari eloquentia*—arguing that this shared language was "the root and bark of the politics, law, poetry, and theology of the whole of Italy." Some time between 1309 and 1317 he wrote a defense of the imperial mode of government, *De monarchia*. And most importantly, though he set the *Comedy* in 1300, throughout these years in exile and right up until his death, he forged that masterwork.

His last home, where Dante finally settled in 1318, was Ravenna, the old Italian residence of the Byzantine imperial representative. There, "he was honorably received by the lord of that city, who revived his fallen hopes with kindly encouragement, and, giving him abundantly such things as he needed, kept him there at his court for many years." And there, at last, his sons Pietro and Jacopo, his daughter Beatrice, and possibly his wife Gemma, came to live with him, until he died of malarial fever on his way back from a diplomatic trip to Venice (he was serving as ambassador to that city) in September 1321.

At Last, a Higher Unity

Guiseppe Mazzotta finds in the end of *Purgatorio* and in *Paradiso,* both of which Dante wrote in Ravenna, echoes of that place with its

> dense woods of pine trees near the city; the tombs and reliquaries of the Caesars; the memory of Boethius and of the emperor Justinian; the spiritual presence of the contemplative Peter Damian in the Benedictine abbeys surrounding the city . . . the mosaics of Ravenna's basilicas, with their figurations of the Pantocrator (God as the all-ruling Father) hovering over the hierarchies of angels and saints, the Virgin Mary, the extended narrative of the life of Christ.

These mosaics, like Dante's poetic vision, encapsulated the whole of the cosmos in a beautiful, systematic way. And like those artworks, whose purpose was to lead the viewer into contemplation, Dante's *Comedy* was founded on the contemplative theology of such men as Benedict and Bernard of Clairvaux. As these contemplatives fully understood, and as Dante shows in his poem, while politicians and patriots remain mired in their own partisan interests, poetry and theology celebrate universal human experience.

This, indeed, was the last of the three distinctive redemptions Dante found in exile and wrote about in his *Comedy*. Dante was deeply patriotic, loving his city-state of Florence in something of the same way he loved Beatrice and Lady Philosophy, and he yearned to return from his exile, even when it became clear that this homecoming would never happen. This civic loyalty had mired him in party passion and made him willing, with his fellow conspirators, to go to almost any lengths to regain his beloved city. When those efforts failed, while the conspirators around him wailed that all was lost, he slowly emerged from the dark tunnel of their despair.

He realized that this passion for "home and native land" had also been out of balance in a sinful way. Patriotism can be a good, but not when it stands in the way of a proper theological vision of the universe as a single, all-encompassing, God-breathed cosmos. So Dante raised up his eyes from his beloved Florence and its warring factions, and found that "the way out of the darkness of partial and relative viewpoints . . . is a universal standpoint." This was the burden of his *De vulgari eloquentia* and *Convivio,* and it flavors the *Comedia* as well. And so in that last work, Dante showed his Pilgrim persona being led step by step from fierce, and ultimately sinful, localism to a universal perspective.

Indeed, the poem can be read as a paean to the movement from the narrow, hidebound, provincial, selfish perspective to the irenic, humble, universal, divine perspective, in which all human idolatries, whether romantic or intellectual or political, are swallowed up. Contrary to the uneducated slur that Dante "enjoys throwing his enemies in hell," he in fact makes short work of factional wrangling by having a mix of Guelfs and Ghibellines show up in all three of his afterworlds. Even more vividly, he cuts through theological infighting by having the scholarly disputants show up side by side in "the sphere of the sun" in heaven—a place of reconciliation in which "Aquinas the Dominican extols the holiness of Francis of Assisi; Bonaventure the Franciscan extols the holiness of Dominic"; and "St. Thomas shines and circles side by side with Sigier of Brabant, whose opponent he was in the schools, and with them too is Joachim of Flora, who is pointed out to Dante by his opponent

Bonaventure." As one who seems to have studied at both Dominican and Franciscan schools, Dante "probably amused as well as delighted himself by thus proclaiming the heavenly concord of the doctors, for he must have known as much as most people of the disagreement of theologians." If ever a thinker in the church practiced boundary-crossing as a healthy theological discipline, it was Dante.

A Triune Salvation

Dante begins his poem with the confessional midlife crisis: "Once upon a time he had known the right way, *la diritta via, la verace via;* but he lost it, let it get overgrown and rank." But as we get deeper into his epic poem, he mounts a sharp critique on his own irresponsible devotion to romantic love, his own intellectual pride and his own loyalty to party and to Florence. Dante the poet makes these character traits of Dante the pilgrim look less and less appropriate as he nears the Beatific Vision of God's own person. In a stunning moment toward the end of *Purgatorio* Dante meets Beatrice again after a long separation. But the tender scene the reader expects (after all, it was Beatrice who arranged for this whole supernatural tour, in the interest of Dante's salvation) does not come. Instead, shockingly, Beatrice lashes out, accusing Dante the pilgrim of gross sin and unfaithfulness to her memory in the period after her death. It is simply amazing that Dante would write this scene.

We will never know the exact nature of the sin. He does not tell us, but we may guess that he lost the cardinal virtue of hope—which is the very definition of hell—and even considered suicide. But Dante's midlife sin was no single sinful act. Rather, it was a complex of habits and characteristics leading him off of the "straight and narrow road" and on to the broad way to damnation. These habits stemmed from his "disordered loves," his pursuit of right ends—love, knowledge, citizenship—by wrong means and to wrong degrees.

Having used his own poem to critique himself on all three of these fronts, Dante comes to the central question of his life: if God's grace could free him from these partial loves, how could he then, with all of his talents, best serve God and love—and lead—others? To answer this question, he tells a story about the wrong sort of leader, the character Ulysses from Virgil's epic *The Aeneid*.

Ulysses, in an imagined dialogue with Dante, tells what had happened to him after the exploits recorded by Virgil. Back from the Trojan War, Ulysses became bored with normal life and convinced his shipmates through his powerful rhetoric to abandon their families and sail with him once more—to their collective doom. This last quest was the very epitome of a leader's selfish abuse of his exceptional talent with words and with people, and it deprived his nation of their king. In fact, Dante's portrayal of Ulysses is clearly also a portrayal of himself: a talented, charismatic person who is good with words, but who has misused them in idolatrous service to romantic love, philosophy and party. Now he must decide how to use his gifts properly.

A New Kind of Leader

As a mature, brilliant and well-educated leader in exile who is still well-placed in Italian society, Dante has (1) access to the ear of those involved in the factionalism, (2) the rhetorical and poetic ability to put things in persuasively striking ways, and (3) the long experience of exile in which to think about how to frame his persuasion.

The climactic moment comes in *Paradiso* 17 and 18. There Dante meets his great-great-grandfather Cacciaguida—a martyr in the Second Crusade. Cacciaguida offers Dante a "new crusade," a war of peacemaking and perspective to be waged not with the sword, but pen: he is to describe for the good of the world all the people he has met in the three afterworlds—their stories, sins, virtues. Through their stories, Cacciaguida is saying, all parties will learn a new and compelling "universal view," indeed, a God's-eye view, compared with which their petty squabbles are like so many paths to misery both for themselves and for those caught in their intrigues and vendettas. Dante accepts Cacciaguida's proffered quest, thus inheriting a mantle of prophecy from the Old Testament prophets themselves.

And so the author Dante, in one brilliant flash, illuminates both his salvation at last from all forms of self-interest and party-interest, and the purpose and vision of this, his greatest literary work. For all the wrong paths, disordered loves and wrecked lives we find in the *Comedy*, if we stick with Dante through the three realms of the dead, we come at last to this calling: to rise above pettiness and be a new kind of person, and a new kind of leader.

Margery Kempe

WEEPING OVER JESUS' BODY

AND PRAYING HIS HEART

In 1373 was born a remarkable person, destined to become a flashpoint of controversy. Her emotionally expressive piety would attract crowds, divide religious leaders and expose her to persecution for supposed heresy. Today, as many have reconnected with the humanity of Christ and the emotions of his suffering and death through Mel Gibson's movie *The Passion of the Christ,* this "weeping saint" can help us explore the medieval roots of cross-centered piety.

Margery Kempe came into the world in Bishop's Lynn, England, the daughter of the town's five-time mayor. Her eventual husband, John Kempe, was also a well-known figure in town, though he was often troubled by debt. By both birth and marriage, then, she belonged to the middle class. On the other hand, she was illiterate—though not entirely uneducated or unfamiliar with books; she had clergy and monastic friends read aloud to her. She was also a woman, which automatically put her at a disadvantage in the social world of the Middle Ages. And although she became an intensely devoted

Christian, she was never a nun. She was a layperson, a business-woman and a mother.

All of those qualities lowered her spiritual status in the English church of the late Middle Ages where the ideal Christian—the person who everyone figured enjoyed a close connection to God—was a literate man, cloistered in a monastery or convent, who abstained from sex, kept his hands clean from the things of the marketplace, and devoted his time to prayer and good works. Margery Kempe was thus an unlikely saint, and in fact the only reason we do know about her is that she dictated her life's story to several priests. Even then, her book was lost for some six hundred years. It was rediscovered only in 1934, hidden away in the library of an old British Catholic family.

The Book of Margery Kempe is several things: the first extant biography in the English language; a precious, rare window into the piety of a late-medieval English laywoman; and an illuminating spiritual guide to disciplines and forms of prayer. Ironically, it is now *because* she was an illiterate, low status, married lay mother that many modern Christians—especially modern Christian women—have become fascinated with her. They want to know how this unlettered townswoman gained, in her time, a reputation as a holy person of spiritual power and discernment.

Distanced but Devoted

In 1373 Bishop's Lynn was a bustling port town with a cosmopolitan flavor. Its merchants traded profitably with other North European ports, and more and more citizens were aspiring to something approaching modern middle-class status. While many still labored on the land, the old feudal system with its serfs and warrior nobility was crumbling. And though most folks were still illiterate, reading and writing were on the rise among laypeople, increasingly educated in church schools. Change was in the air.

Fourteenth-century England had inherited a curiously divided religious scene. For some time the parish church had failed to meet most of the spiritual needs of the people. Whereas the early medieval

Mass had been a powerful, intimate and participatory experience, the service was now becoming remoter. As early as Charlemagne's ninth century, Latin had become a scholar's tongue, inaccessible to most layfolk. Yet the service continued in that language. The central ritual of the bread and wine no longer drew the congregation into a personal participation in the saving mystery of Christ. As the centuries passed, many people avoided the heavy pre-Communion penitential requirements by receiving the sacraments infrequently. Four times a year at Christmas, Easter, Pentecost and the festival of their parish church's saint's day seemed ample, and many received only once a year, at Easter. Sunday after Sunday, the Mass was presented to passive audiences as a sacred drama, an allegorical ritual act to be seen and meditated upon, rather than participated in. Week after week, the mystical component of liturgy—the promised *union* with God in Christ through the Lord's Supper—was experienced only by the officiating priests and bishops. Not surprisingly, clergy became increasingly a professional class, separate from and powerful over ordinary, nonordained folk.

In the high medieval period (1000–1300), the distancing trend continued. The altar table receded further and further from view until it finally became lodged against the east wall of the church. The bishop or priest, who formerly had faced the people across the altar, now turned his back on them. From the twelfth century on, a "rood screen" separated the altar area from the main area of the sanctuary, so that the only thing most people could glimpse was the elevation, when the priest raised the consecrated bread above his head.

In the face of these changes, the English layfolk of 1373 were seeking other ways to an experience of union with God in Christ. The road many chose ran through intimate devotional exercises centered on the humanity of Christ. Under the encouragement of the "preaching friars" (Franciscans, Dominicans and Augustinians), fourteenth-century English folks took the Gospels as their canon within a canon. They chewed and savored its vivid stories in their hearts and imaginations, ruminating deeply on its scenes and entering them spiritually through their own emotional responses. Late-medieval English devotional writers wrote manuals, meditations and poems marked by deep feeling, often focused on the sufferings of Christ.

In this, English devotion followed the path laid out by Anselm of Canterbury (1033–1109), the French Bernard of Clairvaux (d. 1153) and the Italian Francis of Assisi (1181–1226). In his *Prayers and Meditations,* Anselm had prayed plaintively to Christ for forgiveness "for not having kissed the place of the wounds where the nails pierced, for not having sprinkled with tears of joy the scars." Bernard had contributed an intense Marian devotion in mystical bridal language about the relationship between the believer and Christ, rooted in the Song of Songs. And Francis and his followers had spread a Christ-centered devotion (including Francis's special emphases on Christ's infancy and passion) to the towns where they preached.

Francis's disciples did more than anyone to bring the humanity and sufferings of Christ into the mainstream of devotion. From portable outdoor pulpits and within chapels whose walls were often covered with life-sized passion scenes, the preaching friars stressed as never before the emotions of Jesus himself during his ordeal and prescribed the answering emotions of the worshiper. They also championed an ascetic lifestyle modeled on Paul, who said, "I fill up in my flesh what is still lacking in regard to Christ's afflictions, for the sake of his body, which is the church" (Col 1:24). Especially in England, the centuries between Anselm and 1373 had seen a flood of passion poetry, characterized by "an intense, intimate relationship to Christ, deep emotionality tempered by a reflective framework, vivid details of the passion, and the fact that Christ's suffering signifies his personal love for each individual, demanding a reciprocal response." In the late-medieval heyday of passion piety that followed, monks, nuns and layfolk alike tried to imitate Jesus' passion or to experience something of the same extreme suffering as had their Lord. Margery's account of her life brings this passion piety home vividly to modern readers—not as the rarified exercises of the cloistered saint, but as the earnest, conflicted, shocking and life-giving experiences of an ordinary layperson.

No Plaster Saint

Margery begins her book at a point of crisis. Some time in the mid-1390s, after the birth of her first child, she descended into a postpartum depression that took her into madness and very nearly to suicide. At the brink of this abyss, Jesus, "in a mantle of purple silk," came and sat "upon her bedside, looking upon her with so blessed a countenance that she was strengthened in all her spirits." The Lord gently chided her: "Daughter, why have you forsaken me, and I never forsook you?" At once, she regained her reason.

In the story of many saints, this would have been the moment of glorious and conclusive conversion. But Margery is brutally honest: Yes, she gained from this miraculous vision and healing a lifelong desire to know and to follow Jesus. But for several years following her vision, she did not live with any kind of Christian consistency. Old habits of pride and materialism pulled her away from God, and she launched into business to support her social aspirations. In her own words (she refers to herself throughout the book in the third person): "She was enormously envious of her neighbors if they were dressed as well as she was. Her whole desire was to be respected by people. She would not learn her lesson from a single chastening experience, nor be content with the worldly goods that God had sent her—as her husband was—but always craved more and more. And then, out of pure covetousness, and in order to maintain her pride, she took up brewing."

The brewery operation failed, and Margery started a mill. Soon this venture failed too. She found herself returning to God in desperate prayer. And she had a series of spiritual experiences that gave her another taste of heaven. These built her up again in the faith, and she got on a kind of spiritual high. She resolved to live in celibacy, in imitation of the holy nuns and monks, and focus entirely on God as they did. Of course, it wasn't that easy. When she tried to get her long-suffering husband to renegotiate their marriage contract, he not surprisingly "insisted on his rights." Celibacy wouldn't be an option at least for some time.

This hindrance aside, Margery felt spiritually powerful—indeed invulnerable to sin. As she tells it, "She hated the joys of the world. She felt no rebellion in her flesh. She was so strong—as she thought—that she feared no devil in hell, for she performed such great bodily penance."

The older, wiser Margery knew what had come next. What happened was that she suddenly fell into a strong temptation. And ironically, considering her desire to live in a chaste marriage, this temptation came in the form of lust for a man who was not her husband: "A man whom she liked said to her on St Margaret's Eve before evensong that, for anything, he would sleep with her and enjoy the lust of his body." As she tells the sordid tale, she is again stunningly honest, revealing damning details few would willingly share. She proceeded to have several contacts with this man, who at first told her he wanted to have an affair with her. Finally, consumed with lust, Margery went to meet him in secret, telling him she wanted to sleep with him. But at the last minute, he backed out. As she would later come to see this series of events, Jesus rescued her from her illicit passion, drawing her back to him. Most importantly, Margery believed God used this time of temptation to break her of the horrible sin of spiritual pride, which was for medievals the fountain of all other sins, far worse than mere lust.

Having weathered those early storms, Margery did at last begin a lifelong habit of intensive prayer and meditation, and began to grow into a steady and mature devotion of Christ. Also, at the age of forty (in the summer of 1413), after having borne fourteen children, Margery's struggle to live a life free of sexual intercourse concluded successfully when she prevailed on John to take a vow of celibacy with her.

Disturbing the Peace

Margery then began extensive travels on pilgrimage. She wanted, for one thing, to get out and meet and fellowship with other spiritually minded folks. Pilgrimage was a common technique for medieval laywomen, in particular, who wanted to expand their spiritual and intellectual horizons, since the social circles of women were more limited than for men and educational avenues were entirely closed to them. But deeper than this, like so many of her time she wanted to get as close as she physically could to the historical Jesus.

Most late-medieval adults went on pilgrimage at some time in their lives, if only a day trip to a regional saint's shrine. Between the eleventh and fifteenth centuries, hundreds of thousands made the long, expensive and dangerous pilgrimage to the Holy Land, and from the late 1200s on, the Jerusalem tour featured a series of special locations connected to Jesus' life: the place where Simon of Cyrene was forced to take the cross, the spot where Mary swooned on meeting her son, the house of Mary. So powerful was the experience of these places that people began setting up replicas of them back home, starting the tradition of the Stations of the Cross.

When Margery took one of these Franciscan tours, she "wept and sobbed as plenteously as though she had seen our Lord with her bodily eyes suffering his passion at that time. . . . And when they came up on to the Mount of Calvary, she fell down because she could not stand or kneel, but writhed and wrestled with her body, spreading her arms out wide, and cried with a loud voice as though her heart would have burst apart, for in the city of her soul, she saw truly and freshly how our Lord was crucified."

The emotional intensity of this Jerusalem experience became a spiritual motif for her, weaving itself into the fabric of her life. Forever after, whenever she saw or heard something that reminded her of Jesus, she wept and cried out loudly and uncontrollably. This often happened in church services, when she heard the preacher talk about Jesus' suffering for his people or when she saw the bread and the wine being blessed and lifted up by the priest, transformed into Christ's body and blood.

Obviously Margery's antics proved disturbing for many, and they repeatedly got her in trouble—some priests even had her barred from their church services. In fact she was herself embarrassed by her weeping and prayed more than once that God would take it away from her. Surprisingly, however, "preachers generally tolerated her loud sobbing; they simply waited for her to quiet down and then went on." Indeed, if not the parish priests, then at least many of the itinerant preaching friars might well have appreciated her expressive response, since they typically preached from the Gospel texts in lively, emotional ways. The best

preachers of her day were known for drawing large crowds and stimulating "explosive reactions of repentance and religious exaltation." (Not
too different from, say, American revivalism of the frontier era.)

Many in that time also saw Margery's tears as much more than a momentary, uncontrolled response, but rather as a special sign of God's work
in her—a "gift of tears." It is hard for us to understand how spiritually
valuable and desirable such an experience of tears seemed then. In fact,
though at times mortified by her inability *not* to cry in public, Kempe took
on "intercessory weeping" as a kind of vocation. At one point she believed
Christ himself spoke to her, ordaining her to pray for the whole world and
saying that many would be saved through her tearful prayers.

Dallying with the Lord

Whatever else they were, Margery's tears were tied strongly to her particular devotion to the humanity of Christ. Wherever she went, the ordinary things she saw reminded her constantly of the events of Jesus' life.
Margery "saw Christ, not as an ancient historical figure, but in the fields
and streets; she saw him in all people—especially 'male children' and
'seemly men.' . . . The events of his life and passion took place eternally
in the streets of Lynn as truly as in Palestine." We see this special affin-
ity for Christ's vulnerable, suffering humanity at many points in her
book. Once, for example, her confessor came to her and, finding her
weeping, said, "Damsel, Jesus is dead long since." She responded to him,
"Sir, his death is as fresh to me as if He had died this same day, and so,
methinketh, it ought to be to you and to all Christian people." I think of
how the story of the crucifixion affected me when I read C. S. Lewis's
death-of-Aslan scene in *The Lion, the Witch, and the Wardrobe* for the
first time in light of the gospel. Suddenly the story of the incarnate Son
of God, which I had heard so many times until I had become dulled to it,
was *fresh* to me. I imagine this to be something like what Margery experienced again and again in her daily life.

Margery did not spend all her time crying. She also developed a vibrant prayer life. She describes often experiencing inner conversations
with Christ—and at times with Mary. A favorite expression that Margery

uses for some of her times of intimate prayer was "dalliance." This homey, down-to-earth term, meaning "warm, affectionate conversation between two people—often two lovers," was Margery's way of pointing to "the rich freedom, the perfect understanding, which expresses the joy of true friendship with Christ, and in Christ." In these times of intimate prayer she would sometimes imagine herself in Bible scenes, for example helping Mary at the birth of Jesus—boiling water, bringing towels, comforting her and witnessing Jesus as a baby. This, too, was part of the spiritual tradition she had inherited, especially from the Franciscans.

A word more on Mary. We hear Margery praying to "the Mother of God . . . amiable lady, humble lady, loving lady," and beseeching her, "Please offer thanks and praise to the blessed Trinity for love of me," and some of us get nervous. Yet it's worth remembering that historically many Christians such as Margery have not found that their devotion to Mary detracted from their devotion to the Trinity. Rather, Mary's story has captivated them with the central, flabbergasting fact of Christianity: that God himself came down and chose to be conceived and carried to term and born the son of a real, living woman. Mary bore our savior, suckled him, clothed him, taught him and followed him. Then, at the cross, she sorrowed over him. And then at last, in the upper room, she participated in the birth of his church. No wonder his church has dwelt on her so lovingly. She reminds us that Jesus arrived on this earth the same way we all do: through pregnancy, labor, birth, infancy. And that fact elevates not only all humanity, but especially all womankind. In the incarnation, as in all human births, nothing happened without the loving, sacrificial participation of a woman. "Be it unto me according to thy word," said Mary. So the angel called her "highly favored." Elizabeth called her "blessed among women." And much later, Martin Luther found her the chief example of human obedience to divine command.

What may be even more disturbing to some readers than the Marian content of some of Margery's visions is the very *fact* of them. They may seem delusions of an unbalanced mind. But Margery tells us that she knew these visionary conversations were usually more imaginative exercises than real visions. She was not seeing these things as we would see a hallucination. They were simply a familiar and expected part of her devotional life—how *she* connected with God. And when she engaged in this kind of vivid prayer, she was acting within an accepted medieval tradition of "imaginative meditation" that would come to fruition in the sixteenth-century Jesuit founder Ignatius Loyola's *Spiritual Exercises*—still used today by countless Christians worldwide in retreats and personal devotions. If we want to write off Margery for the vividness of her prayer life, then we need to discard a longstanding mode of visual/imaginative piety along with her.

Discernment and the Daily Grind

Along with visionary experiences, Margery also began to receive prophetic understandings about other lives and events. But consistently, whenever her prayer brought her to a prophetic sense on some matter, she battled doubt. Unlike so many who become convinced they are "hearing from God," Margery was always careful about such directions and premonitions. Because of her own sin or the deception of the devil, she knew well enough her own capacity for misinterpreting what she thought she had heard from God. "As a prophet," Martin Thornton concludes, "she is extraordinarily free from arrogance."

Her usual practice when she received a spiritual impression about something was to go to others whom she trusted as spiritual mentors and ask them to test what she thought she had heard in light of their wisdom and their scriptural knowledge. (She herself also, like many illiterate English folk of her time, clearly had both reverence for Scripture and an ample store of Scripture passages in her retentive memory. Throughout her book we find allusions both to Scripture and to a variety of known devotional writers, all of which she would have heard from preachers, monks and friends willing to read to her.) She kept careful track of when such prophetic words did not come true—when she had been confused or led astray—as well as when they did. Again, this is an instance of Margery's honesty—one of the things that make her book such a compelling read to a modern church culture that is too often dishonest with itself.

Margery's devotional life was not all about visions, imaginations and prophetic revelations. More central was the way she always brought each of her troubles or concerns, no matter how small, to Jesus in prayer. And her book contains, along with joyful passages describing fulfilled prayers, accounts of frustrated prayer. Among these are several instances in which she heard specific directions for her life but failed to obey—thus suffering hurt and a sense of distance from God. A life that includes such accounts can be both refreshing and challenging to read— at least for mere mortals willing to assess their own spiritual life in an appropriately critical mode.

Contrary to the opinions of her medieval and modern critics, Margery's visions and prophecies, like the weeping and intimate prayer life, do not seem to be the products of an imbalanced mind. I have worshiped in charismatic church settings where exuberant, emotional worship and words of prophecy from the congregation were the norm. Once in a while in those settings you run into imbalanced individuals who interrupt the service by yelling and crying and calling attention to themselves. What you generally find with such folks is that they are trapped within their own minds and emotions. They have become convinced that everything in the church and the world has its ultimate reference in them—their troubles, their spiritual experiences and so forth.

Margery doesn't strike me like that. Really, she knew her own spiritual life too well to think herself the center of the universe. Unlike the cloistered supermystics of her age, Margery's spirituality was of the gritty, everyday type. While the cloistered mystics followed prescribed steps—seeking first purgation from sin, then spiritual illumination and finally union with God—Margery practiced a hodgepodge of spiritual disciplines and prayer forms in the midst of her busy life. She knew and admitted that she wasn't always climbing the ladder of devotion. Rather, she went up and down in her prayer life, sometimes slipping back and struggling with temptation. I'd say that sounds a lot more like the prayer life I experience. Throughout her book, she refers to herself humbly as "this creature." Though her book contains passages, to be sure, clearly intended to vindicate herself, what emerges by the end is a portrait of a down-to-earth, struggling regular person who often needed forgiveness, and whose peak spiritual experiences were tempered by the fallenness of her earthly nature. We can read her—and I think this was her intention—without the pressure of feeling we don't measure up to yet another saintly mystic with his or her strenuous teachings about ascetic purgation. Thornton concludes that Margery's book should be read today as a guide to the many forms of prayer and devotion appropriate to the active life of those unable to retreat to monastic silence and solitude. This is prayer for those who sweat out the spiritual life in the workplace, the marketplace and the busy home. Margery's record of her own devotional life shows us the phases of prayer in the midst of life's challenges and failures, rather than a single, fixed unattainable ideal.

Persecution and Community

Soon, ordinary folk from her hometown and the surrounding area became impressed by Margery's life of prayer and devotion and her seeming special connection with God in Christ. They came to her as a holy woman and an intercessor, for direction and prayer. They trusted her devotional advice, and as the accuracy of many of her prophetic understandings became known, they increasingly sought these from her as well.

Both at home and away from home, however, Margery was always dogged by controversy. All along her thousands of miles of pilgrimage, opinion was divided about her. As she traveled to famous shrines in England, to Jerusalem, Assisi, Rome and Santiago de Compostela (in modern-day Spain), she continued to weep and cry loudly every time she attended Mass, and she was often criticized and even threatened because of this behavior. She was called a disturber of the peace and a charlatan. She was arrested several times and examined as a heretic. At Canterbury she was chased by a crowd threatening to burn her as a Lollard—that is, a follower of the pre-Protestant reformer John Wycliffe (1330–1384), who pitted Scripture against the church in fighting various clerical and theological corruptions of his day. (Margery was examined and proved orthodox on all counts because of her devotion to the sacrament, her frequent confession, her fasting, her pilgrimages and her veneration of holy images—all of which were questioned in Lollard writings.)

In the face of such persecution, she retained a remarkably solid sense of vocation. One day, as she was being marched toward the English town of Beverly, under arrest on suspicion of heresy, bystanders offered her kindly-meant advice: "Woman, give up this life that you lead, and go and spin, and card wool, as other women do, and do not suffer so much shame and so much unhappiness." Margery responded, "I do not suffer as much sorrow as I would do [that is, as much as I want to do] for our Lord's love, for I only suffer cutting words, and our merciful Lord Christ Jesus . . . suffered hard strokes, bitter scourgings, and shameful death at the last."

At Lambeth Palace in London, however, Archbishop Arundel affirmed Margery's calling, granting her permission to wear white clothes, a sign of her so-called new virginity. He also granted her permission to receive weekly Communion and to choose her own confessor. These were special, unusual privileges that were challenged repeatedly throughout the rest of her life.

Margery also found churchly support in the local pastorate and monastic establishments, forming warm relationships with an array of priests and friars who heard her confession, helped her discern God's work in her life, read devotional books to her and supported her against her detractors. A number of these Godly men functioned as "spiritual directors." These included the learned Alan of Lynn, a friar from her hometown, who held a Cambridge Doctor of Divinity degree and had authored a number of influential books. Alan was Margery's constant friend and champion throughout her life. At one point Margery and Alan were forbidden to see each other for a long time. When they were finally reunited at a dinner at a noblewoman's house in Bishop's Lynn, Margery rejoiced, "There was a dinner of great joy and gladness, much more ghostly [spiritual] than bodily, for it was sauced and savored with tales of Holy Scriptures. And then he [Alan] gave the said creature a pair of knives, in token that he would stand with her in God's cause, as he had done beforetime."

We can see that Margery's spiritual life was never the kind of Lone Ranger affair we may associate with cloistered medieval mystics (or modern charismatics of the more intense sort). Though she was emotionally focused, she was not individualistic—turning, rather, to her clerical and monastic friends again and again both for fellowship and for help with spiritual discernment. In other words, despite her clearly strong, independent (and some thought, obnoxious) personality, Margery lived her spiritual life in accountable, joyous interaction with a network of godly friends.

Margery's story can and should make us yearn for such churchly accountability—not instead of, but as a necessary and corrective check on, our individual experience. American evangelicals have worked hard in the past two centuries to continue a move arguably started back in the Reformation, stripping away all the traditional, communal dimensions of their religion—in other words, all mediation—leaving the individual Christian face to face with God. This is often an intensely lonely and terrifying thing. But this is not Margery's way, despite all of her direct, unmediated religious experience.

After her many pilgrimages, Margery settled back in her birth town of Lynn, where she had more visions and conversations with the Lord. In one particularly vivid series of meditations, she imagined herself present at the events of Christ's passion—right through to the resurrection. During these years back home, she deepened and developed in her Christian life, especially in the area of practical charity. She began to desire to kiss lepers, and she helped a woman suffering, as she had once suffered, from a postpartum psychosis. She also now was reunited with her husband, who was incapacitated by illness, and she began to act as his caretaker. This was a difficult role that demanded a lot of patience, and we hear her ambivalence about it as she complains frankly, for example, about the huge amounts of laundry she had to do after he became doubly incontinent in his final years.

The last few chapters of Margery's autobiography, tacked on years after she had dictated the rest, begin with her prayers for one of her sons—then records her joy at his conversion from a dissolute lifestyle.

After this son died (shortly after his conversion, and around the time of her husband's death—probably 1431), she decided to accompany her widowed daughter-in-law back to her childhood home in Danzig, Prussia. (It seems Margery couldn't stay still for long.) The final chapters detail her travels—old and infirm—back from Danzig to England by way of the major pilgrimage sites of Wilsnack and Aachen. These were exhausting and harrowing trips. She traveled poor, often alone, at times in fear for her life, and repeatedly rebuked and abandoned by other pilgrims for her "weird" religious behavior. Then, her account simply stops. There is no artful conclusion wrapping everything up. It just ends.

God in Flesh and Bone

At the start of the chapter I made a connection between Margery and Mel Gibson's *The Passion of the Christ*. What was it about Gibson's movie that has galvanized so many modern (or if you like, postmodern) Western Protestants? After all, of representations of Christ's life there has been no end. Why did this one, in particular, speak so deeply to so many? I think there are two answers to this question, and that both of them can help us understand and benefit from the life of this odd English mystic, Margery Kempe.

First, Western Christians today need to hear Margery and the medievals on this: we tend to hurry over the incarnation—seeing it as a necessary step to get Jesus to the cross, where he can die as a substitutionary atonement for our sins. In general, we miss out on the rich historical theological resources on creation and incarnation, and we focus instead on sin and salvation. Margery certainly dwelled on the passion and even the resurrection—that can be a bridge over which we walk to meet her—but what captivated her most was not so much the atonement wrought by Christ's death as the fact that God has *really become human* and has *really been tempted and suffered in all the ways we have*. In other words, Jesus' stark human suffering affected her most not by illuminating the legal, substitutionary mechanism of salvation, but by revealing the unimaginable love of a God who would go to such extremes to reach us—even taking on the deepest physical and emotional sufferings to which we fallen folk are heir.

This acute awareness of the incarnation was no theologically fuzzy, inward-turned "mysticism." Medieval scholar Ellen M. Ross argues that, on the contrary, "the believers' alliance of compassion with Jesus enabled them to perceive Jesus in other humans and to act compassionately for their benefit." The resulting works of mercy and practices of confessing one's social sins, Ross concludes, helped build a strong, humane center holding together medieval society. Surely we need something like this again.

A second reason for connecting with Margery is that her affective piety may be a medicine for a peculiar ailment of many (post-)modern Christians: the spiritual torpor and indiscipline induced by lives of material gratification and "amusing ourselves to death." To such inaction and spiritual flabbiness, the ascetic discipline of an Antony or a Gregory may seem (I think, correctly) to offer an intriguing tonic. But our modern malaise—termed by philosophers *anomie*—involves not just spiritual inaction, but also spiritual and emotional *distance*. By this I mean a sort of flat-lining of the spirit. We may so easily fall into an attitude that says, "There may be a God. There may be a Jesus who died for our sins. But though I believe these things, they do not touch my heart." How different this is from Margery, who when the archbishop of York asked her the rough question, "Why do you weep so, woman?" replied firmly, "Sir, you shall wish some day that you had wept as sorely as I."

Margery's life and book remind us that such intensely emotional piety focused on the humanity (and thus also deity) of Christ was not merely an inward-focused "kick." Both intuitive emotion (her weeping) and practical imitation (her late-life acts of mercy) can infuse wisdom into our very hearts and bodies in ways that speculative theology can never do.

Reclaiming the Physical

Finally, among the varied aspects of our human nature, our emotions seem especially closely tied with our physical bodies. We use the same words, "feeling" or "being touched," for the physical senses and for emotional experiences. But reading Margery's book makes me ask, Where has the sense of the spiritual importance of touch or physicality gone in today's culture? Are these human senses now allowed to communicate anything true or spiritual to us? We have plenty of the visual in our TV- and movie-soaked culture, and even in our churches. But how often do we experience anything spiritually significant through touch? The most intense, ecstatic touch-experiences, those of our sexuality, have been devalued and dehumanized through obsessive attention and being made into the commodities of the impersonal marketplace. I think that like *The Passion of the Christ* Margery's life of devotion and the whole English mystical tradition can help draw today's Christians back to the sort of visible, physical devotion epitomized in the medieval pilgrimage.

In the midnineties I was giving a lecture on Pentecostalism at an evangelical seminary in New England. I was describing the huge influxes of eager believers that traveled every day to the Azusa Street Revival in 1906, launching Pentecostalism, and the similar crowds that flocked to the modern Toronto Airport Vineyard Revival and the Brownsville/Pensecola revivals. One student put up his hand and asked with skepticism in his voice, "Why do Pentecostals and charismatics feel that it's so important to actually go to the place where a revival is supposedly happening, to *'bring back'* that revival to their home churches?"

At the time, I didn't have an answer to that. Now, having encountered Margery and studied her context, it seems to me that these trips to modern charismatic revivals resonate with medieval pilgrimages. People have always gone to places where God is reputed to be moving in a special way *because they recognize the essentially personal, visual, physical nature of this historic faith of Christianity.* That is, they see that the God who incarnated himself in history as the first-century Jewish Jesus continues to make himself incarnate, though imperfectly, in the *body of Christ*—which is his people, his "living stones" (a very tactile image), wherever he chooses to build them together.

We may not venerate saints today or go on pilgrimages to seek out their relics (which were the focal point of many medieval pilgrimages), but we do crave the kind of contact with Christ that comes to us in special gatherings of his people—his body—where he seems to be doing things uniquely "for our time and place." That we can come away from those gatherings *changed* reflects the fact that the church is the continued incarnation of Christ.

Of course, we will only consider the coolness or emotional flatness of much modern devotion a problem if we agree that our emotions and desires *should* come into play in our faith life. If we do, then we find ourselves in the camp of the "Christian eudaemonists" (the Greek *eudaemonia* refers to well-being, blessedness or fulfilled desires). The classical philosophers asked, what makes humans truly happy? The Christian eudaemonists have answered: we are happy when God transforms and fulfills our desires, by leading us into the bliss of his loving presence. So in his *Confessions* Augustine, the dean of Christian eudaemonists, can pray with fervor, "Inebriate me, O God!" From Augustine through the Middle Ages and on to such modern groups such as the Puritans, the Pietists, and John Wesley's and Jonathan Edwards's early evangelicals, Christian thinkers and saints have picked up this emphasis on the transformation and fulfillment of spiritual desire. Not all Christians share this emphasis, but it is to be found deep in the fabric of Christian history, through all ages of the church.

Of course, other sorts of emotion do show up in our churches: whipped up, self-centered, spiritually and morally useless. But in Kempe we meet a different sort of religious emotion, rooted in a "full boisterous" acceptance of Jesus' real human nature. Her spirituality sprang from a theology that bled to death before her eyes. It drove her not only to strong feelings, but also to strong spiritual action. In our own time, the vision of Gibson's *Passion of the Christ* lies in the same medieval tradition of piety that formed Margery Kempe. If only we could come to the same balanced, physical/emotional/cognitive devotion to the three-person God and the two-natured Christ. For the help toward that goal that Margery gave many in her own time, I would say she is still well worth reading today.

5

John Amos Comenius

LEARNING DIVERSITY

AND TEACHING PEACE

In the best surviving portrait of John Amos Comenius (1592–1670), his heavy-lidded, deeply lined eyes brood. First, he seems to be thinking moodily or anxiously about some crisis—perhaps the dreadful strife of the Thirty Years' War, which had driven him and his people from their homelands of Bohemia and Moravia, or the appalling state of education in Europe, which he was to reform so successfully that he would become known as the father of modern education. Second, as bishop of the Unity of the Brethren—the scattered remnant of Jan Hus's followers that would become the Moravian Church—he seems to dwell with mother-bird-like nurture on his flock.

The gaze of Bishop Comenius seems to communicate something else too. Beneath the sorrow and concern smolder two passions. One is a love for knowledge and for truth. For Comenius was a man of great intellectual curiosity, and coming to adulthood during the dizzying knowledge explosion called the scientific revolution, he was captivated by the possibilities of human learning. Like Dante in his *Convivio* phase, something deep in Comenius's makeup wanted to know everything about everything. Early in his life, he had fallen in love with the new empiricism of Francis Bacon, through which all of the world's secrets seemed open to discovery, classification and control. But deeper still lay Comenius's love for Jesus Christ. We read this in his allegory, *The Labyrinth of the World and the Paradise of the Heart,* which sets against all the proud vanities of human culture the "one needful thing": a personal relationship with Jesus, experienced in a worshipping community.

Brethren Born and Bred

John Amos Comenius was born the youngest of five children to a financially secure miller and his wife in Moravia—part of what is now the Czech Republic. Their town, Nivnice, lay on a rolling plain near a low mountain range. John's father Martin was a well-respected man in the local congregation of the Unity of the Brethren, and naturally John was raised Brethren and got his early education in a Brethren school.

The Brethren was an old evangelical communion with roots among the followers of Jan Hus (1369–1415), a pre-Protestant reformer from Bohemia who was condemned by the Council of Constance and burned at the stake on July 6, 1415. Hus had taught the importance of personal piety, holiness and fidelity to the Bible, and he had critiqued the popes and bishops where he felt they contradicted the teachings and example of Christ. In fact, his Bethlehem Chapel, where thousands came to hear him, was adorned with paintings contrasting the behavior of the popes and of Christ—no wonder he was martyred! In a radical departure from traditional teaching, Hus had insisted that church hierarchs were not needed for salvation, as God alone was head of the church, and he condemned the sale of papal indulgences (long before Luther) and allowed communicants to partake of both the bread and wine in communion, against church practice.

After Hus's death, a preacher of nonresistance and church-state separation named Peter Chelcicky (ca. 1390–ca. 1456) organized the Unity of the Brethren out of the martyr's followers. Then in 1458, twenty-five years before the birth of Martin Luther, a saintly man named Gregory, a nephew of the archbishop of Prague, assumed leadership and relocated the little band to eastern Bohemia. In 1467 the Unity formed themselves as a separate denomination (though they still preferred to think of themselves as a corrective movement) by ordaining three men among them as bishops.

Like the Anabaptists, the Brethren focused not on a distinctive doctrine, but rather on a practical code. While Luther and other reformers dwelt on Paul, the Brethren loved the Sermon on the Mount and "the tender Epistles of St. John." Luther praised the Brethren's *Ratio Disciplinae,* its church constitution, which was less a doctrinal confession (though the Brethren were orthodox) and more a guide to a peaceful, ecumenical and disciplined communal life. For pursuing this life and refusing involvement with all secular power, this band of disciples was persecuted severely—several of their number were even burned at the stake. Nonetheless, the blood of the martyrs proved "seed," and by the early sixteenth century, the Unity numbered some hundred thousand members and exerted an influence in Bohemia and Moravia that rivaled that of the Roman Catholics and Utraquists. (The latter was another group of Hussite descendants, who made certain compromises with the Catholic majority.)

Acquainted with Grief

Raised "in the nurture and admonition of the Lord" among these folks, in 1604, when he was just twelve, John lost both of his parents and two of his sisters—likely to plague. This was one year before William Shakespeare (1564–1616) wrote *Macbeth,* five years before Galileo Galilei (1564–1642) built his first refracting telescope and seven years before King James I of England (1566–1625) published his Bible edition. It was also the dawning of the scientific revolution and the accompanying upheaval in thought and social structure known as the Enlightenment.

With no parents to care for him, Comenius was sent away to live with his aunt in the nearby town of Straznice. Then began a period of bitter hardship. His education was no longer the business of loving parents and fellow congregants. Now instead, John entered elementary school—a system not only outmoded but cruel. Like almost all such schools in Europe, what Comenius called "slaughter-houses of minds," this was a place "where a hatred of literature and books is contracted, where ten or more years are spent in learning what might be acquired in one, where what ought to be poured in gently is violently forced in and beaten in," and where children parroted words whose meanings were never clearly explained.

Not just Comenius but almost all the children of Europe were subjected to programs that ignored the differences between children of various ages, requiring all alike, for example, to learn Latin while reading classical texts far beyond their comprehension. The usual method consisted of a combination of rote memorization (without reference to anything within the child's empirical experience) and brutal corporal punishment. One contemporary observer said that early seventeenth-century schools "seemed to have been the invention of some wicked spirit, the enemy of the human race." Comenius's elementary school experience, though excruciating, proved a moment of calling: it planted in him a strong desire to save future schoolchildren from such a wicked educational environment.

In Love with Learning

Comenius soon found a better education, however. At sixteen, he was sent to Prerov Latin School—one of countless such schools that Europeans used to prepare their more promising young men (though not young women) for college. There he showed "diligence, industry, and genuine love of learning" and "acquired a reputation for quick intelligence and avid thirst for knowledge." These traits attracted the notice of the school's director, John Lanecky, later a bishop of the Brethren, who nicknamed John "Amos" (that is, "loving"). Lanecky brought the bright young student to the attention of the lord of the city, Count Charles of Zerotin, who that year (1608) became the supreme vice regent of Moravia. These two important men became even more interested in young John when he decided to become a priest of the Unity, "for Charles of Zerotin himself, having been educated abroad . . . wished to raise the

Unity to a higher level of learning and, therefore, had an especial care for the training of the clergy."

In 1611, with the sponsorship of his powerful new friends, Comenius began studies at a well-known college at Herborn in Nassau in the Reformed (that is, Calvinist) tradition. The Unity of the Brethren preferred to send their students to the schools of Calvinists—with whom they shared such emphases as a spiritual interpretation of the Lord's Supper and a close attention to a disciplined Christian life—rather than to those of the Lutherans. From there he moved on to theological studies at the University of Heidelberg—also Reformed. The early 1600s were a time of dissension among the churches, foreshadowing the open warfare to come. But the house of Comenius's Heidelberg professor David Pareus was a gathering place for all those interested in Christian unity. Pareus, a leading Calvinist theologian, went so far as to present a proposal to Sweden's king, Gustavus Adolphus, that would have united Europe's Lutherans and Reformed into one Protestant church. Comenius's own Unity background reverberated with his professor's ecumenical spirit, and we can imagine him, like Mary the mother of Jesus, storing these things up in his heart.

The early 1600s were a dynamic period of religious conflict, new knowledge and deeper piety in Europe. Scant decades had passed since Martin Luther measured the church against Scripture and pruned back corruptions and traditions alike with a vigorous hand. Now the brightest scientific minds in Europe, following the Reformation's path of "deconstructing" sacred authorities, were revolutionizing their fields by replacing timeworn assumptions with careful observation. Real progress was evident on every side, and the mood was optimistic. Though Comenius was a "heart Christian" first, trained in the warm-hearted and intense piety of the Unity, he was also an Enlightenment man. How many college students begin, during their undergraduate years, "the colossal task of writing, single-handed, a sixteen-volume encyclopedia, comprising all things from the creation to his day"? This was a quintessentially Enlightenment enterprise (and one he never finished, though it ran to twenty-eight volumes!).

Fleeting Happiness and Gathering Troops

In the spring of 1614, done with his three years of exhilarating study in Germany, young Comenius *walked* back to Prague, the capital of Bohemia (he walked for his health and to save money). Full of hope, he took on a teaching position at the Latin school at Prerov, his own alma mater, and began work on a small Latin grammar. These were happy times for Comenius, in a world of promise both for himself and for humankind. The conflict that would soon engulf Europe was still just a cloud on the horizon the size of a man's fist. In April 1616 Comenius was ordained a minister in the Unity of the Brethren Church, and in 1618 he was appointed pastor of an important church at Fulnek, near the Moravian-Silesia border. This was not an easy job in the shadow of the Roman Catholic majority. Leading local Catholics "bullied and badgered him." But the young pastor bore the insults patiently, and soon it was commonly said that the pastor of the Brethren "had no gall." During this period Comenius also married, and for a few years he enjoyed "the only period of tranquility in his native country which it was ever his fortune to experience."

The groundwork for the Thirty Years' War had been laid in the 1555 Peace of Augsburg between the forces of the Holy Roman Emperor, Charles V (a Catholic), and the forces of the Schmalkaldic League (an alliance of Protestant princes). The peace had instituted into Germany the principle of *cuius regio eius religio*—"Whose reign, his religion," meaning that each prince mandated his people's church affiliation. This carved Germany's many regions into a jigsaw puzzle of Catholic and Lutheran princedoms. Of course, the solution satisfied no one. The Catholics were forced to cede vast territories that once owed allegiance to their church. The Lutherans were forced against their consciences to allow political leaders to determine the eternal matter of their people's religion. And the Calvinists and Anabaptists both found themselves left out of the Augsburg Peace's reckoning altogether.

It was only a matter of time until these tensions came to a boil and broke out into open conflict. In a dark irony, the spark of religious violence was lit in the very country that hosted one of the world's most ecumenical churches—the Unity of the Brethren. In 1618, the year of Comenius's first pastoral appointment, the intolerant Catholic Ferdinand II (1578–1637) was declared king of Bohemia. When two Catholic councilors were sent to Prague to govern in Ferdinand's absence, a group of Bohemian Calvinists met the new king's men with a welcome they would not soon forget: they threw them out the window of a high tower. (Protestant annalists tell us that the men survived the fall, owing to the poetic mercy of a large pile of manure at the bottom of the fifty-foot drop.) This "Defenestration of Prague" ignited the conflict that would drag on for thirty years, engulfing France, Sweden, Spain and Germany in bloody interreligious warfare that spread havoc and depopulated swathes of Central Europe.

After the defenestration in 1618, the Bohemians raised an army, expelled the Jesuits and elected a Calvinist, Frederick of the Palatinate, to their throne. The Bohemian troops confronted the imperial forces, but their resistance was not to last long. On November 8, 1620, the Czech Protestants suffered a decisive defeat at the Battle of White Mountain. Young Comenius witnessed "the weapons for stabbing, for chopping, for cutting, for pricking, for hacking, for tearing and for burning." He saw "the savage hacking of limbs, the spurting of blood, the flash of fire." And he wrote, "Almighty God . . . what is happening? Must the whole world perish?" In the battle's aftermath, Protestant ministers were driven away from their flocks; some were imprisoned and some put to death. Wrote Comenius, "Not a few (of whose number I, unhappy, am one) are miserably in hiding for the fear of human fury." Fulneck was captured, and Comenius's house and all his belongings—including his beloved books and papers—burned. The young minister had to send his wife and young son to his mother-in-law's house in Prerov and, as they thought, safety.

John Comenius was never to see Fulneck, or his family, again. His wife was already sick with the plague when she arrived at Prerov. Soon after, she and his first child died. Within the year, he lost his other child to illness too.

With the Hapsburgs now in power and Catholicism the only legal religion in Bohemia and Moravia, Ferdinand imposed such repressive measures on the Protestants that other European Protestants became alarmed, and both Denmark and Sweden entered the fray. Ferdinand's measures forced the Unity underground, and some fled Bohemia and Moravia altogether, but Comenius stayed in the mountains with a group who decided to ride out the conflict—sometimes living in caves or even trees.

Masterwork from a Hut

After 1622 Comenius's group—twenty-four priests, at least one bishop and their flock—stayed at a town called Brandeis, in Bohemia's far northeast. There they received the protection of the powerful Count Zerotin, who had remained loyal to the Hapsburgs and thus earned their forbearance. Brandeis, with its wide marketplace and small streets, nestled in a narrow river valley surrounded by steep piney hills. Above, on a rocky bluff, loomed the nearly ruined castle of the Zerotins, and across the river from the town sat Comenius's hut, which some believed had been built by Brethren founder Brother Gregory with his own hands. There Comenius wrote for his Brethren a masterful allegory, whose original title suggests its Ecclesiastes-like contents: *The Labyrinth of the World and the Paradise of the Heart; that is, a book that clearly shows that this world and all matters concerning it are nothing but confusion and giddiness, pain and toil, deceit and falsehood, misery and anxiety, and lastly, disgust of all things and despair; but he who remains in his own dwelling within his heart, opening it to the Lord God alone, will obtain true and full peace of mind and joy.*

Like Dante's *Comedia*, the *Labyrinth* is a "philosophical work" and "a book of adventure," and at the same time primarily a theological story. Unlike Dante's allegory, Comenius's is written by a relatively young man and set at that time in its pilgrim's life when the "human mind begins to understand the difference between good and evil"—that is, adolescence or young adulthood, rather than Dante's midlife crisis. This points to Comenius's educative purpose: he wanted to warn especially the young, before they wasted their lives, to look beyond the vain show of the world to the truth of Christ.

The young pilgrim of the *Labyrinth* set out in search of truth yet found that every aspect of society and culture kept him from finding it. Everywhere he saw people chasing material goods and empty self-gratification, and reaping from these only misery, which they hid behind masks of gaiety. Some "did nothing but change clothes, putting on one costume after another." Others "had become accustomed to stuffing and filling their bellies with delicacies." Most found no meaning in their work: "They took up one task, then another, showing fickleness in everything." Even their families did not bring happiness. Couples were bound together with shackles, and attached to many of these were children who "screamed, shrieked, stank, quarreled, and got sick and died." Parents had to restrain them with bridles and "make them follow in their tracks by driving them on with spurs," but the children still "caused such terrible mischief that they drove their parents to exhaustion and tears."

As the pilgrim continued his search for truth, he came to the great universities and centers of learning. There he found people buying books but not reading them, writing books by pouring increasingly diluted stuff from one book into another, purporting to proffer wisdom but in fact selling "as many poisons as medicines," cramming themselves with knowledge like gluttons so that it "came out of them again undigested, either from above or from below," or merely "carry[ing] their knowledge in their pockets." In the end, all of this pursuit of knowledge led only to strife: "The more learned one considered himself or was esteemed by others, the more quarrels he began," and these quarrels proceeded with "unusual cruelty," as the combatants "spared neither the wounded nor the dead, but mercilessly hacked and slashed at them all the more." His conclusion about the learned men of his day has a postmodern ring: "These people are like peasants in a tavern. Each one howls his own song." Churches proved just as alienated from truth. The clergy preached righteousness and the people listened, to be sure, but neither of them lived what they talked about. Meanwhile, worldly leaders gave the worst vices virtuous-sounding names designed to hide their true natures—"merriment" for drunkenness, "economy" for greed, "dignity" for pride and so forth. Even

Solomon, who came to lend his wisdom, was seduced by their lies.

Sick at heart and thinking of ending it all, the pilgrim cried out to God. Immediately he heard a voice, calling "Return!" Though puzzled by the command, he felt he should enter, like Augustine, into his own heart. This he found to be dark, lit only by a dim light from beyond a window blackened by the grime of sin. But into the gloom came Christ, who embraced him like the prodigal sun, kissed him and then promised him joy: "This only I ask of you, that you transfer and turn over to me whatever you have seen in the world, whatever human efforts you have witnessed for the sake of earthly goods. As long as you live, let this be your task and occupation. I will give you in abundance that which people in the world seek and do not find: peace and joy." Then Christ led the pilgrim back to a small, ragtag band of Christians he had seen at the fringes of the marketplace, but dismissed. Now, in their company, he found "things working as they should, free from pride, greed, and lust—a community committed to its Lord." This, he concluded, was "the Paradise of the heart!"

Rebuilding from Exile

By 1624 the persecution against the Brethren had become so intense that Zerotin was no longer able to keep his friends safe. Fleeing their patron's estate, they wandered Moravia and Bohemia, evading Jesuits and visiting their own churches secretly to preach and administer the sacraments. In 1628, with no signs of an end to the war, the Unity was forced to divide, and Comenius was selected to take a large group to Leszno (or Lissa), Poland. As the ragged band of refugees crossed the border, they looked backward into their homeland and sang:

> Nothing have we taken with us,
> All to destruction is hurled,
> We have only our Kralitz Bibles,
> And our *Labyrinth of the World*.

Comenius's allegory had given the community the kind of centering and identity that only stories can provide.

A few—a "hidden seed"—stayed behind. These "buried their Bibles in their gardens, held midnight meetings in garrets and stables, [and] preserved their records in dovecotes and in the thatched roofs of their cottages." Then they read "the glorious promises of the Book of Revelation—a book which many of them knew by heart," and "awaited the time when their troubles should blow by and the call to arise should sound."

Throughout most of Comenius's adult life, the Thirty Years' War swung this way and that; he and his people always hoped for peace and the joyous return to their homeland. The Brethren's hopes peaked after 1630, when the Swedish forces under the Lutheran Gustavus Adolphus II entered the fight by invading Germany and began to turn the tide against the Catholic Hapsburgs. Two years later, however, Gustavus Adolphus died, putting an end to that hope.

In 1632 the expatriate Brethren elected Comenius their bishop, and he continued to work tirelessly on their behalf until the end of his life. But this was not merely the usual ecclesiastical work. Throughout the Leszno years, Comenius fulfilled part of his episcopal duties by teaching at a gymnasium there.

As Comenius thought about the massive reconstruction effort that would be required if his compatriots ever returned to their native land, he realized that education would need to be a major part of that effort. Drawing on his Unity heritage, he outlined a program for educational reform among his people. "They must begin, he said, by teaching the children the pure word of God in their homes. They must bring their children up in habits of piety. They must maintain the ancient discipline of the Brethren. They must live in peace with other Christians, and avoid theological bickerings. They must publish good books in the Bohemian language. They must build new schools wherever possible, and endeavour to obtain the assistance of godly nobles."

Increasingly, as Comenius worked and wrote on educational reform, he thought beyond his own people to the welfare and peace of war-torn Europe. While teaching at Prerov, beginning in 1629, he wrote the *Janua Linguarum,* or *Gate of Languages Unlocked.* This book described useful facts about the world in both Latin and Czech, side by side, allowing students to compare the two languages and identify words with things (in good empiricist fashion). Published in Czech in 1631, English in 1632 and German in 1633—with many more translations to follow—the *Janua* made Comenius a leading educational figure on the continent.

From Pupils to Pansophy

Beyond these grand visions, Comenius revolutionized the practice of education. He was one of the first educators to understand young people as full spiritual and intellectual beings who need to have their natural curiosity encouraged rather than their behinds beaten. He pointed to the Son of God, who "not only willed to become as a little child, but thought children a pleasure and a delight. Taking them in His arms as little brethren and sisters, He carried them about and kissed and blessed them. He severely threatened anyone who should offend them, even in the least degree, and commanded that they be respected as Himself."

From this insight flowed a new, more systematic understanding of how teaching should be adapted to "the age, interests and mental ability of the pupil." Aware of the developmental needs of children of various ages, Comenius divided elementary schools by grades. Believing that children must be wooed rather than coerced into learning, he invented the illustrated textbook and made experience and discovery part of the classroom environment. He taught that corporal punishment, if used at all, should be connected only with moral, and not intellectual, faults. He insisted girls were fully as capable of learning at the highest levels as boys (reflecting the "advanced" views of many humanists in the lineage of Erasmus and More). And he preached that schools should teach all knowledge, including morals and piety.

Comenius began publishing these reforms in a series of books that were praised and implemented all across Europe. Over half of European schools eventually used his textbooks. Cardinal Richelieu sought his services for France (and was willing to overlook the small fact that according to the teachings of Richelieu's church, the Moravian educator was a heretic). The Massachusetts Puritans offered him the presidency of Harvard.

Several principles underlay Comenius's reforms. First, he worked from the empiricism of Francis Bacon (1561–1626)—surely the most influential theorist in the whole period of the scientific revolution: "Why," asks Comenius, "should we need other teachers than these our senses to learn to know the works of Nature? Why, say I, should we not, instead of these dead books, lay open the living book of Nature?" In other words, our children will learn properly only when they cease the empty, parrot-like study of words (the dual legacy of medieval scholasticism and Renaissance humanism's reverence for ancient texts) and turn to the study of the things represented by those words. This applied not only to natural things, but also to spiritual things. As his *Labyrinth* so clearly illustrates, Comenius believed one could truly experience Jesus' presence and power in one's heart. And the truths to be found in that "school of the heart" would be studied side by side with the truths of natural science and human society.

Along with the inductive method, Comenius also borrowed Bacon's "pansophism"—the project to comprehensively organize all truth into one system, reminiscent of Dante's vision of divine orderliness. Those captivated by the pansophic vision, while encyclopedic in their reach, never claimed that humanity could know literally everything. Rather, they aimed at the more modest goals of wisdom and usefulness, along with the higher goals of glorifying God and inspiring humanity to love all good things. Like Bacon, Comenius worked toward the goal of bringing all areas of knowledge together in a scientific system, which would require the work of many scholars over many years. Comenius himself spent forty years compiling the encyclopedia that was to be lost in the 1656 burning of his house.

What a Liberal Education Is For

Against the dark backdrop of the Thirty Years' War, Comenius clung—as an irenic, ecumenical Pietist—to the hope of Christ's redemptive work in the church and—as a man of Reformed convictions and Enlightenment vision—to the hope that this redemptive work could be felt in such "secular" places as the classroom and the international political stage.

Christendom was already breaking up. The days of the "medieval synthesis" between church and culture were clearly numbered. And Comenius, as a Brethren man, was no fan of coercive state involvement in religion. Yet pansophism gave him a Christian hope for Europe's future: a future in which universal, equal-opportunity education grounded in God's truth could foster the work of restoration, unity and peace.

In the 1630s this Comenian vision attracted an influential Cambridge-educated Prussian intellectual living in London, Samuel Hartlib. He and others brought Comenius to England, published (without the Czech thinker's knowledge) his notes on a pansophic scheme, and pressed him to stay in their country and found there an international "college of light"—joining scholars of diverse disciplines and denominational backgrounds in the pursuit of God's truth. The scheme was ruined, ironically, by the civil war then brewing, but it did inspire England's great Royal Society—the coalition of scientists across the bitter divisions of the English Church, embracing Anglicans and Dissenters alike—which became so crucial to the careers of Isaac Newton, Robert Boyle and other fathers of modern science. And the English interlude also allowed Comenius to write a book, *The Way of Light,* proposing "as the remedy of the chief problems confronting Europe at the time, common textbooks, universal schools, a centralized research institution, and a universal language."

As an educator, Comenius saw that much strife arose on the European scene simply because the parties in various debates talked past one another, not understanding the very terms they used. The cause of this communication gap was double: First, people simply were not well enough educated either in Latin or in the various vernaculars to speak intelligently to each other. Second, as the pilgrim in the *Labyrinth* had discovered, people intentionally twisted language to cover up their sinfulness.

Comenius's problem with European elementary education was coterminous with his critique of higher education in the *Labyrinth* and with his grand plans for education at all levels throughout Europe: failure to know things accurately and experientially (after the empirical manner promoted by Bacon) confused relations and caused ill will. This was like the effects caused by God's confusing of human tongues after the Tower of Babel incident: "All were speaking their own language, and no one listened to anything, though they pulled at one another in an effort to gain a hearing. But they were not successful and instead provoked fights and scuffles."

At the same time, in the Europe of the Thirty Years' War and after, Comenius was surrounded and impacted in deeply painful ways by the results of a *spiritual* failure to communicate—the continued breakdown of Western Christendom into warring Christian factions. So through scholarship, knowledge and pedagogy—with the goal of spreading "pansophy" or universal wisdom—this Moravian bishop sought to make the conditions of Europe better.

Disappointment and Renewal

After the English interlude, Comenius was courted by the French, the Dutch and others, but he accepted Sweden's offer of refuge in their territory in Prussia, in the town of Elbing. There he lived and worked from 1642 until the Treaty of Westphalia in 1648, which marked the end of the Thirty Years' War. The Swedish chancellor, Oxenstierna, had promised he would take the side of the Czech Protestant exiles in the peace negotiations after the Thirty Years' War wound down. This had influenced Comenius's decision to put himself under Swedish protection, but when the time came, Oxenstierna reneged on his promise. To Comenius's bitter disappointment, the treaty conceded much to Europe's Lutherans and Calvinists, but nothing to Protestant sects such as the Unity of Brethren. Returning to Leszno, Comenius fell under the sway of an old schoolmate, Nikolas Drabik, who claimed to have revelations from God indicating the return of the Brethren exiles to their homeland. The great educator went so far as to publish a book of these prophecies, but in the end they proved false.

Comenius was now the leading bishop of a Unity that was anything but unified, at least geographically. Scattered through Europe, sheltered in German, Poland and elsewhere, members discussed the possibility of dissolving the church. In 1650 Comenius wrote on the Brethren's behalf a tract called *The Testament of the Dying Mother*. In it, he spoke in the voice of the Brethren Church, admonishing the scattered faithful to serve and minister in whatever evangelical churches wanted them: "Joining a communion in which ye find the truth of the gospel of Christ, pray for its peace and seek its upbuilding in good." Then he addressed, in turn, each Protestant denomination, lovingly expressing each church's strengths. (Although he did acknowledge the Roman Catholic Church as "our mother who has borne us," his only advice to her was that she must "repent of her adulteries.")

Paraphrasing the day's ecumenical slogan, he prayed, "May God give you wisdom to discern the distinction between the things fundamental, instrumental, and accidental . . . then ye all would know what things are or are not worthy of zeal, and which are worthy of greater or less zeal, so that ye would avoid all zeal which is without knowledge and brings no edification." In the end, still speaking in the voice of the Unity itself, he bequeathed to all Christian churches the Unity's "lively desire for unanimity of opinion and for reconciliation among themselves, and for union in faith, and love of the unity of spirit."

Was this ecumenical desire a naïve product of Enlightenment optimism? Did Comenius underestimate human resistance to learning and human potential for evil? Certainly his *Labyrinth* seems a work of Christian realism; in it, he showed that sin would always corrupt and confound human enterprises. Yet as he lived longer and wrote more on education, he always insisted that there is a moral, spiritual quality about learning things accurately about the world around us (God, after all, created that world, so that all its truths are his truths), and that when we truly understand each other's perspectives, we can work together in harmony toward godly goals.

Our own postmodern moment has called into question all systems of knowledge. Yes, such systems have helped us control our environments and improve our lifestyles, but they have also helped some people control and destroy other people. Two modern world wars have demonstrated this with devastating finality. But to give up on the very possibility that all people can share a common framework of knowledge may also be to court the kind of strife that so deeply scarred Comenius's life and times. It may be time for us to recapture some of the values at the heart of Comenius's early modernism, with its delight in systems and confidence in human knowledge. Enlightenment thinkers—many of them committed Christians—saw that clear thinking and systematic exposition are good things. Science is a good thing, and the orderly and tangible principles of scientific experimentation can bring real clarity—again, a moral value—into human understanding and human interaction. Comenius knew that the mastery of knowledge could be harnessed to evil ends, but he would always insist that accurate learning and knowledge also provide a relational good. As the late modernist Dorothy L. Sayers also argued, when people learn shared frameworks and a common store of knowledge, *they can understand each other better.*

Although to elevate education in this way may seem to go against the grain of the gospel, Comenius never separated learning and faith. A good teacher would always show his students how to "distinguish vice from virtue and falsehood from truth"; more than this, he would lead them to turn away from the former and embrace the latter. Education could therefore function as "a form of repentance." In *The One Thing Necessary,* Comenius described his educational innovations as "reforms intended to lead others out of the labyrinth." That only Christ can lead us out of worldliness and sin he makes clear in the climactic section of the *Labyrinth.* From the story's beginning, the truth-seeking pilgrim had toured the world with guides named "insatiability of Mind, which pries into everything, and Custom, which lends a color of truth to all the frauds of the world." He had also been fitted with a bridle and a pair of blurry spectacles: "The bridle is Vanity, and the glasses are constructed from the rims of Habit and the lens of Assumption." But when at last, at the story's climax and turning point, the pilgrim finally found Christ, the Lord gave him "new lenses" to replace the old ones and give him clarity of vision.

Comenius saw education as a pastoral work—"the process by which people could be trained to see beyond the apparent chaos of the world and discover the underlying harmony of God's universe." His hope was securely rooted in a Christian understanding that despite the depths of human sin (and he was very Reformed on sin) and the futility of human enterprises apart from Christ, God had not abandoned his creation. Better days could yet come if people were willing to learn and work together under the tutelage of Christ.

As with Pope John Paul II in our era, Comenius experienced the horrors of war and oppression, yet he would not let fear and despair rule him. He reached the highest level of his church and used that position to work for international understanding, peace and Christ-centered learning. He truly stands to be a Protestant "patron saint" for modern Christians. We can still learn something from his life and his life's work—not just in education, but in ecumenism, international affairs and indeed Christian spirituality.

At the most basic level, I believe Comenius bequeathed to Europe and the world a Christian reminder of that particular benefit of a broad liberal education—the tolerance and generosity of spirit it can instill in its students. "If all men understand each other," he wrote in *The Way of Light,* "they will become as it were one race, one people, one household, one school of God." Focused as we are on schooling ourselves toward technical mastery and economic ends, we may overlook that deeper mode of education. For Comenius, writing in the midst of a bloody religious war in a fractured Europe, a Christ-centered liberal education was not just a "nice-to-have." It was a matter of life and death.

Paradox Lost

Here are two central paradoxes in this remarkable Moravian thinker, both representing a kind of balance we have lost today. First, there is his response to the Enlightenment vision. The expansion of knowledge in his day electrified him, but he also portrayed its limits with devastating clarity in his *Labyrinth.* He recognized that human reason and human enterprise could not provide either truth or happiness—at least, unaided. But he did not retreat into an irrelevant pietism either. Rather, he believed and taught that the new discoveries of his age were fully compatible with the ancient moral law and the gospel of Jesus Christ. And he staked his life on the possibility of a truly Christian pedagogy and a Christian culture.

The second paradox of Comenius's life lies in reaction to the slaughter and exile of his small, fringe Christian community by others bearing the name "Christian." This sectarian leader certainly could have done what so many others persecuted Christians have done: retreated in rage and bitterness, licked his wounds with his people and set up legalistic fences to keep outsiders out. Instead, he insisted on the ecumenical slogan: "In essentials, unity; in non-essentials, liberty; in all things, charity." And he poured his life out for church unity and international peace.

Before his often tragic life was done, John Amos Comenius created a breathtaking vision of international peace and cooperation. At the heart of this vision was a comprehensive educational program that had already, in his lifetime, begun to transform the way Europe's children were taught. We have asked how Comenius could possibly do this, given his background in a small persecuted group who were hounded, killed and exiled by fellow Christians. It seems a paradox that a persecuted, pietistic sect could form a person such as this.

The key to this paradox seems to be something that had happened to the Unity of the Brethren by the early sixteenth century. Now flourishing and increasingly influential, the Brethren were forced to confront the perennial question of the relationship between Christ and culture. Many devout Christians believe that if the church in any time or place grows and gains cultural power, it will inevitably compromise the radical nature of the gospel among them. The church must, such folks argue, forgo all attempts to "transform culture," for such attempts inevitably suck the life out of the church. Was this the case with the Brethren and Comenius? Certainly in the decades of their peasant origins, the Brethren had distrusted all people of other classes and all the trappings of culture. But as a new diversity of folks—even nobles such as Count Zerotin—were drawn by these people's strong devotion and joined with them, the group moderated its views. Inevitably, some Brethren felt this moderation as a betrayal. They pushed the group to "hold up its ancient standard" of enmity against all structures of worldly culture. But this group of world-renouncing conservatives did not win the day. Instead, a schism occurred, with the majority taking the socially progressive (though still theologically conservative and experientially pietistic) position.

It is worth considering that had this social widening not occurred among the Brethren, Comenius would likely have never developed his unique mix of deep piety and broad ("liberal") culture. Nor, very likely, would the European Union today be acknowledging Comenius as its teacher in this matter of international liberal education. But in fact, it is doing so: the European Commission of the EU has created a government-supported, pan-European elementary education initiative involving around thirty European countries, named "Comenius" after the Brethren bishop and educator. The program promotes the same values that drove its namesake's reforms of the 1600s: pedagogical innovation, transnational cooperation and equal opportunity for all students. Comenius, and his Lord, seem still to be at work.

6

John Newton

In 1765 the sixty-two-year-old John Wesley, father of evangelicalism in England, wrote a letter to the forty-year-old John Newton, a Church of England clergyman of evangelical persuasion whose star was rising within the movement. Some twenty-five years earlier, Wesley had joined his friend George Whitefield in preaching to Bristol coal miners, and their work had launched the Methodist (or "Evangelical") Revival in England. Wesley was an Arminian, emphasizing God's love and humanity's free choice of salvation; Whitefield was a Calvinist, emphasizing God's sovereignty and humanity's inability to achieve salvation. Together, these men and a growing group of other leaders had pioneered world evangelicalism by preaching passionately for conversion, teaching brilliantly from Scripture, dwelling lovingly on Jesus, and seeking to change individuals and the world for Christ.

Even as he penned the letter to Newton, the small Methodist "societies" Wesley had erected on the fringes of the Church of England's parish structure were proving an engine of tremendous growth, although almost no Church of England clergyman yet professed to be evangelical. Despite this growth, however, not all was well. A virulent pamphlet war had arisen between Arminians (those who emphasized God's loving invitation to all people, and humans' answering decision in their own salvation) and Calvinists (those who emphasized God's sovereign choice of his "elect," and his irresistible grace in saving them). The dispute was threatening to tear the infant movement apart. So, weighed down with the fractiousness of his spiritual children, the old lion had taken up his pen to praise his younger colleague. Wesley wrote with gratitude because, in the midst of the strife, he recognized that Newton was "designed by divine providence for an healer of breaches, a reconciler of honest but prejudiced men, and an uniter (happy work!) of the children of God that are needlessly divided from each other."

Maybe Newton flushed with pride at this endorsement. Certainly, his newfound leadership position among the evangelicals must have seemed a dizzying height compared to his condition just a few years before. Bluntly put, Newton had spent his young adulthood cursing Christ (fighting his childhood faith and actively trying to deconvert others from it) and trading slaves. Now, however, like Saul become Paul, he had undergone a complete transformation. By God's grace, he was becoming a Christian leader loved and trusted by thousands. Young ministers were competing to lodge with him and learn under him. By 1800, nine years after Wesley's death, John Newton would be recognized as British evangelicalism's leading clergyman. And although he would not live to enjoy it, he would also become known as the author of the most popular English-language hymn ever—"Amazing Grace."

And John Wesley was right: Newton was the sort of healer and reconciler that a troubled evangelicalism needed. Having experienced God's grace, he consistently showed it to others, as he reached out across all of the barriers that ran down the middle of early British evangelicalism: He was not only a Calvinist who accepted Arminians but also a state-church pastor who encouraged independent churches, and a friend of prominent personalities while pastoring the working poor. He was, in short, a bridge figure in a troubled time.

Newton, however, would never let himself forget those earlier years of sin. If he felt, at the peak of his powers, a momentary pride at Wesley's words of praise, in the very next moment he would almost certainly have brought himself back to earth. He would have told himself that no matter what success he had seen and no matter how much fame he was gaining, he was still that same "old African blasphemer" (he often called himself this) who had plied the seas, trafficking in human lives. Newton knew well the darkness at the heart of every person. It was deep in the fabric of his own life.

A Fair Beginning

Newton had begun well enough. He was born in London, an only child, in 1725. His mother was a pious Dissenter—that is, one of those descendents of the Puritans who felt that the Church of England had been insufficiently reformed (along Calvinist lines) from its Catholic roots under Henry VIII, and who worshiped in their own independent churches apart from the Anglican parishes. She taught John to read Scripture and memorize Calvinist catechisms and hymns. Together they attended an Independent Congregationalist church in London, at a time when barely 1 percent of that city's population associated with such bodies.

At age seven, however, Newton's mother died, and he fell under the less religious and more distant care of his sea-captain father. From age eleven to seventeen John accompanied his father on five sea voyages that proved a stern and thorough education in seamanship. In the long interims between these trips, he was allowed by his stepmother to run free, and he got himself into ample adolescent trouble. After each fall he would rise again, resolving afresh to live the life his mother had shown him. He would turn with renewed vigor to prayer, pious reading and spiritual journaling. Yet, in all of these activities, as he later admitted, his boyish aim had been not to please God, but to escape damnation.

In 1742, soon after John's father retired from the sea and took a shore job with the Royal Africa Company, he announced the good news that John would soon make his fortune. Captain Newton had arranged for his son passage to Jamaica on a ship owned by a Liverpool man who had interests in slaves and sugar. Once in Jamaica, the plan was that John would work as a slave overseer. From this humble beginning, John's father foresaw a rapid rise to a planter's estate—and then, in time, to a seat in Parliament.

His father's dreams for John soon hit a snag. On a family visit, the seventeen-year-old sailor met Mary Catlett, the daughter of friends, at the Catletts' substantial estate in Kent. John not only fell hopelessly in love with Mary but decided he could not bear to leave for Jamaica when the important work of wooing the apple of his eye remained. And so he deliberately missed his ship to Jamaica, hiding out instead at the Catletts'.

When John could no longer put off his return home, weeks after the Jamaica-bound ship had left, he found his father furious. The elder Newton had had enough. His son *would* learn discipline, one way or another. So off John was sent, on a months-long voyage. Though his father could have used his influence to secure John a more comfortable position, he had him shipped as a common sailor, with no paternal protection from the harshness of the seaman's life.

In the company of the rough crew, Newton soon lost the last of his former religious resolve. He took up smoking and swearing and indulged his lusts at the journey's end in Venice. The God he had learned to worship at his mother's knee seemed a distant being with no claim on his life.

His "Precious"

On the way back from Venice, Newton had a striking symbolic dream. He saw himself pacing on deck when a stranger approached and gave him a valuable ring. The stranger cautioned him to guard it well, for it was the key to all happiness. No sooner, however, had Newton slipped on the ring than he faced another stranger. This man ridiculed his faith in the trinket.

As he listened to this second man's persuasive words, the young sailor became more and more embarrassed. At last he turned, wrenched the ring from his finger and dropped it overboard. The instant he had done so, the tempter told him he had in fact cast away God's mercy and must now be consigned to fire.

But the dream did not end there. As Newton awaited his fate, terror-ized, another stranger (or was it the first man?) came and recovered the ring for him. This man, however, would not give it back, saying he must now keep it in trust, for John was still too foolish to have it.

For a few weeks after the dream, Newton was shaken enough to sepa-rate himself from the rough company of the other sailors and resume something of his earlier religious observance. But by landfall in Decem-ber 1743 he had once again put such disciplines aside.

In the following months Newton missed a second voyage—on which he would have been an officer—again by overstaying a visit to Mary. Then on March 1, 1744, as he was traveling to see Mary, John's life took an unexpected turn. Strolling in town with the unmistakable gait of a sailor but no papers as a legitimate merchantman, Newton was set upon by a naval pressgang.

This time his father, knowing well the risks of naval life, did his best to intervene. But it was to no avail. Within days, John found himself a lowly crewman aboard a man-o'-war of the Royal Navy, the *Harwich*. From the first, he was driven, half-starved, and "broken" from dawn till night. In short, he was treated as were all young men in the eighteenth-century navy. Severe discipline seemed the only way young sailors could be prepared for the extreme hardships and dangers of life in England's floating military.

As bad as the physical privations aboard this ship were, the voyage's effect on Newton's spirit was worse. The captain's clerk, a man named Mitchell, was a free thinker and only too happy to share his convictions with a young friend. Life, said Mitchell, was for the taking. God was a phantom invented by killjoy religious types. We must eat, drink and be merry, for tomorrow we die.

Newton had long desired to escape the constraints of his mother's religion. Now, under Mitchell's influence, he took the precious ring of his dream from his finger and threw it overboard.

Enjoying the heady release of his new creed, Newton struck up a friendship with a younger man, midshipman Job Lewis, who still clung to enough religion to keep him steady against the low morals of the crew at large. Newton was a clever and persuasive speaker and a forceful personality, and he had soon turned young Lewis from the Christian faith and driven away the last of his compunctions.

Just Deserts

At Christmas 1744 the *Harwich* moored north of the straits of Dover, preparing for its next voyage. With horror Newton learned this would take them not, as before, to the Mediterranean for a year, but instead to the East Indies, for five long years. By the end of that time, John was convinced, his Mary would belong to another. Distraught, driven by passion and no longer checked by scruples born of faith, Newton resolved to find some way off of this ship. When the opportunity came on a trip to the market for provisions, he slipped away, determined to quit the navy forever.

Unfortunately, a party of marines he encountered the day after his escape had other ideas. They arrested the deserter and dragged him back to his ship in chains, where the captain had him stripped and flogged with a cat-o'-nine-tails. Newton now faced the universal scorn of the crew, five years of misery and the near-certain loss of Mary. Only the secret hand of God, he later claimed, kept him from killing either the captain or himself.

By a remarkable coincidence, however, Newton was soon able to secure a transfer to another vessel—the *Greyhound*—bound for the Guinea coast and the slave trade. The captain of this vessel was a friend of his father's, and before long Newton was well-established in the trade, working under the ship's part owner, a Mr. Clow, at a slave "factory" on the Plantain Islands near Sierra Leone.

The arrangement proved disastrous. As biographer Bruce Hindmarsh tells it, "During the next two years [Newton] suffered illness, starvation, exposure, and ridicule as his master's black mistress used him poorly, and as he lost his master's trust." In what was scarcely better than rank captivity to this mistress, Newton became lower than a slave, a servant to the human chattel in which his master traded. A few of the slaves, taking pity on him, snuck food to him and ferried a series of desperate letters to his father onto ships bound for England.

Miraculously, a captain deputized by his father did actually find Newton at the end of these two years of misery. But by that time, the younger Newton had found a new master and was set again on a course to financial success as a future owner of his own slaving operation. His father's friend had to lie, claiming Newton was to come into a handsome inheritance back home, before John would return to England with him. On this voyage, Newton surpassed his earlier immorality and impiety, blaspheming to a degree that shocked even the older men—crude parodies of the Gospels were his favorite form of humor—and once narrowly escaping death by drowning as he fell overboard during a party.

A Cry in the Dark

Just as Newton seemed irrevocably lost to the faith, he picked up, for lack of other shipboard reading material, Thomas a Kempis's *Imitation of Christ,* a Catholic devotional guide that had also deeply influenced John Wesley. At first, the book's words meant little to him. But then came the first pivot point of his life's voyage.

The *Greyhound*'s voyage from Brazil to Newfoundland, laden with slaves, led them on March 21, 1748, into a violent storm. In poor repair, the ship soon began to split and take on water, and Newton was awakened from sleep to find that a crewmember had been swept away in the raging sea.

"Tied to the ship to prevent being washed away," relates Hindmarsh, Newton "pumped and bailed all night until he was called upon to steer the ship. All the while he reviewed his life: his former professions of religion, the extraordinary twists of past events, the warnings and deliverances he had met with, his licentious conversation, and his mockery of the Gospels."

At first Newton was convinced that he had sinned too much to have any hope for God's forgiveness. Yet at last, when the storm did not recede and he really felt he would soon meet his God, he clung to Scriptures that taught God's grace toward sinners, and he breathed his first weak prayer in years. In the phrase of his own famous hymn, this was "the hour he first believed."

Yet Newton's new faith would not find a solid footing for some months. Indeed the very next year, on a voyage as mate of the slaving ship *Brownlow,* Newton backslid entirely, giving his lust free license. It was only when he became sick with a violent fever while visiting the place of his previous captivity—Clow's Plantain Island "factory"—that he came to himself.

Feeling that, as biographer John Pollock puts it, he had "crucified the Son of God afresh and thus had shut and locked the door of hope," Newton nevertheless mustered enough faith to creep to a "remote corner of the island," where "between the palm trees and the sea he knelt upon the shore and found a new liberty to pray."

After this episode, Newton never again went back on his faith. He developed a consistent habit of prayer, and his watchword became humility. "What a poor creature I am in myself," he wrote, "incapable of standing a single hour without continual fresh supplies of strength and grace from the fountain-head." He looked back across his life's story, which featured a series of miraculous rescues from death by storm, starvation, mutiny plots and slave uprisings, and his sense of that grace grew even stronger.

On the matter of slavery, Newton's progress was slow. Though he disliked the inconvenience and dangers of the trade, for years he still accepted it as an honorable profession, as did the rest of "polite" eight-eenth-century society. In the end, he would turn against the slave trade as the worst kind of sin, but it would take him a sinfully long time to do so.

Just before he received his first command as captain of a slaving vessel, with a bright future ahead of him, Newton at last succeeded in winning Mary, whom he had now loved for seven years. They were wed on February 1, 1750, and were soon devotedly attached to each other. Indeed Newton came near to idolizing her, as their relationship began to overshadow his nascent faith. He still found it embarrassing to talk about faith with Mary or her relatives, and he could not yet bring himself to pray with her.

In the years following his marriage, Newton captained two slaving vessels, the *Duke of Argyle* and the *African,* on three voyages. During the long months he began to pray for his slave cargo—mere distaste for the trade was beginning to dawn into something more.

A Sad Reunion

As Newton prepared for his second voyage as captain, aboard the *African,* he encountered the young man he had once "deconverted" from Christianity—Job Lewis. Reforging their acquaintance, he invited Lewis aboard as "volunteer and captain's commander." This was a decision he would soon regret, for the once clean-living young midshipman was now a hardened sinner. He not only fouled the air with his cursing and inflicted his cruel bad temper on the crew, but also flouted Newton's authority.

When in January, having reached the Guinea Coast, Newton found a way to get for Lewis another ship, he did so with orders to trade on the *African*'s account. Before this ship, the *Racehorse,* was launched, Newton came aboard and gave Lewis some final spiritual advice.

But nearly as soon as he left Newton, Lewis began indulging himself in every vice, from drinking to fighting to sleeping with the native women. And when his dissipated lifestyle and the local climate felled him with a fever, Lewis's body could offer little resistance. As Newton soon heard of it from other sailors on the *Racehorse,* Lewis spent his last hours on earth enveloped in despair and rage, screaming that he was going to hell, but unable or unwilling to seek God's mercy. For his part in the shipwrecking of young Job's life, Newton suffered acute and long-lasting remorse.

When a few weeks later Newton himself contracted a similar fever, he had much to think about. His own death no longer held for him the terror it once had. If recovery were denied him, he felt ready to face his end. But he did pray for two things: first, for better understanding of the faith so that he could turn unrepentant sinners onto the path of righteousness, and second, for freedom from the slave trade and the seafaring life.

In the spring of 1754 Newton found at St. Kitts a true friend—a Scottish captain, not engaged in the slave trade, by the name of Alexander Clunie. This was the first close Christian friend Newton had, and he was overjoyed. The two spent weeks together in May and June, with Newton drinking in the things of God as Clunie imparted them. "I was all ears," he wrote, "and what was better, he not only informed my understanding but his discourses inflamed my heart." As Pollock put it, until now "Newton had thought of God as a distant potentate whom he must obey. Now he discovered that God could be very near and his love be warmer than Newton had dreamed."

Newton's prayers as he recovered from the fever were soon answered. After he arrived safely back in England that summer, he never sailed for a living again. Instead, he took a post as a "tide surveyor" in Liverpool, a well-paid government shore job that involved boarding vessels as they entered port and searching for smuggled goods. When in 1756 the Seven Years' War broke out, maritime traffic fell off to the point where Newton had a great deal of free time on his hands. In effect, this allowed him to become the most active layman in the land, touring widely and enjoying the preaching and fellowship of the day's leading evangelicals. He developed lifelong friendships with many of these men, relationships as sustaining and upbuilding as that first friendship with Captain Clunie. He felt such relationships were so vital to the church that in 1756 he wrote a little book called *Thoughts on Religious Associations* and had copies sent to every minister in Liverpool.

Young Whitefield

One of his favorites among his preacher friends was the famed evangelist and evangelical pioneer George Whitefield, whose ministry had helped trigger both the Methodist Revival in England and the Great Awakening in America. In fact, Newton himself became known as "Young Whitefield"—not because he preached like the better-known man (for though he was beginning to speak publicly, he was still a far-from-polished orator), but because he shadowed the great preacher, dining with him when he could and even attending meetings at 5 a.m. in the bitter cold of winter.

Newton's contact with Whitefield gave him an exciting vision of how far "gospel preaching" could go in British life. It seemed that evangelical Christianity would soon cease to be a hidden thing involving a minuscule percentage of the populace, as it had been in the Independent churches of his childhood. It was on its way to gaining a new and significant public profile. And Whitefield, along with John Wesley, was leading the way toward this dream. (It would take until about the 1780s for this evangelical influence to make significant inroads into the Established Church and thus English society at large.)

When not tagging along with Whitefield, Newton spent much of his Liverpool phase attending both the small Church of England "religious societies" that met for preaching, testimony and mutual edification, and any Dissenting or Established church he knew to have a gospel message. Ignoring the ecclesiastical boundaries that separated Baptists, Presbyterians, Independents and Anglicans, he drank in fellowship and spiritual knowledge wherever he found it. At home, he began teaching himself the biblical languages and reading books of divinity.

Slowly there dawned on Newton the knowledge that God did not intend for him to remain in the civil service for his whole life. In 1757 he began formally to seek a "living"—that is, a ministerial appointment in an Established Church parish—and the ordination to go with it. Thus began his struggle, between 1757 and 1764, to become an ordained minister in the Church of England—his own "Seven Years' War."

To achieve that goal, Newton had to press on through the flat refusal of several bishops to ordain him. They wanted no "enthusiast" or "Methodist" in one of their pulpits. When he met with his first refusal from the Anglican hierarchy, he began looking seriously at invitations from a variety of Dissenting churches. When none of these seemed right for him, he began to preach to friends in his own house.

Then at last in the spring of 1764, through the influence of a powerful patron, Lord Dartmouth, Newton found himself the ordained curate of a congregation in the English midlands town of Olney, Buckinghamshire. There he quickly realized that the bishops, failing to keep him out of the ministry, had done the next-best thing. They had exiled him to England's

Siberia—a "low and dirty" country whose inhabitants mostly dwelt in poverty. The lace trade, the area's main industry, provided a precarious living, owing to wildly fluctuating prices in London. The town's men, women and children worked cyclically on the brink of starvation.

And not all the local clergy appreciated Newton. A local parson named Dixie refused the request of one of his parishioners, a Mr. Perry, to allow Newton to preach the funeral sermon for one of Perry's family. Instead, Dixie took the occasion to preach a sermon against "enthusiasm," the belief in direct, extrabiblical inspiration by the Holy Spirit. Dixie's point: Newton was to be seen as one of those wild Methodists.

At Home with the Lowly

Yet Newton established himself in his new surroundings. Having crossed ecclesiological barriers with impunity, he now found ways to bridge another division, that of class. Preferring his old blue captain's jacket over "proper" clerical garb, he hobnobbed with spiritually alive folks wherever he found them, regardless of their social status. He once wrote, "I get more warmth and light sometimes by a letter from a plain person who loves the Lord Jesus, though perhaps a servant maid, than from some whole volumes put forth by learned Doctors."

From the beginning he did his work of soul care with a true pastor's heart, preaching, singing, visiting and establishing midweek meetings of every description. He especially labored for the children of Olney parish. He visited them personally to catechize them. And he founded an annual three-day meeting at which area ministers brought God's love alive to the parish's youth.

Newton was known for his open, emotional manner in the pulpit. Into the middle of a sermon recorded in one of his notebooks from the Olney years, he interjected an impassioned prayer, "The Lord . . . proclaims a free pardon, . . . and will you . . . refus[e] to hear his voice? O Lord God prevent, & rend the heavens & come down, [and] touch the stoney heart, that it may stand out no longer." We can imagine him turning his gaze on his hearers as he delivered the next line: "Let us chide our cold unfeeling hearts & pray for a coal of fire from the heavenly altar to send us home in a flame of love to him who has thus loved us."

He also hosted a continual stream of students, laymen and clergy from surrounding areas eager for spiritual conversation. He toured extensively, preaching in Dissenting as well as Established church pulpits. Back home, he welcomed visitors from all over the country to his own home, where many stayed to dine and talk long into the night. Young preachers stayed at his house and apprenticed under him.

More than just a personal habit, this extensive—and, his contemporaries charged, indiscriminate—networking revealed a deep conviction in Newton about how Christians of different backgrounds and beliefs ought to treat each other. Wesley's assessment still stands: the warmhearted Newton was "an healer of breaches" at a time when such reconciliatory work was deeply needed within evangelicalism.

The Remarkable Life of Mr. ✱✱✱✱✱✱✱✱

To his contemporaries, probably the key moment of Newton's long career was the publication in 1764, just after his thirty-ninth birthday, of his spiritual autobiography, *An Authentic Narrative of Some Remarkable and Interesting Particulars in the Life of* ✱✱✱✱✱✱✱✱. The *Authentic Narrative* told of his early life, with all its adventures and divine mercies. Throughout, its theme was God's amazing grace. And despite the coy omission of his name, everyone soon knew whose "interesting particulars" were recorded here. Thereafter, Newton's fame only grew.

Experience is the touchstone of Newton's *Authentic Narrative*. He shows himself becoming who he was, not because of genetic predispositions, but because of the situations he lived through and the influence of other people. As his empirical data, he laid out before the reader not only these situations and influences but also his states of mind and heart or emotion on the road to conversion. In choosing this approach, Newton wrote under the influence both of John Locke's empiricism and of the heart-oriented John Wesley, who in turn had picked up a kind of "spiritual empiricism" from Comenius's Moravians. (David Bebbington reminds us that the Moravians taught Wesley that Christians can *know,* subjectively, they are saved; they also taught him to value hymn-singing, "firm discipline, warm fellowship, and apostolic zeal for missions.")

Newton's use of poetry and story penetrated not only his autobiography but his preaching too. He "had the eye and heart and tongue of a spiritual poet, and this gave his speech a penetrating power that many Reformed preachers desperately need. . . . Instead of excessive abstraction in his preaching, there was the concrete word and illustration. Instead of generalizing, there was the specific bird or flower or apple or shabby old man."

Newton's empirical, narrative approach clearly met with a receptive audience, illustrating the evangelicals' willingness to find spiritual truth not just (and perhaps not even primarily) in doctrinal statements but also in the earthiness and experiential quality of stories, testimonies and biographies. In the late-eighteenth and nineteenth centuries Newton's conversion story became one of the evangelicals' favorite books.

During his Olney period, Newton also penned many hymns. These he wrote to accompany sermons for the whole church or for one of the midweek meetings. Often—again harnessing the power of story and poetic imagery—he would write a hymn to address the specific need of some member of his congregation. Aware, as Comenius had been, of the special receptivity of children, Newton particularly liked to teach hymns to his youngest congregants and to sing along with them. In 1767 Newton was joined in this enterprise by a dear friend, the brilliant but mentally unstable poet William Cowper. In 1779, as a testament to their friendship, Newton published the Olney Hymns hymnal, which included "Amazing Grace."

Nothing in this hymn's English reception foreshadowed its eventual popularity across the sea in the renegade Americas, where in the nineteenth century it would become the emblematic song of a vibrant church. Little did this ex–slave trader know that his hymn would be set to what may well have been the melody of a slave spiritual. He could hardly have foreseen that in that form "Amazing Grace" would become the most recognizable and beloved hymn of generations of Americans—a favorite at public events, a soundtrack for the Jesus People of the sixties, and even the subject (as America's emblematic hymn) of a 1990 documentary. I remember that Newton in his old age wrote the influential antislavery pamphlet "Thoughts on the African Slave Trade," based on his own experiences in the trade, and testified against the barbarity of the slave trade before Parliament. And I like to think that he would have had great sympathy for this musical setting and these uses of his hymn.

Prophet Without Honor

Toward the end of his ministry at Olney, Newton began to come up against another traditional barrier—the wall between clergy and laity. He established a variety of "social meetings" for prayer, hymn singing, Bible study and catechism of the youth. And rejoicing that "nothing has been more visibly useful . . . to unite the people . . . in the bonds of love," he encouraged his parishioners to lead those groups. But his experiment was not an unalloyed success. He may have failed to sufficiently protect his ministerial authority. He so encouraged parishioner-led prayer groups that some became restive. He had, in effect, established "little churches" within the parish church, an echo of Wesley's Methodist societies. This led some to assume they could flout the church's established leadership—even his.

When, for example, Newton spoke out against the reckless behavior typical of Guy Fawkes Day celebrations, many in the town opposed him. Festivities that day did indeed get out of hand, and Newton had to bribe the mob to avoid having his house burned down. Following this incident, Newton perceived that the townspeople were increasingly afflicted by spiritual deadness. He told a friend that they had become "sermon-proof." So in 1779, when the bluff, warm-hearted ex-captain found himself invited by England's richest merchant, John Thornton, to become rector of one of the most prestigious parishes in London, St. Mary Woolnoth, he accepted.

In London, Newton soon exerted tremendous influence among clergy and politicians, with friends from diverse circles. William Jay, a nonconformist friend, recalled Newton saying, "I am more of a Calvinist than anything else; but I use my Calvinism in my writings and my preaching as I use this sugar." Newton then took a lump of sugar and stirred it into his tea, adding, "I do not give it alone, and whole; but mixed and diluted." As Wesley had observed in 1765, though Newton held fast to his theological convictions, he did not allow them to interfere with Christian fellowship or prevent Christian cooperation. And even in his own faith, despite his essential Calvinism, Newton was something of a spiritual eclectic. "I am," he once said, "beholden to most of the birds in the air for a feather or two. Church and Meeting, Methodist and Moravian, may all perceive something in my coat taken from them."

It was during this period of peak influence that Newton founded the Eclectic Society, a group of like-minded gospel clergy, to discuss the issues of the day. It was, he said, "the society that bears no name, and espouses no party." It included in its membership Anglicans, nonconformists and even a Moravian or two. The agenda of each monthly meeting was driven by a single question, submitted by one of the members at the end of the previous meeting. The members would take turns answering, and Newton kept minutes in a small journal.

The questions spanned theological issues, cultural trends, and the practical trials and dilemmas of church and family life—from How should we reconcile Paul and James on justification? to What are the particular dangers of youth in the present day? Throughout these discussions Newton insisted the group maintain a high tone of gracious humility. In responding to theological error and dealing with ecclesiastical foes, kindness always took precedence over sternness and persuasion over polemics. "If we stretch our authority, we lose it," he observed.

In both its irenic tenor and its extraecclesial format, the Eclectic Society became the model for other parachurch societies (including William Wilberforce's influential Clapham Sect) and agencies (including the great British missionary societies, two of which were birthed out of the Eclectic Society).

As a genial and gregarious—but, even better, discerning and wise—leader during the fast-growing, gawky, painful "teen years" of what became known as the evangelical movement, John Newton helped give the movement its irenic breadth. He knew that networking and fellowship are not optional. They are essential to the church's vitality. And he harbored a deep conviction that all who are saved, regardless of denominational label, belong to the true church and contribute to its health.

John Newton is an example of amazing grace, not only in coming to salvation, but in living it out in fruitful friendships with Christians of differing backgrounds and persuasions. He served Christ in London until his death in 1807, and the list of key Christians he influenced is long. The wealthy and well-connected William Wilberforce had sat at Newton's feet as a child, drinking in his sea stories. When in 1785, as a young member of Parliament, Wilberforce renewed his commitment to Christ, he wondered if he should leave the brutal and worldly sphere of politics. So he paid a surreptitious visit to Newton, seeking the answer to this dilemma. Newton didn't hesitate, but advised Wilberforce to live his witness for Christ in the halls of power. This advice the younger man took to heart, and he dedicated the rest of his life to social reform—most famously, the abolition of the British slave trade. Newton also mentored and encouraged such luminaries of early nineteenth-century evangelicalism as the Cambridge pastor Charles Simeon (see the next chapter in this book), the leading clergyman Richard Cecil, and the author and philanthropist Hannah More, in whose conversion he was instrumental.

By the end of his life, Newton was widely beloved in England and beyond. During his lifetime, evangelicalism began slowly to move out of its "hidden years" as a Puritan fringe relegated to the Established Church's lectureships and private chapels, and into the limelight of prominent churches and reforming agencies. In this fertile period for gospel ministers, gospel hymns, and gospel books and meetings, Newton was everywhere—a trusted father and counselor in the young movement. His hymns were sung, his sermons well attended and his letters of spiritual advice passed from hand to hand, with more than five hundred of them eventually seeing publication.

An Old Sinner to the Very End

Through all the years of ministry and fame, Newton never forgot how far he had come. Over the fireplace in his vicarage study at Olney, where he would always see it as he prepared for Sunday services and midweek meetings, he placed a plaque that read in large letters as follows: "Since thou wast precious in my sight, thou hast been honourable (Isa. 18:4), BUT Thou shalt remember that thou wast a bondman in the land of Egypt, and the Lord thy God redeemed thee (Deut. 15:15)."

When he died, Newton left behind the epitaph that remains today on his gravestone. It returns to this same twin theme of slavery from sin and unmerited redemption: "John Newton, clerk, once an infidel and libertine, a servant of slaves in Africa, was, by the rich mercy of our Lord and Saviour Jesus Christ, preserved, restored, pardoned, and appointed to preach the faith he had long laboured to destroy."

In a funeral sermon for Newton, his friend and fellow minister Richard Cecil quoted him late in life, "Whatever I may doubt on other points, I cannot doubt whether there has been a certain gracious transaction between God and my soul."

Charles Simeon

**OVERCOMING WOUNDS
AND SHAPING LEADERS**

If ever there was an unlikely candidate to lead a generation, it was Charles Simeon (1759–1836). As a young man, he was "proud, imperious, fiery-tempered; a solitary individual, eager for friendship, whom others avoided because of his conceits, eccentricities, and barbed words." Those who knew him in his youth could hardly have guessed that in the course of fifty-four years of ministry at Cambridge University and from the pulpit of Holy Trinity Church, Simeon would mentor some 30 percent of the Anglican ministers of his day (1,100 or more), pull strings to secure pulpits in the languishing Church of England for the most promising of these, send countless chaplains to India and help launch the hugely influential Church Missionary Society. By the close of his life Charles Simeon had almost single-handedly renewed an Anglican Church in danger of losing all the benefit it had gained from John Wesley and John Newton. And all of this he achieved while struggling first with bitter opposition from many in his own church and university, and then with his own temper and temperament.

Simeon was born into a family of means and privilege in England. One of four brothers, he never knew his mother, whom he lost to death when he was still an infant. So Charles grew up in a male-dominated home, under his wealthy attorney father, Richard, who seems to have been a domineering, intimidating personality. Young Charles began his education at England's most celebrated public school, Eton, where he excelled at horsemanship and cricket. Known as "Chin Simeon," he had been extremely ugly as a small boy and seemed ever since to compensate by trying to distinguish himself somehow among his peers—to little avail. He tried too hard to gain friends, tending to smother the hapless objects of his awkward affection. Perhaps in compensation, he gained a reputation as a dandy. Even worse, a bad temper manifested itself often enough to make fellow students wary of him. Ambition and insecurity seemed to wrestle for mastery of him.

Simeon also lacked any notable intellectual talent. Nonetheless, he did manage in 1779 to make his way along the well-worn path from Eton to Cambridge (King's College). There, amid the usual distractions of a college town, including taverns and horse races, he encountered the Christian faith. This encounter seems to have occurred almost despite the religious climate of late-eighteenth-century Cambridge. His college's chapel was well attended, but only because it was required of undergraduates. Uninspired chaplains hurried through the twice-daily liturgy, and every student, whatever his personal beliefs, was required to take Communion. Worse still, most of the faculty, clergy themselves, skipped chapel. Christianity lingered at this famed university where half the nation's ministers were educated, but the atmosphere was one of religious indifference and downright hypocrisy.

Satan Was as Fit as I

As for Simeon himself, nothing in his upbringing had instilled any real faith in him by that tender age of twenty-one. Nonetheless, when he received the official summons to his first Communion service on a cold winter day, three days after arriving at Cambridge, he entered "a state of spiritual panic." Looking within himself, he concluded that

"Satan himself was as fit to attend [the sacrament] as I." He bought a stern book titled *The Whole Duty of Man,* because it was the only religious book he had heard of, and under its prescriptions he proceeded to read, fast and pray himself into physical illness. For all that effort, he still went to his first Communion unrelieved from his acute sense of unworthiness and fear.

Nor did his struggle end there, for he knew he must receive the sacrament again on Easter Sunday. The first book having failed him, he bought a second that specifically addressed preparation for Communion. But this one, too, required more of him than he could bear. So he went to a third book, a small volume by Bishop Thomas Wilson (1663–1755) titled *A Short and Plain Instruction for the Better Understanding of the Lord's Supper.* As he read Bishop Wilson, he continued to review his former sins and weep over them, not only repenting but also making restitution where possible, even in some cases that required great self-denial. Though this process did not yet set him free spiritually, he never regretted it, saying in his *Memoirs* that "it has been a comfort to me even to this very hour, inasmuch as it gives me reason to hope that my repentance was genuine."

At the time, however, the three further months of self-examination and study leading up to the Easter season again brought him no relief. Then, during Holy Week itself, he found in Wilson a passage "to this effect—'That the Jews knew what they did, when they transferred their sin to the head of their offering.'" Immediately the thought flashed into his mind, "What, may I transfer all my guilt to another? Has God provided an Offering for me, that I may lay my sins on His head?" Exhilarated, Simeon decided that he would not bear his sins "on my own soul one moment longer." He sought to lay them instead on the head of Jesus.

At first he felt no change, but on the Wednesday of Holy Week he "began to have a hope of mercy." The hope strengthened on Thursday, and again on Friday, and even more on Saturday, until "on the Sunday morning, Easter-day, April 4, I awoke early with those words upon my heart and lips, 'Jesus Christ is risen today! Hallelujah! Hallelujah!'" Said

Simeon later, "From that hour peace flowed in rich abundance into my soul; and at the Lord's Table in our Chapel I had the sweetest access to God through my blessed Saviour."

Soon the young man was holding prayer meetings in his rooms and writing passionate evangelistic letters to his brothers and father (rebuffed at first). Returning home after for the long summer vacation, he instituted family prayers for the servants, and was delighted when his eldest brother, Richard, joined in.

He Would Serve Him Gratis

By May of 1782, still short of the prescribed age of twenty-three and lacking even a B.A., Simeon decided to enter the ministry and received ordination as a deacon. This was the beginning of Simeon's career as a "gospel preacher," an evangelical after the pattern of John Newton, John Wesley and George Whitefield. He gave his life to the same message that those men had taught: that Jesus both saves us for heaven and changes our lives here on earth; that the Christian Bible contains everything we need to receive that salvation and transformation; and that upon receiving subjective assurance of their salvation, people must set out to change the world for Jesus.

Simeon made his decision to become ordained and preach this gospel without any support from like-minded Christians. His evangelical calling was a lonely one in the less-than-zealous setting of Cambridge. He even thought of putting an ad in the papers, seeking a minister who, like Simeon, "felt himself an undone sinner, and looked to the Lord Jesus Christ alone for salvation, and desired to live only to make known that Savior unto others." His fancied ad would promise that "if there were any minister of that description, he would gladly become his curate and serve him gratis."

Instead, as a young deacon Simeon received his first assignment in 1782 as summer "supply minister" at St. Edward's, Cambridge—the historical pulpit of the sixteenth-century Protestant martyr Hugh Latimer. In between preaching the Sunday services, Simeon went door to door through the small parish. He would say as folks answered his knock, "I

am come to enquire after your welfare. Are you happy?" The parishioners, who were at best ordinarily wary of clerics, were disarmed by this
energetic young man's friendly approach and "began to wonder what
had hit them." A particular incident secured his reputation: On his first
day, as he returned from service along a narrow alley, he heard through
an open doorway the sound of a violent marital quarrel. As one biographer tells it, the zealous young minister entered the house, "solemnly
appealed to them, and then knelt down to pray. The room was soon full
of a respectful group," and word traveled fast that this earnest, loving
young man was no ordinary minister.

The upshot of these early efforts was that the pews of St. Edward's
were soon filled with curious hearers—"a thing unknown there for near
a century." One evangelist wrote to the old lion of British evangelicalism, John Newton, to announce gleefully that "St. Edward's is crowded
like a theatre on the first night of a new play." Soon the crowd grew so
big that the respectable old parish clerk was even ousted from his customary seat. At the end of those seventeen weeks the flustered clerk
greeted the regular vicar on his return: "Oh sir, I am so glad you are
come; now we shall have some room!"

More important to Simeon's future than the overflowing St. Edward's
pews were two new acquaintances who would ease his loneliness and
much more. These were the father and son who would become, respec-
tively, his mentor and his best friend: Henry Venn (1725–1797) and John
Venn (1759–1813). Henry was a prominent minister and author who
served as rector of Yelling, near Cambridge. John was to become the
pastor and guiding light of the circle of influential social-activist evangelicals called the "Clapham Sect." That group of wealthy, zealous Christians, which included William Wilberforce, successfully campaigned
for the abolition of slavery, advocated prison reform and supported
world missions. Simeon's longstanding friendship with both men would
bring him "much necessary wisdom and balance . . . saving him from
the many pitfalls of inexperience and over-enthusiasm."

Venn senior and junior certainly had their work cut out for them. As
it had been in Simeon's schooldays, his personality was still angular and

at times arrogant. A contemporary observed that Simeon's impetuous, haughty manner often resulted in behavior "painful to the feelings of others." What Simeon needed most from the Venns and the few other soul brothers he would meet along the way was the kind of friendship that could confront him with the hard truth about his own personality. And blessedly, he had the very great Christian virtue of willingness to acknowledge his own faults and accept correction. This habit of humility came as little naturally to him as to anyone—perhaps less, given his brash, blustering personality—but he was able to develop in it as he matured. So when he dressed down a servant, for example, his friend Edwards of Lynn wrote to chastise him, signing himself "John Softly." Simeon, reading the letter, admitted his fault and wrote a penitent response, signing it "Chas. Proud and Irritable." His friend Thomas Lloyd, though fiver years younger, proved himself a good friend to Simeon by pointing out some of the latter's failings. And Simeon accepted the criticisms, writing after one honest letter from Lloyd to thank him "for your kind observations respecting misguided zeal," and to say that he hoped he might improve.

The Peach Will Be Sweet

Simeon did indeed improve. He learned especially from observing and conversing with the devout elder Venn. On one occasion, when the young minister visited the Venns at their Yelling rectory, Henry's daughters were struck by his awkward, blustering mannerisms. As soon as Simeon had left, the three sisters hid themselves in their father's study to enjoy a good laugh at the young man's expense. The patriarch, discovering his daughters indulging in this amusement, first reprimanded them, then took them out to the garden. There he told them to bring him a peach. As it was summer and the peaches were green, the young ladies protested, but they brought him one. He took it and said, "Well, it's green now, and we must wait; but a little more sun and a few more showers, and the peach will be ripe and sweet. So it is with Mr. Simeon."

In the time-honored mode of apprenticeship and imitation stretching back to the early desert fathers, not all of the lessons the young minister learned from his mentor came in the form of direct teaching. On one occasion (and only one in the twenty-four years he knew him) Simeon saw Venn lose his temper and speak ill of another person. But Simeon then also got to see the result: "I was particularly struck with the humiliation he expressed for it in his prayer the next day," he said afterward.

Despite the roughness of the younger man's character, Henry Venn loved him and took him under his wing. Even as early as 1786, Venn wrote to his friend Rowland Hill, "Mr. Simeon's character shines brightly. He grows in humility, is fervent in spirit, and very bountiful and loving." Into his old age, Venn welcomed "my affectionate friend Simeon" into his book-lined study and rejoiced that the younger man "calls me his father; he pours out his prayer for me, as an instrument from whose counsel he has profited." What Charles Simeon hadn't found in his father, he now found in Henry Venn—a man who shared his dream, believed in him and fostered his growth in the Lord.

After his summer at St. Edward's, still short of a completed degree, and still lacking experience as a curate (assistant to the senior minister), Simeon asked to have his name put forward for the pastorate of Cambridge's Holy Trinity Church. This was unheard-of impudence. First, he was barely ordained. Second, he belonged to a class—the evangelicals— who were looked upon with extreme prejudice by the bishops and patrons who controlled such appointments. But the bishop decided (probably with some wisdom!) that it would be better for this congregation to have another man as their minister than the person they themselves requested. And so he gave Simeon the parish where he would labor the rest of his life.

The congregants of Holy Trinity were less than pleased to receive this minister who insisted that to be Christian meant being saved by grace and living Christlike lives. They distrusted his ivory-tower background— they were largely artisan families, or more bluntly, in Simeon's words, "very poor church folks." And most weren't used to his kind of fervor; they would have labeled Simeon an "enthusiast," a sort of eighteenth-century curse word aimed at a person who (it was charged) relied so much on religious experience that he believed he was hearing directly from God words of authority as great as Scripture's.

Destined to Wage War

The timing was both auspicious and difficult. If John Newton's time was the gawky adolescence of the evangelical church in England, then Charles Simeon's time was the movement's early manhood—but it was a challenging manhood. During the early 1800s the movement, begun nearly a century before, was sustaining heavy damage from political intrigue within England's state church, from an apathetic and dwindling Anglican membership, and from a continuation of the same internal struggles that had marred Newton's day—Arminian vs. Calvinist, Established Church vs. nonconformist. It was beginning to look as though "gospel Christianity" had seen its day in its birthplace, and the calmer, more reasonable and less activist faith of the Deists and their ilk would swallow up the movement in its very cradle.

But not if Charles Simeon could help it.

Striding resolutely from his rooms at Kings to preach at Holy Trinity, only five feet eight inches tall but "accustomed to 'bearing himself so well he seemed taller,'" Simeon walked with a hint of a swagger. He wore an ensemble on the showy side of formal, including a "short black coat, breeches and gaiters, black gloves, white ruffled shirt and voluminous preaching gown trailing behind." Under his arm he tucked a fancy umbrella. The determination in his jutting chin and surging stride confirmed a friend's portrait of Simeon as a man "destined to wage irreconcilable war with the slumbers and slumberers of his age."

Yet around the flashing eyes were creases telling the tale of a kindly heart. The young pastor was learning to love and to work tirelessly for a difficult people. Indeed, "difficult" is a pale understatement for the harassment and persecution Simeon endured from members of his congregation. Starting from the second week of his ministry at Holy Trinity, a sizeable group of malcontents had simply locked their proprietary pews and walked out en masse—some of them never to return. This forced those who wished to hear the new minister to find standing room as best they could—for the next ten years. Simeon tried to fix this early on by buying and installing benches at his own expense, but church council members promptly tossed them out into the churchyard. Not long after, Simeon started a Sunday evening service to reach lost sinners, but those same members locked the church doors to try to keep them out. In fact, the wardens sometimes even tried to lock Simeon himself out.

When Simeon did reach the pulpit and begin his sermon, people would walk out. Some mornings, students would poke their heads through the back door of the vestry and yell out insults. At one point Simeon resorted to having ushers stand in the aisles with truncheons or clubs to threaten any of these would-be hecklers.

Simeon's reception in town was no happier. The fastidiously dressed minister was pelted on a number of occasions with filth, stones and, at least once, rotten eggs. This was undergraduate behavior, but the faculty at Cambridge hardly treated him any better—they slandered him and excluded him from their circle. Many of the townspeople, too, ostracized him, so that when one day a passing member of the working poor actually tipped his hat to him, Simeon "was so touched that he had to hurry back to his rooms where he broke down in tears of gratitude."

In a time of particularly intense opposition, Simeon wrote in his journal, "In this state of affairs, I saw no remedy but faith and patience." He clung to 2 Timothy 2:24, "The servant of the Lord must not strive [that is, be quarrelsome], but be gentle unto all men, apt to teach, patient" (KJV). Once, when he was feeling all of this opposition acutely, Simeon "went for a walk with his Greek Testament in his hand, and prayed that God would comfort him from his Word." He opened his Bible at random and read, "And as they came out, they found a man of Cyrene, Simon [Simeon] by name; him they compelled to bear his cross." Wrote Simeon in his *Memoirs*, "When I read that, I said, 'Lord, lay it on me, lay it on me. I will gladly bear the cross for thy sake.'" Looking back across his life, he would later write then whenever rejected, "I have wished rather to suffer than to act; because in suffering, I could not fail to be right; in acting, I might easily do amiss."

Simeon would not give up. And after many years, he did begin to see a turnaround. Especially remarkable was his changing reputation among Cambridge undergraduates, who by 1818 filled his nine-hundred-seat church to the galleries, making up about half of his congregation. The persecution did not end, however, even after a decade and more of ministry. Even as late as 1820, his curate, Mr. Scholefield, regularly had to walk guests to Holy Trinity through a gauntlet of "coarse abuse" from "idle undergraduates who rejoiced in nothing more than hooting at Simeon or his curate."

YOU Have Robbed God

The focus of Simeon's life was preaching—first his, and then that of his protégés. While most of his contemporaries in the Anglican ministry read other men's sermons from their pulpits, Simeon spent twelve hours and sometimes more preparing his. Each of the thousands of sermons he gave in his fifty-four years of ministry he read six times before delivering. More than anything, he wanted to let the Bible speak, interpreting only far enough to let its own message shine through. Yet he was no fundamentalist. At a particular Eclectic Society meeting, the group was studying the book of Job. Simeon stated bluntly that the book was a poem, and that Satan's appearance before God may best be understood as an allegorical scene. Other more conservative ministers present took issue with him on this, but he stood his ground.

Though in his early years his own style of delivery was crude and his interpretations sometimes theologically clumsy or inaccurate, he never lacked drama. His manner, according to eyewitnesses, was compelling, if idiosyncratic. Once, speaking from the verse "Will a man rob God?" he turned to his congregation and thundered, "YOU have robbed God. You, you, and you." His first biographer, William Carus, called his style of delivery "earnest and impassioned to no ordinary degree."

Simeon remained for his life, by the rules of the university which bestowed on him a fellowship and thus housed and paid him, a celibate single man. Though his work was officially limited to his pastoral duties at Holy Trinity (he did no official teaching or lecturing), he poured himself into the lives of the undergraduates—particularly those studying for the ministry.

He wanted to provide these future pastors with the thing he himself had never received—decent training in theology and pastoral ministry. For, although a full 50 percent of the university's students were seeking ordination, they were offered almost nothing in the way of vocational guidance. Theological and biblical language courses were sketchy at best, and students received no instruction in the practicalities and skills of preaching and administration. It was assumed they would simply pick these skills up once they entered the ministry—an assumption proved wrong in too many cases. Nor were there any real standards for ordination. "The ordination examination consisted merely of the construing of a passage from the Greek Testament, and was taken on the day of ordination itself so that any thought of anyone's name being withdrawn as unprepared or unsuitable was out of the question."

So Simeon began in 1790 to hold talks for ministerial students in his Cambridge rooms on Sunday evenings—informal seminars on preaching. He would continue these for forty years. In 1812 or 1813 he added weekly "conversation parties," essentially theological and pastoral Q&A sessions open to all members of the university. By 1823 some forty students were attending each of these gatherings, which were both held on Fridays: the conversation parties at 6:00 p.m. and the sermon classes two hours later at 8:00. By 1827 the number edged closer to sixty, keeping two servants busy distributing tea and straining the capacity of even Simeon's spacious front room, with its large semicircular window overlooking a college courtyard. "To this day," says his biographer Hopkins, "one can see the rows of old-fashioned hat and coat pegs which lined the passages to his rooms erected for the benefit of his many undergraduate visitors, and also the substantial shoe-scrapers which he insisted that they use to save spoiling his carpets with the yellow gravel of the college paths."

His mentorship of these students extended well beyond such formal settings. He was concerned that his young charges develop into whole and holy ministers, healthy intellectually, spiritually and physically.

Toward this goal, he imposed on his protégés a regimen of hard work, careful study, obedience to university rules and, above all, exercise. Yet he counseled moderation even in these disciplines. And once his students had emerged into the ministry, he urged them, "Don't let Satan make you overwork—and thus put you out of action for a long period." To an aged bishop he wrote with this congratulation: "It requires more deeply-rooted zeal for God to keep within our strength for his sake, than to exceed it. Look at all the young ministers: they run themselves out of breath in a year or two and in many instances never recover it. Is this wise?"

In his weekly sermon classes, Simeon most often taught the undergraduates such nuts-and-bolts things as preaching techniques and how to construct a sermon: "Never weary your hearers by long preaching." "Endeavour to rivet their attention on your message for a reasonable time; but remember that the mind, and especially among the generality of persons or the uneducated, will only bear a certain amount of tension." "It is the want of a good and impressive delivery that destroys the usefulness of a great proportion of pious ministers." Simeon even "suggested that they might try rehearsing their sermons to a piece of furniture imagining the wooden object to be a listening parishioner." Hopkins adds wryly that this was a task "most parsons would not find very difficult."

Simeon taught his protégés to write out their first three hundred to six hundred sermons in the ministry (that is, the product of their first three to four years of preaching), then after that to prepare outlines and speak extempore. As for sermon preparation, much of what he prescribed has since become standard preaching-class advice: "Scope out the biblical text and analyze it. Look at the context of the passage. Consider the literal meaning, but don't be bound by it. Discuss each part of the text in turn. Develop a unified theme, with an introduction, development, and conclusion. Don't read your own favorite ideas into the text. Avoid overly ornamental language and obscure references. Devise a style of delivery that suits your individual personality."

Soon Simeon began to publish detailed sermon outlines. These were widely used in his time and stayed continuously in print for over a hundred years. In the preface of what became a twenty-one-volume set of "skeleton" sermons—2,536 in all, covering the entire Bible—Simeon said that the preacher should put every one of his own sermons to this test: "Does it uniformly tend *to humble the sinner? to exalt the Savior? to promote holiness?* If in one single instance it loses sight of any of these points, let it be condemned without mercy."

The Truth Is in Both Extremes

Finally, Simeon told his students to preach from the heart, from a genuine love of their congregants. "If a man's heart is full of love, he will rarely ever offend. He may have severe things to say, but he will say them in love." Even the very words of each sermon should be invested with the preacher's own feelings and should elicit responding feelings from the listeners. In such a way could "the presence of God the Holy Spirit" be invited into each service. Such advice mirrored the philosophical sentimentalism that Simeon's age shared with Newton's—that characteristic late-eighteenth- and early-nineteenth-century attention to emotion, experience and honest expression, rooted in John Locke's empiricism.

As each gownsman entered Simeon's rooms for his weekly conversation parties, Simeon would offer his hand, bowing and smiling in a kindly way. He kept the name and a few notes about any newcomer in a pocket memorandum-book, sometimes making a humorous comment on the name to set everyone at ease. When the students had gathered and the servant was busy bringing around the tea, Simeon would sit on a high chair near the fireplace. Every inch of the great front room was arranged with benches, and the window seats were often crowded too. Simeon would then, a student remembered, fold his hands on his knees, turn his head slightly to one side and "encourage us to propose our doubts."

This low-key approach soon had its desired effect, as students opened up with their questions. One thinks, reading about these "parties," how presciently similar they were to such modern free-form, question-based modes as the Alpha program or campus ministries like InterVarsity (of which these meetings were actually the precursor, via the 1848 founding of the Cambridge University Prayer Union). In fact, Simeon's approach shares much with Newton's Eclectic Society. This is not coincidental, as Simeon himself was involved with that society, attending at least thirteen times between 1798 and 1811.

Like Newton, Simeon was not dogmatic or sectarian, but sought to embrace what he felt were legitimate differences in opinion over the interpretation of Scripture. The division between Calvinists and Arminians that Newton had faced still troubled Simeon's time. But Simeon famously stated that he wanted to make "Bible Christians, not system Christians." He recognized in the Bible certain paradoxes and antinomies that simply could not—and must not—be reconciled. We can eliminate neither divine sovereignty nor human responsibility, he insisted, since the Bible teaches both. He imagined the first-century Calvinist or Arminian sitting at St. Paul's elbow, recommending that the apostle to change one or another of his expressions to make his theology more "consistent." In response, Simeon professed, "I have read Paul, and caught something of his strange notions, oscillating (not vacillating) from pole to pole. Sometimes I am a high Calvinist, at other times a low Arminian, so that if extremes will please you, I am your man." For Simeon, "it is not *one* extreme we are to go to, but *both* extremes."

Yet despite this "extremism," Simeon's position was a crucial and a healing one for evangelicals of his day. Handley Moule, a graduate of Cambridge and later bishop of Durham, went so far as to claim that it was Simeon more than anyone else whose therapeutic influence eased tensions between Calvinists and Arminians. Simeon, like several of the other saints in this book, acted as a barrier-crossing and bridge-building figure at a crucial moment in the church's history.

By 1811 Simeon was spending two-thirds of his time and energy on the undergraduates at Cambridge. His disciples, in turn, began to be labeled "Simeonites" and "Sims" by the other students. These monikers they wore as badges of honor, although predictably their other-worldly devotion made them the butt of much campus amusement (one 1822 college ditty distinguished between "some carnally given to women and wine," and "some apostles of Simeon all pure and divine").

Mr. Simeon Watches over Us

Looking back over the life of Charles Simeon, we face a kind of paradox. There's no denying that he was a broken person with some serious personality flaws. It seems reasonable to say that he was scarred early on both by a domineering father and the derision and rejection of his schoolmates (and we know that no one can be crueler than school-aged children!). Out of these early experiences came a man who for his whole life put on an affected, punctilious manner. He seemed at pains to be recognized as a gentleman. A friendly critic, Sir James Stephen, remarked that Simeon carried himself with "a seat in the saddle so triumphant, badinage so ponderous, stories so exquisitely unbefitting him about the pedigree of his horses or the vintages of his cellar," that he seemed to be "studying in clerical costume for the part of Mercutio, and doing it scandalously ill."

Beyond such affectations, Simeon had more serious rough edges. His biographer, Hopkins, called him "his own worst enemy when it came to establishing close friendships." His personality, angular and at times arrogant, stood in the way of satisfying fellowship. "Though highly sensitive himself," said Hopkins, "it was a long time before he learned sensitivity to . . . others."

How could someone with such personality flaws inspire loyalty and form character in so many young men? How could he become a successful and well-liked mentor? On the deepest level, we would probably have to say: "By the grace of God." But how did that grace manifest itself in his life, so that he became one of the most beloved and influential men in his generation of evangelical Anglicans?

First, Simeon loved his students genuinely and sacrificially. His care for his young charges was transparent. He called the conversation parties "a foretaste of heaven," saying, "They diffuse a spirit of love amongst us. I would I could have them oftener." "Having gathered you all together on my hearth," he told the assembled students at one of these affairs, "I warm myself at your fire, and find my Christian love burn and glow." One of the students, Thomas Thomason, wrote in a letter to a friend, "Mr. Simeon watches over us as a shepherd over his sheep. He takes delight in instructing us, and has us continually at his rooms. . . . His Christian love and zeal prompt him to notice us."

Second, he called his church back to basics (a common theme of every age's prophetic patron saints): in particular, to a high—and realistic—view of the calling of full-time Christian ministry. He believed that of all vocations the ministry was not only the most vital but the most difficult, because it demanded both self-denial and "spiritual affections" from its workers. He knew that "many mistake their calling and with devoted hearts are nevertheless out of their sphere when they enter the ministry." So he counseled divinity students that their calling would likely come, not in a blinding flash of revelation, but "partly from a sense of obligation to [God] for his redeeming love, partly from a compassion for the ignorant and perishing multitudes around us, and partly from a desire to be an honoured instrument in the Redeemer's hands."

Third, he exercised two qualities most crucial in any mentor: wise discernment and a willingness to help his charges in practical ways, at any cost to himself. As for discernment, he was known as an insightful and sympathetic spiritual director—often, as had Newton, providing this service through the mail. By 1829 he had copies of more than seven thousand letters of counsel filed in his sideboard.

As for willingness to provide practical help, his biographer says that "as soon as he was convinced that a young ordinand had true potential and was fully committed to Christ, there was nothing he would not do for him." This help extended beyond his charges' Cambridge days to the financial and political support he provided to those seeking ministerial positions after their graduations. In that day, clerical positions were bought and sold, given often to unqualified and undevout sons and relatives by laymen descended from medieval landlords. Many an on-fire young divinity student emerged from his degree and from Simeon's mentorship to find himself unable to secure a pulpit. Simeon, wealthy from both family money and the sales of his famed sermon outlines, addressed their dilemma in the most direct way possible: he paid out of his own pocket to buy many of them "advowsons"—coveted clerical positions especially in the day's growing urban areas. Soon many of his fervent pupils found themselves preaching in influential city parishes long accustomed to slumber under the ministry of untalented sons of privilege. As more and more of his protégés made their way out into the ministry, Simeon founded a trust drawing on other sources of funds to help them in this way.

Perhaps the most important aspects of Simeon's character as a mentor—certainly one most often noted by his devoted flock of gownsmen—was his willingness to acknowledge his own faults and accept correction. By the example and counsel of those around him, Simeon seems to have grown a great deal in his character, knocking off many of the rough edges and mellowing with age—and this endeared him to many. The longer he lived, the more he knew his own shortcomings—that they were not surface blemishes, but deep issues of character. Even eight years before his death, he wrote in his diary on his birthday, "I spent this day as I have for these forty-three last years, as a day of humiliation; having increasing need of such seasons every year I live." Elsewhere in his diary he wrote, twice, in large letters, "TALK NOT ABOUT MYSELF."

And he continued to accept correction and discipline, not only from his Lord but also from his friends—people who got to see that Charles Simeon struggled with habits and issues that might have stopped another person from being useful to God. Writing to the Reverend Mr. Stillingfleet of Hotham in 1795, Simeon admitted how different was the public perception of even a supposedly "great man of God" from the reality: "It is well that our fellow-creatures do not know us as God knows us, or even as we know ourselves; for they could not possibly bear with us: but the patience of God is infinite." He admitted that his own character was far from perfect, but even in the face of his continued struggles, he professed hope.

At the heart of Simeon's willingness to be transparent with friends like Mr. Stillingfleet, and even with his students, was the spiritual virtue of humility. This did not come naturally, but he developed it as he matured. And in his heart, Simeon knew *this* virtue, among all others, was of the very essence of a Christian's life. He had been with many professed believers and heard them speak many words about religion, but what he treasured above all was "to be with a *broken-hearted* Christian." Transparent brokenness was a keynote of his ministry.

In 1808, upon falling ill for eight months, Simeon faced probably the greatest test of any man's humility when his protégé and curate Thomason took over his pulpit, coming nearly up to Simeon's mark as a captivating speaker. On hearing of this, Simeon simply quoted the scripture "He must increase; I must decrease." To a friend he said, "Now I see *why* I have been laid aside. I bless God for it."

Simeon stands as an encouraging example of how God uses broken vessels to accomplish his work. For those of us (I certainly include myself) who want to serve God, yet also recognize the ugly forms that brokenness has taken in our hearts and lives, the story of a man such as Simeon can be a reviving thing. Though he struggled throughout his life with the scars of sin in his personality, he was enabled by grace to show loving kindness to others, to treasure the ministry of God above all else, to give of himself constantly ever in the face of ingratitude and persecution, and to continue throughout his life not only teaching but also being taught. While many people "harden" in unpleasant ways during their later years, people who knew Simeon talked about how he kept on sweetening right up until the end, like the peach in Henry Venn's parable: "As he grew older, although the eccentricity and punctiliousness remained, humility and love triumphed over pride and harshness, so that during the latter part of his life there can have been few men who had more friends."

May God work such obvious fruits of the Spirit in my own life! And yours!

Amanda Berry Smith

STANDING TALL AND

BREAKING DOWN BARRIERS

Amanda Berry Smith is one of the least known and most courageous "barrier-crossing prophets" in American history. At various times an evangelist with the African Methodist Episcopal Church, the white National Camp Meeting Association for the Promotion of Holiness and the largely white Women's Christian Temperance Union, Smith rose from slavery roots, through years of menial service, to prominent pulpits and platforms both white and black, national and international. Throughout her career, her life and message were complicated by the big three barriers of race, class and gender. But she also saw the Holy Spirit operating to heal the wounds caused by these barriers in some amazing ways. To Smith, a staunch advocate of the Wesleyan holiness doctrine and experience of entire sanctification, that experience was the final solution *on the personal level* for racism. A preacher at largely white camp meetings in the 1870s through the end of the century, Smith taught that the Holy Spirit working in sanctification could both release the black person from the pain of the experience of racism and release the white person from racist attitudes against others.

Smith's life was complicated from the very beginning by race. Born Amanda Berry in Long Green, Maryland (just north of Baltimore), on January 23, 1837, she spent her earliest years as a slave child on a dairy farm. She was to be the oldest of thirteen children, only five of whom would be born in slavery (her father would earn enough to secure the family's freedom and move them to Pennsylvania). As a little girl, Smith attended the Presbyterian Church with her masters, who spoiled her, as she later said, with dresses and delicacies. But as she would realize, "They were getting me ready for market." While still enslaved, Smith's father, Sam, worked for other farmers in the area after hours to earn the money that would eventually free his family. After he had earned his freedom, these same farmers were ready, on at least one occasion, to make him a slave again over the fact that he had broken a discriminatory travel law.

Praying Together Across the Color Line

Despite the obvious barriers, Amanda, like many Southern blacks, experienced a certain degree of spiritual mutuality and even a sort of spiritual equality in biracial church settings. As a girl she often heard the story of how her mother, Mariam, had been instrumental in the conversion and Christian life of her white "mistress" (that is, her master's daughter), Celie. Mariam had prayed for Miss Celie's conversion, and when Celie went forward at an "old-fashioned, red-hot Camp Meeting," her "staunch Presbyterian" family deeply disapproved and ordered her not to return to the "hollerin'" Methodists. Mariam supported Celie during this time, meeting with the girl in secret in an old dairy, praying and singing with her. Soon, however, Celie fell ill. On her deathbed, the girl first requested that Mariam sing and then demanded of her family that Mariam and her children be released to the children's father. This the family later did.

Upon their emancipation, Amanda's family moved north to Pennsylvania. There they worked tirelessly on the so-called underground railroad. Their white landlord, John Lowe (after whom the local Methodist campground was likely named), "would allow my father to do what he could in secreting the poor slaves that would get away and come to him for protection." For the rest of her life, Smith carried with her the memories of her parents' courage as they worked to help slaves escape across the Maryland border into the free North.

Smith also continued throughout her life to experience the crossing of racial boundaries, both in practical and spiritual ways. In Pennsylvania, other "good white people all over the neighborhood" were solicitous of the welfare of runaway slaves. One night when the slave catchers came at about midnight and knocked on their door, Mariam Berry was so put out she stormed downstairs in her nightdress, took up a cane containing a hidden sword (the very presence of such an object in their house suggests the father's reasonably comfortable economic and social status by that time) and would have attacked them had Amanda's father not restrained her. The next morning Mariam trooped into town and told, to anyone who would listen, her story of being hounded by these men. A number of the white townsfolk encouraged her to make her complaint public ("All the rich respectable people . . . backed her up"), and so she declaimed for an hour in front of the town's largest tavern, as townspeople cried, "Shame! Shame!" and "the [slavecatchers] skulked away here and there."

Smith's own initial "trip to the altar," though she did not call it her conversion, was a biracial experience. It took place when she was thirteen, in a white Methodist church in Pennsylvania. The person who led Amanda forward was a white girl, Mary Bloser. Smith reminisced: "she came to me, a poor colored girl sitting away back by the door, and with entreaties and tears, which I really felt, she asked me to go forward. I was the only colored girl there, but I went. She knelt beside me with her arm around me and prayed for me. O, how she prayed!"

As a young woman Smith continued to spend much time in a multiracial (though largely white) setting. Her mother and family "arranged to keep a boarding house during the camp meeting time." She associated those times with food, friends, warmth and bustle. "It was white people's camp meeting," she recounted, "but colored people went as well." Despite all of the well-documented use of the Bible and church by ruling whites in the slave South as tools with which to control the black population, still many pre–Civil War blacks received their salvation, sanctification and Christian nurture as did Smith, in largely white church and camp meeting settings.

Yet, on the other hand, racist attitudes persisted even in those integrated settings, both before and after emancipation. Smith related numerous stories of such prejudice and admitted she especially struggled to accept the reality of "full sanctification" (on which, more in a moment) against evidence of racism even in supposedly sanctified folk. For example, in the months after her first commitment to Jesus at thirteen, she attended a largely white Bible study. There, the leader made it a rule to speak to all the whites before getting to her—no matter in what place Amanda sat in the order. This meant that Amanda was kept late from her duties to the white household in which she was working at the time. Finally, her white employer demanded she give up on this religious exercise or lose her job. Needing the money, Smith left the Bible study, and she soon drifted away from the church altogether.

Northern whites' antislavery sentiments were also at times as much politically motivated as born of real compassion and a sense of equality of blacks with whites. Many whites who fought against slavery felt the final solution to the issue was to send all the Africans back to their native lands—never mind that they had worked to improve huge swathes of American land by the sweat of their brow and had put down roots in this country, into which many had in fact been born, never having seen Africa in their lives.

In ways like these, Smith's experiences continued to teach her that although whites could sometimes be genuinely solicitous and helpful, their underlying motivations were often tainted by racism. And although she was later able to overcome these early experiences and form true friendships with whites, she often had to do so in the face of lingering racism. Not surprisingly, even as she went on to a ministry career in white circles, she would always feel the black community was her true home.

Saved amid the Storm

As Amanda grew into womanhood, she faced many trials. She was married to two difficult husbands—the first one spent much of his time drunk and finally went away to join the Union army and never returned, and the second one lied about wanting to become a minister so he could convince her to marry him, then spent much of his time arguing with her. She also bore five children, of which only one, her daughter Mazie, survived into adulthood. Her second husband died early, and she lived the remainder of her life as a single mother.

In 1855, at the age of eighteen, Amanda fell seriously ill. The doctors gave her up, and she began slipping into exhaustion, with her end seemingly near. Suddenly she saw a vision of herself at "a great Camp Meeting" preaching to "thousands of people" from a high "platform" as tall as the trees. She recalled, "I was on this platform with a large Bible opened and I was preaching from these words:—'And I if I be lifted up will draw all men unto me.' O, how I preached, and the people were slain [that is, experienced the charismatic "falling in the Spirit"] right and left." The vision led her to dedicate herself to Christ and to the ministry of the gospel, though she considered her conversion not to have taken place until the following year.

The conversion happened like this. In 1856, after the birth of her first child, Smith was struggling in prayer in the basement of a Quaker family for whom she was working. All of a sudden, she felt she had broken through and received salvation. Her response was immediate and characteristic: "Hallelujah!" she cried out, "I have got religion; glory to God, I have got religion!" She soon joined the African Methodist Episcopal Church (AME) in York, Pennsylvania. Though she would spend much of her ministering life in other settings, she retained membership in the AME until her death.

When she moved with her husband James to New York City so he could take a hotel job, Smith began a stretch of domestic work. New York had once been a land of opportunity for blacks, but by the time James and Amanda moved there, opportunities were dwindling, race riots had erupted, whites were accusing black workers of being scabs and union-busters, and many jobs that had traditionally been held by blacks (for example, barber, caterer) were now being taken by European immigrants such as the Irish. James, who by the 1860s was a Master Mason and Odd Fellow, joined the local Masonic chapter and several similar fraternal groups. Having (as she said) "high-toned" aspirations at that point in her life, Amanda joined several affiliated women's groups, although she had trouble coming up with the monthly dues.

In 1866, as Amanda and James were struggling to make ends meet in this setting, they were evicted from their rooms and were forced to spend time in the public Colored Home. Conditions there, however, proved unlivable. Now pregnant, Smith found brief relief when a friend from Philadelphia took her in until the baby was born that September. By then the marriage had been rough for some time, and she was living apart from James. So from her friend's house, Smith moved to a damp basement apartment advertised as furnished. The landlord, however, had deceived her, and he soon began moving the furniture out from under her in the small, cramped apartment. The dampness in the place likely worsened the arthritis and a string of respiratory ailments with which she had been struggling. In those conditions, the baby, a boy, sickened and died.

Though James was sporadically helping with her rent, in order to keep going financially Smith began to take in others' washing. Sometimes she worked twenty-four hours at a stretch, stopping only to lean occasionally on the windowsill. Soon, too, she was pregnant again, but with no hope in sight for an improvement in her living conditions.

The Holiness Experience

It was at this point that Smith, having heard holiness preaching in various settings, began to seek entire sanctification. This was a teaching forged in the 1700s by John Wesley out of his reading of Scripture. It was revived in the 1820s and 30s by teachers such as Methodist laywoman Phoebe Palmer. The central experience of entire sanctification meant two things for holiness believers. Entire sanctification or "Spirit baptism" in the holiness movement could be thought of as a sort of "negative" event—that is, an event that removed something from a person, i.e. sin. But holiness folk spent a lot more time talking about sanctification as a "positive" event. For holiness folk, entire sanctification meant recapturing the "first love" of your conversion, and reorienting and stabilizing your affections toward God.

This was the experience for which Smith began to yearn. Entire sanctification had been considered the special emphasis of Methodism in its early years both in England and America. However, times were changing. From the 1840s on, Methodists seeking holiness began to charge that many of their denomination's churches were becoming too wealthy and spiritually sluggish to preach the doctrine. In fact, by Smith's day two major "come-outer" churches had already separated from the main body of Methodism over that issue, among others (the Wesleyan Church and the Free Methodist Church). And as white Methodism had gone, so too black Methodism. American Protestants on both sides of the color line seemed bent more on respectability and comfort than on spiritual growth. And the holiness movement, including Smith as one of its key spokespeople, brought the message of a loving, active God who waited like the father of the prodigal son to take his children in his arms, cleanse them of their sins and give them the inheritance that was rightfully theirs.

This is all very well, but what about the triple prejudice Smith faced as a poor black woman? She had found her place in the holiness movement. But this movement, for all its radical traits, was still overwhelmingly middle-class, class-conscious, accustomed to the privileges (and cultural blindness) of white folks and largely biased against women in leadership—despite the fact that its most famous and influential leader, Phoebe Palmer, was a woman. Smith indeed felt these prejudices deeply; at times they drove her nearly to despair. How could she overcome such hurtful attitudes among the sanctified? The answer to this question is that even then, before she experienced it, Smith saw the experience of sanctification as a balm for the heart-wounds of racism, classism and sexism. She wrote, "[My] hunger [for sanctification] went on, and when I read, 'Rejoice when men persecute you,' I felt that was *not* my experience; there was a feeling of retaliation. And when they spoke about me and blamed me, I wanted to justify myself instead of leaving it all with God. *Then* I read, 'This is the will of God, even your sanctification.'"

Then at last, in 1868, Smith visited the church of the white Methodist holiness leader John Inskip. Inskip had just cofounded the National Camp Meeting Association for the Promotion of Holiness. This was a rapidly growing organization whose annual summer camp meetings had already begun to draw thousands of seekers. In the service, Smith felt Inskip was "preaching right to me." And she began to feel the Holy Spirit working in her, like waves rolling over her. "The vacuum in my soul began to fill up; it was like a pleasant draught of cool water," she wrote. Three times this sensation welled up in her, and three times she felt like shouting right there in the service. But "just as I went to say 'Glory to Jesus!' the Devil said, 'Look, look at the white people, mind, they will put you out,' and I put my hands up to my mouth and held still, and . . . I felt the Spirit leave me and pass away."

When Smith at last gathered the courage to shout, however, "Brother Inskip answered, 'Amen, Glory to God.'" Her heart soared, and she felt that God himself had affirmed her and had great things in store for her. As she left the church building, overflowing with joy, her thoughts burned within her: "O . . . if there was a platform around the world I would be willing to get on it and walk and tell everybody of this sanctifying power of God!"

This was clearly a turning point. Up until now she had worked for whites as a washerwoman and had often been mistreated by white landlords and neighbors. She testified, "I always had a fear of white people—that is, I was not afraid of them in the sense of doing me harm, or anything of that kind—but a kind of fear because they were white, and were there, and I was black and was here!" But now, standing on the street outside of Inskip's church, with his "Amen" ringing in her ears, she heard other words, seeming to come from the northeast corner of the church, slowly but clearly: "There is neither Jew nor Greek, there is neither bond nor free, there is neither male nor female, for ye are all on in Christ Jesus" (Gal 3:28 KJV). And as she looked at the crowd of white

people leaving the church—the people she had always been afraid of—
"they looked so small. The great mountain had become a mole-hill.
'Therefore, if the Son shall make you free, then you are free, indeed.' All
praise to my victorious Christ!"

A Speckled Bird Among My People

In a sense, Smith was now picking up again the thread of biracial religious experience she had learned at her mother's knee and in her experience as a thirteen-year-old religious seeker who had wept and prayed
with the white girl, Mary. At first, she testified of her sanctification at
the African Methodist Episcopal (AME) churches, but the message was
often not welcomed. AME bishops and pastors in the 1870s were becoming increasingly concerned to separate their religion from the religion of slavery days. To demonstrate that they were educated, rational
people, worthy of the respect of the whites who controlled the culture all
around them, black church leaders in the North condemned the emotional expressiveness of holiness worship. It just looked too much like
the exuberant, physical practices of dancing, swooning and shouting
that slave Christians had picked up both from white Methodist and Bap-
tist evangelists and from their own African roots. Among Northern
blacks with these concerns, Smith again had three strikes against her as
a potential leader: she was a woman, she belonged to the domestic class,
and she brought a message and a religious style that seemed too strongly
connected with the old slave religion.

She tells in her *Autobiography* how, in the first flush of her sanctification, this stigma attached to her: "I had become a speckled bird among
my own people on account of the profession of the blessing of holiness."
In Sullivan Street AME Church, where she attended, the Reverend Nelson Turpin was fiercely opposed to the doctrine, and "we poor souls who
dared to testify definitely in a Love Feast, or in a General Class, might
expect a raking; and especially on Sunday nights, when the church
would be crowded, he would take especial pains to tell some ridiculous
inconsistency about some sanctified sister or brother that he used to
know." She tells also of having gone to Union Church, an "uptown . . .

colored church," in which "there was not a member . . . that believed in the doctrine of holiness; and from that church there had been great criticism in regard to my professing such a blessing." Knees trembling, she went there to testify to her experience. Although the meeting yielded good results, these came only in the face of great resistance.

In contrast to these scenes of black resistance to holiness, Smith soon found herself in an uptown New York church of the Free Methodists—a white holiness group that had seceded in 1860 from the main body of Methodists over issues of slavery, class prejudice and the Wesleyan message of sanctification (they were on the pro-holiness side). There the minister, a Mr. Mackey, was "a good friend to the colored people," and the congregation treated her much better than had her own people at the black Sullivan or Union churches. She was ready to join the Free Methodists on the spot: "Though I had been a member of the African Methodist Church for years, I was willing that morning to join without a letter, on probation." Soon, however, she uncovered prejudice among these folks, and so her quest for a church continued elsewhere.

During this early postsanctification period, though she spoke at a variety of churches and attended the "Tuesday Meetings for the Promotion of Holiness" in the home of Phoebe Palmer, she could not yet enter full-time ministry, the path of her childhood vision. She was still a mother, caring for her young teenager Mazie and her fifth child, the infant William Henry. Her marriage was also in deep turmoil as James did not approve of her holiness beliefs, which led her among other things to quit the fraternal societies she had joined, feeling they were not compatible with a holy life. But within months, her situation changed. In the winter of 1868 William Henry came down with bronchitis. He worsened slowly, and Smith struggled with the ultimate test of her consecration. Would she be able to say to God, "Thy will be done," even if that will meant taking her child? At last, after long struggle, Smith found herself able to do so. Within hours, little Will died in her arms. She received twenty dollars from a friend and was able to bury him (Smith did not have and James did not provide any money for the purpose). Nor did James show up at either the funeral service or the cemetery, though the latter was near his house. Within four months, James too was dead of stomach cancer, and buried alongside Will.

Although a harsh reality, the deaths of Will and James freed Smith to increase her evangelistic work in the holiness cause. In October 1870 she began traveling as an evangelist. The first place she visited to minister was a black church in Salem, New Jersey. She later recalled how the minister had introduced her: "'There is a lady here, Mrs. Amanda Smith . . . she says the Lord sent her,' with a toss of his head which indicated he didn't much believe it." Despite this less-than-auspicious start and fear so severe that she was "trembling from head to foot," by the second night she presided over "souls convicted and converted," and soon the meetings erupted into full-scale revival. This spread, Smith noted, "from the colored people to the white people."

A Tall Black Woman in Quaker Dress

Her evangelistic career was launched, and as she travelled from place to place, bringing the message of holiness, she found herself moving increasingly "from the colored people to the white people." For the rest of her life, she would receive an increasing flow of invitations from whites— first at churches, then at camp meetings and then abroad. An important part of this shift was her first holiness camp meeting.

This was in July of 1870, in the fourth year of the National Camp Meeting Association's operation. The meeting that summer was in Harford County, Maryland, near the town of Oakington. Though they had started only four years previously, the camp meetings were already becoming major national events, drawing tens of thousands of people each summer. They were very different from the wild, emotional camp meetings of the frontier period. The largely middle-class, white attendees who rode the trains out of New York, Boston and other urban metropolises to the beautiful wooded retreats chosen for these camp meetings had little taste for the sorts of extreme physical manifestations that had characterized those earlier gatherings.

Nevertheless, as historian Melvin Dieter puts it, the atmosphere at these meetings was "packed with emotion, Methodist enthusiasm, and spiritual expectancy." At the huge Manheim camp meeting in 1868 (over 25,000 attendees), when a respected minister began to pray aloud, "as sudden as if a flash of lightning from the heavens had fallen upon the people, one simultaneous burst of agony and then of glory was heard in all parts of the congregation; and for nearly an hour, the scene beggared all description. . . . Those seated far back in the audience declared that the sensation was as if a strong wind had moved from the stand over the congregation. Several intelligent people in different parts of the congregation spoke of the same phenomenon. . . . Sinners stood awestricken and others fled affrighted from the congregation." The sea of weeping, praying people was galvanized, convinced they were "face to face with God."

The 1870 Oakington meeting featured 150 ministers and over eight thousand attendees, including not only Methodists but Presbyterians, Quakers and others. All of these braved one-hundred-degree heat to be part of the ten-day event. Though clergymen were the most prominent camp meeting figures, at Oakington "an unusual lay person stood out." It was the fourth day of the camp meeting, in the early afternoon, in a secluded grove near the head of the grounds. All of the camp meeting's official venues were in use, but here "four clergymen and a tall black woman in Quaker dress gathered with 'a large company' to pray." The black woman, Smith, was "urged to take part in the meeting," and she gladly complied, giving a long "oration," which was later printed in full in the camp meeting report.

This was the beginning of Smith's decades-long camp meeting ministry. Her simple Quaker dress and plain scoop bonnet set far back on her head dated from soon after her sanctification. It was no doubt a visible sign of her intention to keep herself separate from the pride and social-climbing of the fraternal societies to which she had once belonged. It may also have marked her affection for the Quakers themselves, who had been so sacrificially involved in the underground railroad of her childhood. She was indeed a commanding presence—nearly six feet tall, dark brown skin, a deep contralto voice and disarming smile. When she spoke, it was with humor, picturesque illustrations and a clear, biblical presentation of her message.

We get a sense of the impression she left on so many of the thousands who attended these white camp meetings from the white Methodist bishop James Thoburn, who in his introduction to Smith's *Autobiography* recalled the first time he had seen her, at a camp meeting in the mid-1870s. Kneeling near her at a prayer meeting on a rainy night after a relatively unsuccessful day at the camp, Thoburn was sinking under the general mood of discouragement. Suddenly, he was startled by the sound of singing. "I lifted my head, and at a short distance . . . I saw the colored sister . . . kneeling in an upright position, with her hands spread out and her face all aglow. She had suddenly broken out with a triumphant song. . . . Something like a hallowed glow seemed to rest upon the dark face before me, and I felt in a second that she was possessed of a rare degree of spiritual power."

Grace to Be a Gazing-Stock
As a barrier-crosser, Smith would need every ounce of that spiritual power. Her first experience as a featured camp meeting speaker (that is, someone who was "on the program" and spoke from one of the meeting's official platforms) would be at the Kennebunk, Maine, camp meeting in 1871. When she arrived at Kennebunk, Smith found herself followed by crowds of curiosity-seeking whites. "The people followed me about," she later remembered, "and just stared at me. Sometimes I would slip into a tent away from them. Then I would see them peep in, and if they saw me they would say, 'Oh! Here is the colored woman. Look!'" Then they would rush to see her. Upset to the point of wanting to leave, Smith had to pray herself through: "I told the Lord how mean I felt because the people had looked at me. I prayed, 'Help me to throw off that mean feeling, and give me grace to be a gazing stock.'" Sure enough, by the end of her prayer, the Lord had dealt with her feelings and allowed her to be comfortable in that setting. It was such a huge relief, "I laughed, and cried, and shouted."

Locked out of leadership within her own denomination, which wanted no part of having women serve as ordained ministers, frequently snubbed among both blacks *and* whites for her relative poverty and plain dress, Smith would become the only black and the only woman member (that is, leader) of the National Camp Meeting Association. From that position she continued her ministry for years within the largely white setting of the holiness camp-meeting circuit, singing, exhorting, testifying and leading meetings.

Eventually Smith became so well known that opportunities opened to her to travel abroad and minister in England, India and Africa. This she did for several years before returning home to found an orphanage and "industrial school" for abandoned children in Chicago. And then, in her mature years, she settled down to write her *Autobiography*. This book, which she sold in support of her perpetually near-insolvent orphanage (like many powerful evangelists before and since, she was no administrator), exemplifies Smith's unique ministry. She not only preached the born-again, sanctified, experiential faith of the holiness movement, she also spoke frankly and directly to her reading audience as well as her live audience about the realities of racism in postbellum America.

For example, she recorded in her book a conversation with a white lady who asked her one day if all blacks wanted to be white. Smith replied that she had only wanted to be white once in her life, at a white Methodist church meeting in Lancaster, Pennsylvania, where she got stirred up and felt like shouting, but was conscious that she would open herself to criticism should she do so. She concluded her story about this meeting by affirming the God-given dignity and nobility of her people. "No," she wrote, "we who are the royal black are very well satisfied with His gift to us in this substantial color." Then she concluded with another reminder to her largely white reading audience of the results of their racism. "I, for one, praise him for what He has given me," she wrote, *"although at times it is very inconvenient."*

Sometimes her stories along these lines could be even more pointed. She related, for example, a time when she was asked bluntly by another white lady at the Ocean Grove camp meeting whether, if she could be, she would rather be white than black. Answered Smith, "No, no, . . . as the Lord lives, I would rather be black and fully saved than to be white and not saved; *I was bad enough, black as I am, and I would have been ten times worse if I had been white."* Her interrogator proceeded to "roar laughing," showing perhaps that she was aware of the foolishness of her own question.

At times in her personal dealings with whites, and very often in her *Autobiography,* Smith used such moments to pierce her white audiences with an awareness of racism and its effects. Warm memories and positive relationships with whites notwithstanding, she ministered always in the face of prejudice, and she continued, even after her fame, to know the pain of racism. To those whites who remarked to her how well she was treated by all, Smith replied, "If you want to know and understand properly what Amanda Smith has to contend with, just turn black and go about as I do, and you will come to a different conclusion." Driving the point home, she concluded: "I think some people would understand the quintessence of sanctifying grace if they could be black about twenty-four hours."

As one student of Smith's life remarked, those white readers who bought her *Autobiography* in droves must have been more than a little discomfited by such reminders that the problem of racism still loomed in their own society—indeed their own churches! Though they were no doubt expecting in Smith's book something in the familiar genres of "ministerial biography, travel narrative and success story," what they found was also "an unfamiliar story about what it meant to be black in America." What a wonderful use of story this was, to challenge whites with their own presumptions about blacks—to show them the realities of the situation from the perspective of a black person whom many of them were learning to trust and love as a spiritual leader.

Healing for Racism

Where, then, did Amanda Berry Smith get the courage and strength to persist in talking about this painful subject? To the end of her evangelistic career Smith taught that sanctification was the way out of the personal effects of racism, classism and other corrosive prejudices, for both the perpetrators of prejudice and their victims. Sanctification had taken away both her own fear of whites and her desire to be white. She had also seen it completely remove the racism of whites. One example of this was a man named Jacob C. Jacob. He had seen Smith at the Kennebunk camp meeting and been overcome by feelings of prejudice against her. But in that holy setting, Jacob recognized his sin and retreated to the woods to pray about it. Smith rejoiced to tell her readers what happened next: "It was a wonderful meeting that afternoon. The first thing Jacob saw when he got up and stood on his feet, he said, was the colored woman standing on a bench with both hands up, singing 'All I want is a little more faith in Jesus.' And he said every bit of prejudice was gone, and the love of God was in his heart, and he thought I was just beautiful!"

In Amanda Berry Smith we have someone who could easily have nursed anger and resentment against those who throughout her life put her down—for her race, her class and her gender. Having been treated poorly throughout her life, she could have descended into bitterness. But through, as she believed, the work of the Holy Spirit in her heart—her sanctification—Smith was able to transcend her anger. And Amanda Smith found her calling in working for the greater good of all people, including her oppressors, reaching out to them with a universal message. That message was the blessedness and irenic power of sanctification.

Did her message ultimately heal all ills? Not demonstrably in any historical sense. We can't point to American race relations after her life and say, "Her ministry changed everything." But we have plenty of individual people's testimony that her very presence, as a sort of barrier-crossing exilic prophet, worked a change in people—gave them a compelling vision, rooted in Christ, that promised the possibility of better ways of relating to each other.

And one may also say that she left a concrete legacy in the dynamic holiness movement that exploded across America and fed the even more explosive Pentecostal movement. Though of course this cannot be attributed wholly to her influence alone, she was constantly mentioned in the white holiness newspapers as a key figure in the movement. Smith was clearly a special person, whose tenacity of vision and clarity of purpose led her to persevere through a life of suffering under the prejudices of other people, yet who poured back into the lives of her persecutors a worthy balm.

Was she naïve in believing people could change? It doesn't seem so. On many occasions she communicated frankly, though tactfully, the brutality, small-mindedness and deceptiveness of the human heart. Yet she also preached a better, higher way, which her oppressors could and should reach out for because it had been made available by the grace of God.

From Amanda Smith's remarkable life and ministry, we can learn both about the need for change in our churches and our society, and about what it takes to make real change. If we are to address areas of need in the church and world, then these are likely also to be areas where we feel the brunt of sin's power to wound and destroy lives. We don't have the privilege of living above this reality. It's all very well to launch crusades for change, peppered with such buzzwords as *innovation* and *creativity,* planning our approach like a business climbing its way toward success. It will very likely be quite another thing to step into the areas where God is actually calling us. There, in the midst of a humanity—whether churched or unchurched—scarred deeply by sinful social attitudes, those of us seeking to become change-agents may find, as Smith did, that the trait most required of us is the old-fashioned virtue of *courage.*

9

Charles M. Sheldon

KNOWING OUR NEIGHBORS
AND SERVING THEM WELL

It is near the end of the 1800s, Sunday morning, in the comfortable upper-middle-class "First Church" in the fictional Midwestern town of Raymond. Halfway through the service, a tired, sick tramp walks into the church, up the aisle to the front, and begins to speak.

What I feel puzzled about is, what is meant by following Jesus. What do you mean when you sing "I'll go *with* Him, *with* Him, all the way?" Do you mean that you are suffering and denying yourselves and trying to save lost, suffering humanity just as I understand Jesus did? . . . I get puzzled when I see so many Christians living in luxury and singing "Jesus, I my cross have taken, all to leave and follow Thee," and remember how my wife died in a tenement in New York City, gasping for air and asking God to take the little girl too. . . . I understand that Christian people own a good many of the tenements. . . . I heard some people singing at a church prayer meeting the other night, "All for Jesus, all for Jesus, All my being's ransomed powers, All my thoughts, and all my doings, All my days, and all my hours." And I kept wondering as I sat on the steps outside just what they meant by it. It seems to me there's an awful lot of trouble in the world that somehow wouldn't exist if all the people who sing such songs went and lived them out. I suppose I don't understand. But *what would Jesus do?*

The pastor of First Church, the Reverend Henry Maxwell, stands transfixed at his pulpit. The tramp's question echoes insistently in his ears. It continues to echo as the tramp collapses at the front of the church. It echoes as he dismisses the service hastily. And as he brings the man home to his own house. And as the tramp lingers and finally dies—in good Victorian-novel fashion. Finally, the next Sunday, at the end of his sermon, Maxwell challenges his comfortable congregation to ask themselves that same question, "What would Jesus do?" He instructs those who are willing to come to him after the service and to bind themselves by a solemn declaration that they intend—for at least a trial period—to live by this four-word question. Each time they enter a serious situation or face a momentous decision, they are to ask it to themselves while praying and seeking discernment, looking for the Spirit's answer. And when they think they discern the answer to this question, for them, at that juncture, they are to act accordingly, regardless of potential cost, embarrassment or loss of social status. And many of the members of First Church respond—many more than Maxwell has dared hope.

So begins the story of one of the most-read religious novels of all time, *In His Steps,* by the American Congregational minister Charles M. Sheldon. The novel goes on to detail the revolution that ensues in First Church—and the town of Raymond—and eventually other churches and towns all over the country, when people begin living by this question, what would Jesus do? During the sixty years after it was first published in 1896, *In His Steps* sold more copies than any other book in the United States after the Bible: more than eight million.

What kind of man was the author of one of the most popular religious novels of all time? Though it has inspired countless readers, few have confused Sheldon's novel with great literature. Today its ideals seem naive and its programs unrealistic. And we might expect that the writer of a novel such as this was something of an impractical dreamer—a man who spent most of his time in his study, thinking up stories. But when I started to look into his life, I was delighted to find a man who wasn't contented just to preach at people through the pages of novels—or even from his own pulpit. This was someone who put his money—and his hard work—where his mouth and pen were. He was above all a practical man, passionate about being Christ's hands and feet wherever he could.

Unorthodox Beginnings

Sheldon was born February 26, 1857, in Wellsville, New York, and died February 24, 1946, in Topeka, Kansas. His life of ministry, writing and crusading for "godly causes" thus spanned the period from just after the Civil War to the Second World War. Sheldon's father, a Congregational minister, served as that denomination's first home missions superintendent, and young Charles grew up in the mission field of the Dakota Territory, in a log cabin he helped build. From the time he could hold a hammer, the boy loved the daily toil of the homesteading life, and throughout his life he felt affection for folks who worked with their hands. He once expressed wonder over "the stupidity of those who regard physical toil as something to be avoided as a burden and even a disgrace." Laboring on his parents' Dakota farm had taught him, he said, "the dignity and joy of work with our hands."

As a teenager on that farm, Sheldon "hunted with the Dakota [Indians], fished with them, slept with them on the open prairie, and learned some of their language." In other words, during those youthful years when we all absorb so many of the social cues that shape our lifelong attitudes, Charles Sheldon gained an appreciation for people who didn't look or act like his own family. He also drank in the Bible from an early age. "Each morning, the family would sit together in an open 'parlor' area of the log cabin and read aloud, each member of the family old enough to participate taking two verses in turn." And although his conversion as a teenager was unemotional, Sheldon's new life in Christ made him, as he said, "strangely happy." He said he felt that "a great burden had been rolled off my back." From then on, he worked to avoid, as he said, "anything possibly offensive" to Christ.

Sheldon went on to receive his education first at Phillips Academy, a prep school in Andover, Massachusetts; then at Brown University; and finally at the Andover Theological Seminary. The latter was a Congregationalist institution founded as an orthodox counterweight to Harvard's slide into Unitarianism, but by the time Sheldon arrived, it was enduring its own theological conflicts. A "controversy between old-line Calvinists and new moderates" came to a head in 1886, the year Sheldon graduated. In a heresy trial the school charged a number of its professors with teaching that there were errors in the Bible and that there was a "probation" after death, during which those who had not accepted Christ while alive could get a second chance. The so-called new theology taught by these professors also involved "accepting modern biblical criticism, adopting a relatively optimistic appraisal of human nature, and seeing God as immanent in human affairs"—all facets of the new "liberal" or "modern" trend in late-Victorian Protestant theology. Importantly, the form of this liberal teaching that Sheldon was exposed to was still robustly Christ-centered. One of the professors charged with heresy, Egbert Smyth, taught that "a theology which is not Christocentric is like a Ptolemaic astronomy,—it is out of true relation to the earth and the heavens, to God and the universe."

Upon graduating, Sheldon followed his father into the pastorate, taking a small church in Waterbury, Connecticut. This was a "New England classic, with about 175 members and a white frame building." From his first day in that first Connecticut pastorate, the young Sheldon attended to not just the souls but the daily needs of his congregation and their town. His people must have suspected that this was not your garden-variety pastor when Sheldon launched into his new ministry by "boarding around," as he called it. "Starting on Sunday he would go home with a family, eat dinner with them and spend most of the afternoon with them; and then after the evening church service he would return and visit until bedtime." He would sleep in the hotel room where he had boarded since arriving in Waterbury, then throughout the following week eat "lunch and dinner with the family and then stay for the evening, perhaps helping the children with their homework or amusing them with magic tricks." In this way, he lived week by week with forty-five different families of his mountainous parish's 175-member church.

There was nothing, it seemed, that Sheldon wasn't prepared to do to meet the practical as well as the spiritual needs in his community. He planted a vegetable garden on church property and sold the produce for the church. He helped promote neat and attractive housing, small-business assistance and a good local newspaper. He took up a collection for a town hearse. He launched Bible study groups. He organized a reading club for young people, ending up with some one hundred participants. They read *A Tale of Two Cities* aloud the first winter, and interest ran so high that Sheldon launched a successful drive to create a town library. More seriously, when more than two dozen townspeople died of typhoid, Sheldon, ignoring those who called it "an act of God's providence," began working together with a young physician. The two men showed the community that the real problem was—their wells were too close to their pigpens. They moved the wells away from the pigs, and the typhoid epidemic stopped.

Many of his parishioners appreciated these activities, but some of the more tradition-bound weren't so sure. His "eccentricities" made them uncomfortable, and they began to block his efforts in various ways. Eventually in 1889, two years after coming to the town, Sheldon felt hemmed in enough by this conservative element in the church that he resigned as Waterbury's minister.

He immediately moved west to accept the founding pastorate of the Central Congregational Church in Topeka, Kansas. The new church was a mission parish of just sixty members. They met in a small room over the local butcher shop. Sheldon was paid a salary of one thousand dollars the first year, which though a hundred dollars more than he had earned at Waterbury, was low even for those days—and he would earn not much more than that for the remainder of the fifty years he spent as Central Congregational's minister.

Crossing Class Lines

From the first, Sheldon did well for his new church. The upper room over the butcher's shop was often full, and soon the group was building a big stone edifice. When the new building opened, on June 23, 1889, Sheldon preached a defining sermon to what would be his lifelong flock. We can imagine their mix of pride and discomfort—what had they gotten themselves into?—as the young pastor announced that he would always preach "a Christ for the common people. A Christ who belongs to the rich *and* to the poor, the ignorant *and* the learned, the old *and* the young, the good *and* the bad. A Christ who knows no sect or age, whose religion does not consist alone in cushioned seats, and comfortable surroundings, or culture, or fine singing, or respectable orders of Sunday services, but a Christ who bids us all recognize the Brotherhood of the race, who bids throw open this room to all." Little did those unsuspecting congregants know what concrete shapes their activist pastor's dreams would assume in the years to come. The very next year, Sheldon was confronted with an issue that would loom large in his life, even as it became a flashpoint for the young social-gospel movement (on which, more in a moment): the destitution of many among the working classes. This happened when a tramp came to his house, seeking work, and he had to send him away empty-handed. The incident (echoed in the catalytic appearance of the tramp in *In His* Step) bothered him enough that he felt he must prepare himself to do something about the conditions of the day.

By the 1890s America had slid into desperate times. It had started in the 1870s—Sheldon's formative teens and twenties. The booming railroads had stretched their tentacles throughout the nation; thousands of young men and women were riding the rails from their small towns to the industrializing urban areas to seek their fortunes. Christian parents concerned for the safety of their migrant children's souls amidst the temptations and alienation of the big cities supported such agencies as the Young Men's Christian Association, which attempted to keep young people off the streets and involve them in "wholesome" activities.

But the sins of saloon and brothel were not the cities' only dangers. The 1870s were also the beginning of the "Gilded Age," in which industrial capitalists bankrolled corporations that, by the end of the century, would combine into monopolies who kept an iron grip on the means of production—and tended to overlook the humanity of their growing workforce en route to making their large profits. Long hours in poor conditions, child labor and pitiful wages kept the working classes in a perpetual state of bare survival. Many of the poorest workers were immigrants and blacks—the scorned, feared, "indispensable outcasts" of industrial America. And this class began, soon enough, to lash out. In 1877 wage cuts were announced in Baltimore and Ohio, and a wildcat strike spread, causing riots and looting, suppressed by vigilantes and militia.

Living conditions of the working poor were made infinitely worse by the state of city politics. The bosses of city wards and their political machines amassed support and money by helping some to find jobs, others to explain away minor crimes and so forth. But having gained power, these corrupt governments failed to ensure even minimal standards of fresh water, sewers, transportation and other infrastructure. And so this urban corruption combined with low wages and cyclical unemployment to keep a large percentage of the working classes in near-unlivable conditions.

The middle classes were aware of what was going on but not inclined to intervene. A horrified and titillated public couldn't keep their eyes from the photo-essays of Jacob Riis *(How the Other Half Lives)* and the writings of sensationalist journalists and authors. These exposed the degradation of slum housing, the squalor of the urban poor, and the crime and iniquity that festered in the dark warrens of the "sinful city." The dislocation, bewilderment and suffering that growth, mechanization, urbanization and runaway capitalism were causing so many displaced, oppressed people seemed unimaginable—and for the most part, despite their appetite for sensational reports of urban squalor, the middle classes seem to have preferred not to imagine it. Most, if they thought about economics at all, took a laissez-faire view that combined a Darwinist creed of survival of the fittest and a Christian providentialist belief that God would somehow ensure that the self-interest of the financiers and bosses would eventually trickle down to the good of the masses.

In the 1890s all of this worsened as economic depression returned. Thousands of men began losing their jobs, and they usually could not find other employment—much like the broken-down tramp of *In His Steps*. The unemployed were suffering, and more strikes were launched. Some of these turned bloody, sparking terror in the growing late-Victorian middle class. Rather than coming to the workers' aid, however, the comfortable Christian majority continued to overlook the growing ranks of the unemployed and indigent or blamed them for their supposed laziness.

Sheldon didn't buy this callous explanation. Instead, he placed the blame squarely on the laissez-faire capitalist system that cared little for the welfare of its workers. Sheldon preached on "the horrible blunder and stupidity," as he called it, "of our whole industrial system that does not work according to any well-established plan of a Brotherhood of men, but is driven by forces that revolve around some pagan rule of life called supply and demand."

But, never one to stop at explanations, the young minister decided to see for himself what the unemployed were experiencing. With his congregation's blessing he left the pulpit, put on his oldest clothes and set out in search of work. "He tried stores and factories, coal yards and flour mills," with no success. "He walked into every store (except for the to-bacco shops and theaters, of whose business he disapproved) on Kansas Avenue, Topeka's main business street . . . and was turned down at every door." This the young pastor kept up for nearly five days, without being recognized. Finally, "he saw a crew shoveling snow from the Santa Fe railroad tracks, and asked the foreman if he could help them without being paid. The bemused foreman agreed." With a borrowed shovel he went to work, and kept at it for the rest of the day. The next morning he happened on a job unloading a car of coal, which he finished by noon, earning fifty cents.

The Tennesseetown Experience

The experience moved him, and he preached eight sermons on its basis. But the effects of the poor economy and unfair labor practices stretched beyond the unemployed, so Sheldon set out on a new experience. This time he targeted social groups he felt could show him both the problems and the solutions facing Americans of all walks of life during that volatile time. In a new version of his "boarding around" practice, he ate, talked, worked and slept for one week each with people from eight different Topeka social groups: streetcar operators, college students, blacks, railroad workers, lawyers, physicians, businessmen and newspaper men.

The most radical of these experiments, and the one with the strongest impact on his ministry in Topeka, was his time in the black community at Tennesseetown, right up the street from the church. The families of Tennesseetown had come from the South as part of the "exoduster" migration—the thousands of formerly enslaved black Americans who fled the South during 1879 and 1880 and headed for Kansas, which they had heard was more tolerant than many other states. Some forty thousand of these freed slaves had passed through Topeka, and about three thousand had made their home there, comprising, by 1880, nearly one-third of Topeka's population.

The Tennesseetowners' houses were dilapidated, their poverty abject. When this idealistic young white minister arrived in their midst, they were no doubt wary, but they took him in. Sheldon stayed several weeks here—the first week trying to understand the roots of the town's poverty and to help find them work, the second visiting their schools, and the third week traveling with a black man to experience how residents and business owners in the surrounding communities treated him. Sheldon concluded from this experience that the people of Tennesseetown were not suffering because of their "incompetence," as local newspapers insisted. Rather, in a time when white repression against blacks was rising to outright disenfranchisement and segregation, racist whites who refused to employ or help blacks were effectively burying these newest citizens of Topeka in a deepening cycle of poverty. Sheldon

was the first local white to point the finger back at the white establish-
ment for the problems of these black residents.

Being who he was, Sheldon did not content himself with rhetoric. After a survey of some eight hundred residents revealed the need for basic
social services, he took action on several fronts. First, he discovered an
educational opportunity in the community's young children, ripe for the
recent German innovation of kindergarten. Sheldon talked the owner of
a local speakeasy into leasing him his building, and in April 1893, with
the help of some (but owing to racism and apathy, not nearly all) of his
congregation, he opened the first black kindergarten west of the Missis-
sippi. Within four years the school had attracted 287 pupils, and Central
Church had built a training school for kindergarten teachers whose
graduates fanned out across the country. Then Sheldon moved on to
catalyze a PTA, a library, an integrated Sunday school, crafts programs
for children and other initiatives. Other churches soon joined in his efforts, many of which included a significant self-help component. Tennesseetown crime rates fell; prosperity increased. One Tennesseetown
resident, a man named Minus Gentry, who had been a "Sheldon kinder-
gartener," was interviewed in adulthood. He remembered Sheldon with
these words: "Everybody loved him, everybody. I'm sure nobody ever
resented him." Nor was Sheldon content sticking with local efforts.
Seeking to address the racist roots of the community's problems, he became an early civil rights advocate. He stood up against antiblack activities and spoke out against the Ku Klux Klan when it reared its hateful
head.

Sermon Stories and Youth Clubs

But Sheldon always saw himself first as pastor of Central Church. After
In His Steps spread his fame throughout the English-speaking world, he
could have written his ticket anywhere. But he stayed. Later he wrote,
"One had better stay in an environment to which he is accustomed and
with people who are familiar with his peculiarities" than go far and wide
initiating "experiments." Throughout his pastoral life, his daily regimen
included writing personal notes and letters to his congregants, answer-

ing two or three dozen phone calls a day, and entertaining a steady stream of callers at his office. He also served his congregation of eventually two thousand people (he could have parlayed his prominence into much greater growth, but never saw the need) by making frequent pastoral visits and officiating at countless weddings, funerals and meetings.

In 1891 Sheldon began writing serialized stories to read to his congregation at the Sunday evening service. He did this "to inspire church members to love and good works" as well as to attract them to church. Both goals seem to have been fulfilled; in any case, rarely was there an empty pew—it may have helped that each week he left his hearers with a cliff-hanger. By the time he retired in 1919 he had written over thirty such stories, including *In His Steps*—the seventh in the series. Sheldon was not the first to write such "social-gospel novels," but with *In His Steps* he became easily the most famous. The novels are perhaps overly formulaic: invariably, "white middle-class characters come face to face with hypocrisy in themselves or in their churches, against the backdrop of a pathologic social environment." Then their thinking is revolutionized as they truly encounter the commands of Jesus, which leads them to "personal growth as they pursue social betterment." But there is something captivating and deeply human in their pages. We find here the insight and warmth of a minister who "boarded around" with the families in his town, tramped the streets with the unemployed and fought for the dignity of his African American neighbors even when to do so was unpopular with many in his congregation. There is something incalculable in a story told from such a heart as this.

Sheldon particularly dedicated himself to the youth and children of Central Church. He loved their energy, spiritual hunger and openness to people who didn't look like them. When asked about his obvious preference for youth work, he pointed out that when many of the adults of the congregation revealed their racial prejudice by refusing to help the people of Tennesseetown, the youth had readily stepped in and done much of the work. The Sunday evening services where he read his "sermon stories" were especially popular with the church's youth, and he oversaw a large Sunday school, a Christian Endeavor group and "The Young People's Good Citizenship Federation of Topeka," which published its own newspaper.

The most important of these youth groups was "the Altruist Club." Founded in the early 1900s, the club at first consisted of "high school and college girls and women who helped out in the Tennesseetown kindergarten." Later the group helped Sheldon in many other initiatives, becoming a sort of Jesuitesque special force under the minister's direction. Not surprisingly, Sheldon's heart and efforts for the young also resulted in a remarkable number of Central Church young people dedicating their lives to missions. These were so numerous that biographer Timothy Miller finds credible Sheldon's claim that his church produced "more missionaries than any other church in America."

Liquor, Cops and World Peace

Other innovative Central Church programs included a free cemetery plot open to all church members; a funeral expense fund; a lavish alms program (generously supplemented from the pocket of Sheldon, who was so notoriously free with his family's money that his wife was eventually forced to give him an allowance for his beneficences); and an "Open Door" program founded in imitation of the Catholic confessional, but presciently similar to modern pastoral counseling.

As Sheldon's fame grew, people looked to him more and more as a reforming figure, wanting to know what he thought about this or that social initiative. His favorite causes were a typically eclectic late-Victorian mix of moral crusades and pioneering social programs. Among the former sorts of effort, he spent much effort fighting Sunday labor, clubs and pool halls, long work hours, and the many other centrifugal forces that threatened the health of families and communities. Foremost among these was the temperance crusade in which a very high percentage of Protestants of all denominations and theological viewpoints were passionately involved throughout the late-nineteenth and twentieth centuries.

In the social realm, Sheldon was sometimes presciently innovative and sometimes culpably naïve. We have seen his efforts for race equality, and as a Christ-centered egalitarian throughout his life, he also publicly supported the movement for women's equality. Also exemplifying Sheldon's social activism were his ideas on civil order. In 1913 Sheldon (acting as Topeka's police commissioner) had recommended the kind of community policing that has now been implemented across America: "The policeman . . . is in a position to be the greatest human 'mixer' in the city. He is the one man in all the town who knows the inside life of all the people. . . . He can touch life at its most intimate points of interest in the city. He is in a position to meet the people day and night, to see them from every point of vantage for getting acquainted with them first hand." The policeman—who he felt should more usually be a woman—should see his or her job more as one of saving lives, preventing crime and protecting the populace than as a punitive role. He or she should of course be a Christian and should pray for people as well as serving and protecting them.

Sometimes, however, Sheldon was led astray by the optimism that he shared with other liberals. In a 1936 article in which he was called on to tell what he would do if he were president, he exclaimed that he would "veto every war budget" because "no nation on earth is planning to attack us." He felt America could easily "create friendship with the world," and therefore, he said, "I see no reason for big army and navy forces." Within five years, in the aftermath of the Japanese attack on Pearl Harbor, America had entered World War II.

For the most part, Sheldon was what historians have called a "social gospeler." While late-Victorian American evangelicals such as the evangelist D. L. Moody did tend to focus on saving souls, their social-gospel coreligionists like Walter Rauschenbusch and Washington Gladden put their energy into fixing the systemic evils of American society—especially those that resulted from uncontrolled, greedy big-businessmen and industrial tycoons. As solutions to the various abuses of industrial capitalism, the social-gospel leaders posed a kind of public Jesus-ethic. They preached Christian political action targeted at changing legislation. They challenged comfortable, middle-class Christians to apply the golden rule to the downtrodden and marginalized workers of their cities and towns. And they founded inner-city ministries, especially the so-called urban settlement houses and institutional churches. These were ministries equipped with soup kitchens, work-skills classes, babysitting programs and similar services for the working poor, aimed not just at meeting their immediate needs, but helping them on the way to a ful-filled humanity.

Broadly put (using the ecclesiastical categories of that wise Jesuit, Avery Dulles), while the evangelicals tended to see the church as called to be a "herald" of the gospel to the wider world, these social-gospel liberals saw the church as a "servant" to the world. Of course, we can recognize that these two aspects of "being the church" should not be mutually exclusive. But we might be willing to admit that in recent memory, at least, evangelicals have tended to be stronger heralds than servants. This has not always been so. In fact, Nazarene historian Timothy L. Smith has argued in his landmark 1950s book *Revivalism and Social Reform* that it was not the theological liberals of Sheldon's era but rather the pre-Civil War evangelical holiness movement, with its strong commitment to abolition and other social causes, that founded the American Protestant tradition of activism and reform—an argument accepted today with few qualifications.

Sadly, by the turn of the twentieth century, evangelicals were entering into what sociologist David Moberg has called the "Great Reversal." Because of the theological furor over such liberal-conservative issues as higher criticism of the Bible and the implications of Darwin's theory of natural selection for the story of creation, evangelical "fundamentalists" began seeking to distance themselves from the liberal social gospelers. They repudiated the "postmillennial" optimism of the social gospelers—the belief that God would work in and through human culture and human reforming efforts to bring the longed-for millennial (thousand-year) rule of Christ on earth. Instead, they taught premillennialism, the idea that the state of society would only become progressively worse until Jesus returned, which entailed a priority of saving souls over fixing society.

Post–Great Reversal evangelicals, it seems, have something to learn from social gospelers—something in line with their own older reforming heritage. We can read a story such as Sheldon's and be reminded of our own roots in social activism. And we can see in Sheldon himself a model of a Christian in the modern world who extended those roots and applied them in new ways.

A Personal Social Gospel

The question remains: what were Sheldon's own theological commitments? He certainly drank from the new streams of theological liberalism that were emerging at Andover Seminary during his education there. This is reflected in his later thinking and teaching. To take just one trivial but revealing example: when the tramp interrupted Henry Maxwell's service, that sympathetic minister was preaching a sermon outlining the "moral influence" theory of the atonement—a typically liberal interpretation that saw Jesus' death more as a grand example of suffering and love than as a blood substitution for a sinful humanity. And indeed Sheldon did consider himself a part of his day's liberal social-gospel movement. He visited and endorsed the movement's settlement houses and institutional churches. And his novels became the social-gospel movement's best advertisement.

But in many ways, this liberal troubadour looked like what we might call an "evangelical." The person and work of Christ were his touchstone. While he saw the need to address systemic social evils, he also saw that it was often personal habits—alcohol abuse and patterns of crime—that oppressed individuals and communities. He believed that real change could ultimately come only through a change in individual sinners' hearts. And he believed those individuals could be changed only by the grace of God and the willing, sacrificial work of faithful Christians (two of his famous novel's most sympathetic figures are a tent evangelist and his wife). Only one of the characters in his famous novel seeks to create change through direct political intervention or legislation.

In the end, Sheldon wished to rise above the liberal-evangelical dichotomy (which by the 1920s had become both rancorous and fruitful with church splits, as the fundamentalist controversies heated up).

What we can say for sure is that throughout his life, Sheldon simply refused to become drawn into theological controversy. He saw such disputes as a waste of time when Christians were so often failing to live like their Master—and when so many sinners (and he does not hesitate to use that term in his novels) had not heard the good and transforming news of the gospel, and when so many of God's good creatures were living in abject poverty and moral darkness. He believed those troubled people could be changed only by the willing, sacrificial, Spirit-guided, *personal* work of faithful Christians—not by mere social theorizing and political process, as helpful as those might sometimes be.

Above all, Sheldon was activated by a profound sense of Christ's love for every person, and he felt that such a love demanded nothing less than a life of total dedication.

In the end, who can doubt that Charles M. Sheldon lived, and wrote, in grateful love to his Lord? We get this sense from his own words of anticipation as he grew older: "It is not death but life I greet . . . when he who loves me calls me home."

On February 24, 1946, at the age of eighty-eight, Sheldon answered that final call, resting at last from his many labors. Who among us could not be proud to share the name *Christian* with a man such as this? Evangelicals today still too often draw lines of exclusion, to keep out "the liberals" and other riff-raff. The story of Charles Sheldon is a reminder to us that, when we exclude those not like us, we often end up the poorer for it.

Dorothy L. Sayers

KEEPING IT REAL

AND WAKING THE CHURCH

England's Dorothy L. Sayers (1893–1957) was a prolific scholar, novelist, essayist, playwright and translator. Those who know about her today have usually met her through her detective stories and their memorable hero, Lord Peter Wimsey. But there is much more to her story. In a time of spiritual confusion, she emerged, almost despite herself, as an unlikely voice of clarity and a compelling lay preacher of the gospel.

Sayers's England was a much different place from Charles Simeon's or John Newton's, not to mention Margery Kempe's. The industrial juggernaut had transformed sleepy medieval towns like Sayers's Oxford into thriving manufacturing centers. Urban populations grew and sprawled. World War I marred Sayers's girlhood, World War II her middle age. The greatest change, however, was less visible. C. S. Lewis once divided all of Western history at Jane Austen (1775–1817), saying Austen lived in the twilight of the old West's Christian tradition, after which we entered the age of modern materialism. This "materialism" was (and is) the belief that everything we are and experience is a mere mechanical dance of atoms, and any supposed spiritual or moral verities are thus illusions. Though its deeper background may be found in such Enlightenment figures as Isaac Newton, this worldview arose most directly from the works of Karl Marx, Friedrich Nietzsche, Charles Darwin and Sigmund Freud. And it left tremendous spiritual confusion in its wake—including the confusion of the Church of England that tried to reformulate the gospel in the light of the new materialism, so that by the turn of the century, bishops who doubted Christ's resurrection were called "courageous."

Into this world was born Dorothy L. Sayers. The daughter of a clergyman, she would grow to see for herself that indeed God was "a fact, a thing like a tiger, a reason for changing one's conduct." And she would become an important voice to bring this truth to a struggling church and a skeptical culture. Unorthodox (as we will see) in her personality, but passionately orthodox in her faith, Dorothy Sayers would find herself almost by accident blessing a generation sunk in the spiritual doldrums. By her life's end, as a public Christian of the stature of G. K. Chesterton or C. S. Lewis, she would make the historic creeds, the gospel story and Dante's *Divine Comedy* come alive as few have done before or since.

Of No Mean City
Oxford. City of faith and scholarship. Though her parents moved away when she was still young, Sayers was indelibly marked by this, her birthplace. Before the automobile factories encroached, the Oxford of her earliest memories, with its venerable university, was "a beautiful little medieval city, all tall spires and gray gothic towers." To her, those towers guarded and exalted learning and ideas. As she had one of her characters say, "It might be an old-fashioned city, with inconvenient buildings and narrow streets . . . but her foundations were set upon the holy hills and her spires touched heaven."

When Sayers was four and a half, her father, an ordained clergyman and Oxford graduate in classics who had taught Latin to boys in that city, accepted a parish called Bluntisham in "the Fens" (marshlands) in eastern England. This was a landscape full of romantic historical tales "about Boadicea, the Briton Queen who defied the Roman legions, or outlaws like Hereward the Wake, who held off William the Norman Conqueror." Rising from the mists was the Victorian rectory, where Dorothy would now spend her girlhood listening to her father tell these stories and reveling in a romantic sense of the living past. Even the rectory itself seemed a thing of the legendary past: lacking the modern gas lights and running water of their Oxford home. Instead, primitive plumbing, oil lamps in wall brackets, fireplaces for heating and candle-holders to bring up to bedtime.

The Fens did not offer many companions of her age, and Dorothy spent much of her time reading alone—none of her parents' many books were off limits to an inquisitive child. Everyone else in the rectory was an adult, and her parents talked to her as though she were one of them. Of course, as the only child in the household, Dorothy received doting attention from relatives and servants alike (the latter included the cook, stable boy, gardener and maids), and she made the most of it. She was certainly precociously bright—reading, for example, by age four—and as she portrayed herself in her unfinished novel, *Cat o' Mary*, something of a "prig" too. Her parents likely planned from early on that she would go to university, though this was unusual for girls at the time, and she enjoyed the Latin lessons from her father because she felt they would make her superior to her less-learned relatives, including her mother. Photos from the time show her with a round face and thick black hair, all in all as biographer Alzina Stone Dale describes her: "a cheerful little tomboy, ruler of her own small world and much amused by it."

When she wasn't learning Latin from her father or practicing the violin, which he also taught her, Dorothy loved to swoop about in the costume of Dumas's musketeer Athos—her father indulgently in tow, false beard and all, as Louis XIII. This early passion for swashbuckling tales developed her tastes for both the historical and the romantic. Tales like *The Three Musketeers*, rooted as they were in other periods, were "meat and drink" to her, and she strove to live in their world, attending to every detail.

Sayers's romantic streak seems to have emerged much as it did for C. S. Lewis in his own childhood: snippets of legend and romance opened the windows of her soul to another, more spiritual world. In an unfinished autobiographical novel, Sayers shows us a young girl who discovers the wonder of creation through a line from a Molière play. She reads *"La pâle est aux jasmins en blancheur comparable"* (a lover's fanciful description of the whiteness of his beloved's cheek), and "it was as though the whole scent of summer had poured suddenly through the open window and intoxicated her. For the first time she heard the mower, smelt the roses, noticed the rich buzz of the satisfied bees, became aware that the sky was blue and drenched in sunlight." Cheeks flushed, joy surging up within her, "she held the world between her hands and turned it over and over, like some curious jewel."

Through the ups and downs of her life—and there would be many— Dorothy L. Sayers never stopped being that young lady intoxicated by summer, or the girl with the plumed hat and rapier: imaginative, irrepressible, pouring herself into her enthusiasms, so powerful a personality as to leave her friends exhausted after each visit. "Except ye become as little children," she said, "except you can wake on your fiftieth birthday with the same forward-looking excitement and interest in life that you enjoyed when you were five, 'ye cannot enter the kingdom of God.' One must not only die daily, but every day we must be born again."

The two frameworks that shaped and directed this passionate romanticism were the English Church and English social conventions— though as a teenager and young adult, she strained against the limitations of both of these. As a minister's daughter, Dorothy dutifully went to church, sang in the choir, and absorbed catechism and creed, Bible and Book of Common Prayer. She would remain a lifelong high-church Anglican, "going on silent retreats, making auricular confession, observing the great feasts of the church, crossing herself before meals, keeping a crucifix on her desk." She was also raised in the English ethos of the day, learning early to "keep a stiff upper lip, never cry in public, and never let your side down." The latter surely contributed to her lifelong distaste for making her inner emotions known to those around her.

Drama, debate and satire all came naturally to her, but her true feelings were her own business and hers alone.

Not-So-Golden School Days

By fifteen Sayers had her sights set on Oxford University. To get there, she would need better teaching than was available locally, so her parents sent her to the Godolphin School in southern England. Parents of the girls at Godolphin tended to be lawyers, teachers and such—of comfortable, middle-class professional backgrounds and means. They also tended to be "advanced" in their thinking about gender roles, preferring that their girls train for careers rather than learn the genteel arts of young women being prepared only for marriage.

For many reasons, the school was not a happy place for Dorothy. She arrived midyear and found herself unable to break into the cliques that had already formed. She loathed athletics and was thus cut off from that important center of belonging. She wore glasses and was "tall and plain and lanky, with a long neck which made her fellow students nickname her 'Swanny.'" And since she was behind in mathematics, she also started in a lower grade than did most of her age group—only advancing after much hard work. (Yet her future promise emerged already in her first year: while her schoolmates struggled to translate a French sonnet into rough English prose, she rendered it in fluid English *poetry*.)

Another cause for dismay was the religious atmosphere of Godolphin. There was a sentimental, moralistic piety that seemed to sink under an oppressive reverence. She remarked on "the awkward stutter and hush" that accompanied such words as "God," "Communion" and "sacrament." Like sex, the mysteries of the faith seemed to be considered both "exceedingly sacred and beautiful," yet at the same time somehow "indelicate, and only to be mentioned in periphrastic whispers." As she would later say about this sort of overdone churchiness: "At the name of Jesus, every voice goes plummy."

This perceptive—and, she would later admit, pretentious—schoolgirl may have been saved from an adolescent falling-away from her faith by her encounter with the books of G. K. Chesterton, especially his *Ortho-*

doxy. "It was stimulating to be told," she wrote, "that Christianity was not a dull thing but a gay thing; not a stick-in-the-mud thing but an adventurous thing; not an unintelligent thing but a wise thing, indeed a shrewd thing." There were also bright spots in her time at Godolphin—once she settled in, she joined the debating society, edited the school magazine and acted in the school plays. But when it was all over and her performance on the final exams won her a highly competitive scholarship to Oxford, she was glad to move on.

Oxford: There and Back Again

Sayers went "up" (as the British say) to Oxford as a second-class citizen—an exile from the main life of the institution. This was because she was a woman, and during the time that she studied there Oxford still did not grant degrees to its woman students. Nonetheless, her college, Somerville, was the most competitive of the women's colleges, and the work was as exacting and exciting as anywhere at Oxford. And Sayers entered the scholarly life with gusto, immersing herself in her studies and haunting Oxford's ancient Bodleian Library (and getting in trouble for talking loudly there). She focused on modern languages, which meant "any language that appeared after Latin and Greek," and specialized in medieval French. Conscious always of the demand to prove herself as a woman scholar, she did so with distinction on the "battlefield" of the examination hall.

She also found at Oxford, at last, kindred spirits with whom she could stay up into the small hours discussing life, sex, politics, religion and art—a number of whom would remain her friends for life. She liked especially to talk about Christianity, and she began at Oxford to do this more in terms of creed and theology than in the sentimental and ethical mode she had so disliked at the Godolphin school. With some of these friends Sayers formed a sort of Inklings group, called the Mutual Admiration Society (M.A.S.). About a dozen members strong, the group gathered in each other's rooms, much as Lewis's group would do, to read their writings aloud for "mutual entertainment and criticism." They wrote in every genre, and all but one of them later published books.

The fairyland towers of Oxford could not protect those within from the cataclysm of the First World War. It broke out on August 4, 1914, and by the following year, the ranks of Oxford's young men had been reduced to a third. Of those who left for the front, many never returned—dying in the trenches and fields of foreign lands. Back home waves of grief broke on the young soldiers' families and friends as the casualty reports came in. Misery of a less intense sort battered the home front as food supplies and manufacturing capacity were diverted, and drills and blackouts intruded on life at every hand. But Sayers pressed on, writing poetry in the chinks of her study schedule. At last she wrote and defended orally her Final Honors examinations, earning a First Class in modern languages and eliciting superlatives from her examiners.

Out from the medieval city and into the modern world, Sayers started her career years in a customary field for university-educated women: teaching at girls' high schools. But she also managed to publish her first volume of poetry in 1916 at the age of twenty-three. Called *Op I,* it was filled with heroic figures from myth and history, wartime meditations and a few poems on gospel themes. Within months, however, she had the predictable rude awakening: one could not live off of the royalties of one's published poetry. Having soured on teaching too, she lugged many unsold copies of *Op I* home and lived for a few months with her parents. Her father had switched parishes and moved to the small town of Christchurch, and the townsfolk there, "dismayed by a rector's daughter who spent hours reading novels in her room or walked about smoking," gossiped about her behind her back.

Soon however, to her great relief, a job with her publisher, Basil Blackwell, allowed her to move back to her beloved Oxford. Blackwell himself admitted that to have this talented young woman copyedit manuscripts all day while learning the printing trade was like "harnessing a race horse to a plow." She chafed at having to read other people's work when it was so clear to her that she should be writing her own.

During her off hours the social scene in Oxford was bleak. As the war continued, it seemed the few men left in town were veterans in the local hospitals. She did, however, reconnect with Oxford friends. They were all working toward careers in writing, while also coping with a changing world. The new philosophical winds of scientific materialism had stretched old moral boundaries, and the war lent a poignant urgency to the business of finding happiness for oneself. "The life expectancy of a young officer in the army was two weeks, and everyone Dorothy knew had lost friends and relatives or . . . were marrying soldiers who probably would not return." At war's end, a "frantic search for pleasure" among the young continued, as many returning soldiers could not find jobs in an economically drained England.

Meanwhile, in 1918, Sayers published her second book of poems with Blackwell, *Catholic Tales and Christian Songs.* This book is Chestertonian in subject and tone, and it includes a short satirical play, *The Mocking of Christ,* which foreshadowed many of her later critiques of the poor state of the church in England. In this play, "Christ is mocked daily by ecclesiastical wrangling, by insistence on certain details of ritual, by arguments about the choice of church music, by religiosity, trivialities, respectability, muscular Christianity, self-righteousness, war, sentimentality and the facile identification of Christianity with pagan faiths and Greek philosophy."

Degrees and Careers

This book sold little better than the first, and Sayers began considering doing a very different kind of writing. The market for even badly written mysteries was growing. And in detective fiction she could do what she loved at last, write. And she could get paid enough so that she could stop receiving the modest allowance her father had been patiently sending her during her post-Oxford years. It would be several years, however, before Sayers launched her career as a mystery writer. In 1918 she spent time teaching in France. Then in 1919 she heard that a bill had passed Parliament that now allowed women to receive university degrees, with all the titles and privileges that had until then been reserved for male scholars. "When she heard the good news, Dorothy shouted for joy. Now she could become a real Bachelor of Arts and in fact, at the same time, a Master of Arts, or in the Latin, *Domina.*" This she did, at a grand ceremony in Oxford's Sheldonian Theater the following year, at which for the first time in university history, a group of women received the garb, regalia and titles associated with the B.A. and M.A. degrees.

Still unemployed, Sayers returned to teaching at another girls' high school, but teaching was just a stopgap for her. When in 1922 a job opened up at S. H. Benson's advertising agency in London, she jumped on it. Here was a business in which word-craft was well rewarded. "Even before World War I, many of its copywriters had been university graduates who knew the classics, quoted and wrote poetry, and could come up with witty slogans." She felt at home in the environment of creative camaraderie. In times of client crisis or looming deadline, "the whole agency became frantic, but with a sense of theater, the idea that the 'show must go on,' which made it hard work but fun." This combination of disciplined, heady work and high spirits was reminiscent of Oxford's pressure-cooker exams and midnight coffee sessions, and Sayers flourished at Benson's, staying there for nine years and originating some of the company's most successful campaigns.

A number of her Oxford friends were near enough to her London flat to provide welcome company during her leisure hours, and Sayers kept her mind busy with a slew of new hobbies, from crossword puzzles and photography to jazz saxophone (gone was her girlhood violin) and motorcycle riding. On her visits home to Christchurch she attracted local attention with her motorcycle gear and short, mannish haircut. She was also gaining considerable weight, owing partly to the new pleasures of Soho's ethnic restaurants.

Early in this London phase, in 1923, when she was thirty, she at last published her first mystery, *Whose Body?* The book was one of the first in that field by a woman, before the day of Agatha Christie or Ngaio Marsh. It premiered her famous aristocratic detective, who continued to star in a series of books to follow: Lord Peter Wimsey, "a slim, rabbity fellow with a monocle, a beak of a nose, and handsome hands." Lord Peter would prove the financial key to her eventually being able to quit advertising and enter the life of a full-time writer.

The moral world of her Wimsey books was recognizably Christian,

involving everyday choices for good and for evil, which met their fit re-
ward or punishment. Yet she reached out, too, to the conventions of
mainstream literature, giving her characters complexity and moral ambivalence. The stories also allowed her to indulge her passion for patterns and puzzles—following, for instance, her own "fair play" rule, according to which the reader must be given the same chance as the
detective to solve the mystery.

Wimsey's character was everything Sayers was, down to "his bubbling cheerfulness, his habit of literary quotation, his manner of prat-
tling, sometimes wittily, sometimes foolishly, his tendency to burst into
song or whistle a passage of Bach, his blithe impetuosity, his mental
agility and energy, his untiring capacity to engage in exuberant flights
of fancy in pursuit of an idea." Yet he also struggled with the postwar
depression so common in his generation, and he grew through the series
of books, becoming less a Bertie Wooster–like caricature and more a
three-dimensional romantic lead. Indeed, Harriet Vane, the woman
Wimsey would later meet in *Strong Poison* (1930) and woo through
Have His Carcase (1932) and *Gaudy Night* (1935), was enough like Dorothy herself that many have said Lord Peter was the man Sayers would
be unsuccessful in finding in her real life—even in her husband, whom
she married in 1926.

Love in the Modern World

Before her husband came a pair of ill-fated relationships. During 1921
and 1922, when Sayers was living in London, teaching and beginning
work on her first mystery novel, she was also seeking love in a city whose
male population had been decimated by the war. The young women of
that time were engaged in the fight for women's rights, seeking new
freedoms previously reserved for men—including the freedom to experiment sexually. These young people read Freud's work on repression and
the need for healthy sexual expression and lived Bohemian lifestyles in
garrets and artists' colonies.

During these years, Dorothy fell passionately in love with a man
twelve years her senior. His name was John Cournos. He was a Russian

Jew who had risen from impoverished factory hand to celebrated young novelist and was at home in the Bohemian circles of heroic artists and writers. Handsome and well-traveled, he fancied himself a tragic figure: he was perpetually poor and relied on Dorothy often for meals and lodging as he worked on what he was sure would be the next great epic novel. He was also "an adherent of the philosophy of free love, so much nobler, in his view, than matrimony, with its legal trammels and signing of documents."

Sayers's romance with Cournos escalated to a series of sexual encounters, stopping short of intercourse. He pressured her to use contraception, and she refused, perhaps believing she could convert him to marriage and parenthood. Predictably enough, he would not consent to this, and in the end he not only broke her heart but also wrote what was transparently an unflattering portrait of her in one of his novels, *The Devil Is an English Gentleman.* He even went so far as to weave into this pretentious tale details of her intimate letters to him. This, however, may have been something of a settling of scores. Sayers seems to have struck first in her 1930 novel, *Strong Poison,* in the person of a character named Boyes, whom she dismissed as "rather a defeatist sort of person . . . apt to think people were in league to spoil his chances . . . his idea was that great artists deserved to be boarded and lodged at the expense of the ordinary man."

In December 1922, newly employed at Benson's, still suffering from her rejection by Cournos, Dorothy wrote home to her parents about a man she was bringing home for Christmas. This was Bill White, a car salesman and motorcycle racer whom she had met through neighbors. She cooked him meals (he was out of work), and they went dancing and motorcycle riding together. She found his manly directness refreshing after Cornous's tortured Bohemianism. Though not in love with him, she was, at twenty-nine and after the frustration of her previous unfulfilled relationship, ready for sex, and "they were sufficiently attracted to each other to make it agreeable to both of them." Ironically, though she now used the contraception she had refused for Cournos, she accidentally became pregnant.

She carried the child to term, giving birth to John Anthony during a leave of absence from Benson's she had arranged on the excuse that she needed to finish a new detective novel. "Society in general still had heavy penalties, legal and social, against unwed mothers." If she wanted to keep her advertising job and succeed in the future as a public figure such as a writer, she could not afford for her situation to become known. She also felt that her mother and father, then in their seventies, would be devastated, and she could not tell any of her friends because of the chance the news would get back to her parents.

Bill left the picture, and Dorothy arranged to have John Anthony raised by her cousin Ivy, who worked as a foster mother. Sayers carried on a lifelong correspondence and enjoyed regular visits with her son, working hard to support him financially through boarding school and Oxford, and following his career from afar with parental pride (he became a successful economist). At last, years after her later marriage, she was able to adopt John Anthony. It was not, however, until a 1975 biography that anyone beyond her son, her husband and her cousin Ivy knew the truth about her relationship to John Anthony.

The seeming paradox of a woman who would become a Christian apologist and spokesperson, yet who had an illegitimate son, has led some to speculate that Sayers must have carried a tremendous load of guilt.

As an Anglo-Catholic she initially, during the relationship with White, withheld herself from the Communion table. She understood herself to be in a state of sin. However, as she worked through the aftermath of the pregnancy, she came to repentance and, soon, confession. And she understood the priest's absolution as communicating Christ's unreserved forgiveness of her sin and the complete lifting of any burden of guilt. Of course, she still had to deal with her sin's consequences, and she clearly continued to struggle with the emotional brokenness left in her by these failed relationships. But her conscience had been freed. And she was freed, too, to return to her church (St. Thomas, Regent's Street), and to take Communion on a regular basis, though it is unclear how regular. Alzina Dale suggests that "for the most part she probably kept the habit she had most of her life of going to church alone and getting up to go to the early service of Holy Communion."

Yoked and Running

At last in 1925 Dorothy met the man who would become her husband, a Scotsman named Oswald ("Atherton") Fleming, whose friends called him "Mac." Like Bill, a handsome and rugged man's man, Mac was a divorcee and an army veteran who had risen to the rank of captain. When Dorothy met him, he was working as a journalist, writing about crime and motor-racing, and freelancing in the news and advertising worlds. He was an accomplished storyteller, a pleasant companion and also a man of the world who had no problem with Dorothy having had a child out of wedlock. When they were married on April 13, 1926, the "racehorse" entered a yoke that, though it had its affection and rewards, would prove in many ways more difficult than her stint at Blackwell.

In the early years of her marriage, Sayers continued at Benson's, churning out at least one Lord Peter book a year on the side. She also entered into the life of a number of literary clubs, wrote speeches and articles, and engaged in a staggering amount of correspondence with her friends and fans. On top of all this, she began to write and speak for the BBC, including a series of talks on being a writer. How she managed this level of productivity is a mystery, but those who saw her home said that the papers and books (and cats, which she loved) overflowed from her study into the bedroom and other rooms until they were full too. Even in the bathroom, she had a rack built across her tub so she could read or make notes as she bathed. The racehorse was in her element, and she would run at a torrid pace for the rest of her life.

In 1931, the year after her first Lord Peter/Harriet Vane story, *Strong Poison* (1930), was published, Sayers was doing well enough financially from her books that she was able to quit Benson's. From 1932 through 1935 Sayers continued producing Lord Peter stories. These included the next two books in the Peter/Harriet series, *Have His Carcase* (1932) and *Gaudy Night* (1935), and the book some feel is her best detective story, *The Nine Tailors* (1934), whose unorthodox subject is the art of church-bell ringing, or campanology. Her productivity in these years is more impressive when you consider that for three of them (1933–1935) she was reading an astounding two novels a day as detective fiction reviewer for the *Sunday Times.*

By 1935 Sayers's work had become well enough known that a movie, *The Silent Passenger,* had been made about Peter Wimsey, and a number of dramatists were clamoring for the right to adapt him to the stage. With her friend Muriel Byrne, Sayers beat them to the punch by creating her own new Lord Peter play, also featuring Harriet Vane, called *Busman's Honeymoon.* It debuted in London's West End in December of 1936 and succeeded well enough to leave money in her bank account. Sayers had always loved the stage, and the experience of writing and producing for it changed her life. She found in the camaraderie of theater people another vibrant "club" whose company she adored. More than this, to see her own writing take on flesh and blood and to hear the immediate reaction of the audience was intoxicating for her. She would soon experience that pleasure again.

Not all was well during this time of extraordinary success, however. By 1932 Sayers was becoming increasingly concerned about Mac's mental health. He had been gassed in the war and had suffered from the lingering results of shell shock and recurrent depression as long as she had known him. Though he had been relatively successful as a writer in their early years together, he now found himself out of work. At the same time he was acutely aware of the brilliance and success of his young wife. "He bitterly resented being pointed out as the husband of Dorothy L. Sayers. He took petty revenge by making things difficult for her, insisting that meals should always be punctual . . . and his requirements given prior consideration." His problems were compounded by increasing recourse to whiskey, and fits of temper emerged. In the face of this decline Sayers had to find ways of continuing to work productively, including writing long into the night. In these difficult years, Dorothy and Mac only narrowly avoided the breakup of their marriage.

During this time, Sayers slowly came to the realization that "her real vocation and full emotional fulfillment were to be found in the creative life of the intellect." This she communicated brilliantly in *Gaudy Night,* which was set at Oxford University with a plot hinging on the quality of intellectual integrity. In the novel, Harriet Vane, an Oxford graduate and detective writer like Sayers, realizes that she can marry Peter Wimsey only if he is willing to take her as who she is, her writing work and all, for "no relationship can ever be sound that is not founded in the integrity of each party." Barbara Reynolds has remarked that Harriet still serves today as "a recognizable, living example of the modern, creative independent woman, battling to reconcile the conflicting claims of the personal and the impersonal." These many decades later, Reynolds still hears many women respond to *Gaudy Night* with a shock of recognition: "How is it that Sayers knows exactly what I feel?"

An Unasked Career in the Church

Fame leads one to odd—and sometimes providential—places. When in October 1936 the organizers of the Canterbury Cathedral Festival were looking for someone to write a play for them, they hit on Sayers. At the time she was known primarily as a detective writer, and her *Busman's Honeymoon* had not even been performed. But her friend (and member of C. S. Lewis's Inklings group) Charles Williams, who had written the festival play the year before, suggested her name.

The idea of staging a play in a cathedral was quite radical in that time when an aura of the downscale and the risqué still clung to the theater. Canterbury Cathedral was one of the most venerable and beautiful of England's gothic cathedrals. Its dean, George Bell, saw an annual dramatic festival as a way to bring in people who had drifted away from church. The festival had started in 1935 with a tremendous success: T. S. Eliot's *Murder in the Cathedral,* which went on to run in London's West End.

Sayers accepted, and she wrote for the 1937 festival a parabolic morality tale about the architect William of Sens, who had been called upon in 1174 to rebuild part of the cathedral destroyed by fire. Like Eliot's before her, Sayers's play moved from the cathedral to the London stage, and it was a great success in both venues. Pleased by this result, the festival organizers invited her back to write and produce two more plays, in 1939 *The Devil to Pay,* based on the story of Faust, and in 1946 the wartime-themed *The Just Vengeance.*

During the season of Lent in 1938, Sayers wrote an article for the *Times* in Chestertonian mode: "Official Christianity . . . has been having what is known as a bad press. We are constantly assured that the churches are empty because preachers insist too much upon doctrine. . . . The fact is the precise opposite. . . . The Christian faith is the most exciting drama that ever staggered the imagination of man . . . and the dogma is the drama." From then on, she became something of a public theologian, writing essays with titles such as "What Do We Believe?" "The Other Six Deadly Sins" and "The Triumph of Easter." Her opinions were increasingly sought not just on detective fiction, but on matters religious, and she found in this arena of activity something between a vocation and a distraction. She wanted to awaken a sleeping church and insist that it reclaim for its own the doctrines of the historic creeds— strict in form, hallowed by usage and communicating powerful realities that had been lost under layer upon layer of well-meaning but stuffy "clergy jargon," putting the congregations to sleep. But she frequently protested that if the clergy had been doing their jobs, a layperson such as herself would not have had to speak on such matters. Their failure to proclaim the gospel clearly had left the people "in a nightmare of muddle out of which [they] have to be hauled by passing detective novelists in a hurry and with no proper tackle."

Haul them out she did, both by writing her theological essays and by answering the hundreds of letters laypeople wrote to her with their spiritual questions. But she insisted that all this "theological writing" was not her proper business. She was a storyteller who had happened to have written a play or two representing a coherent, orthodox view of the faith, and it was *storytelling* that was her true art and vocation.

By mid-August of 1939 it had become clear that Hitler would have to be stopped. He had taken Czechoslovakia in March while the world stood by, and now he was preparing to carve up Poland like a pie, sharing it with Russia's Stalin. By September 1, as Hitler entered Poland, children in England were being prepared for evacuation. On September 3 the British minister declared war. Children were evacuated, historical buildings prepared against bombing, and key organizations moved from London. Soon the blackouts and rationing Sayers had lived through during the first war began anew, and everyone who could found themselves doing "war work."

Christ, Country and Creativity

Publisher Victor Gollancz asked Sayers to do a wartime book (really a long essay) that would project the sorts of reconstruction Britain would need after the war ended. It was published early in 1940 under the title *Begin Here,* and its central point was that in a nation that had lost touch with its own human creativity, the people had abdicated their responsibilities. Buying the lie that humans were just economic animals, the English had let liberal education slip and were training merely for commercial ends. No longer capable of making or understanding a coherent argument, the British people were letting others do their thinking for them, and the results were devastating not only for individual morale but for national life as a whole. (Would Sayers be surprised by the current state of education and public discourse in the West? Likely not, but she'd certainly be disappointed.)

She also set out to tie human labor back to its Christian roots, relating it to the doctrine of creation and the idea of the image of God in human beings. Drawing from Aquinas, she argued that the incarnation shows us that we must be fully responsible for the things we do in this material existence: our arts, crafts, politics, music and everything else. Sayers is famous for saying, "The only Christian work is good work, well done." To respect both creation and incarnation, one must do what one does *well:* if God the Father created this world and then said, "It is good"—and if God the Son found this world precious enough to enter it as a created being—then we must not rush our various crafts with slipshod results. In *our* creations, we must respect the beauty, integrity and dignity of *his.*

The years 1940–1941 saw Sayers publish perhaps her two greatest works: an extended Christian meditation on human creativity called *The Mind of the Maker,* and a serialized play on the life of Jesus, *The Man Born to Be King. The Mind of the Maker* dealt again with the theme of human creativity—what J. R. R. Tolkien had called "sub-creation." When humans create, she said, their creation takes the trinitarian shape taught in the creeds. The creative process starts with the idea, corresponding to God the Father; this is the plan or form of the work. Then comes the incarnation of the idea in words, paint, musical notes or the material of the sculptor, analogous to the Son. Third, analogous to the Holy Spirit, comes the power of the finished work, as it communicates to its audience.

The serialized radio play *The Man Born to Be King* was commissioned during the war years by the BBC as a Christmastime retelling of Jesus' life story. Sayers agreed to write it only after insisting that it be done in modern English and that it include among its characters Jesus himself. At the time (and up until 1968), it was illegal in England to portray Jesus on stage, and it required a special church dispensation even to allow this radio play. In a letter about the matter to the BBC she wrote, "I feel very strongly that the prohibition against representing Our Lord directly on the stage or in films . . . tends to produce a sense of unreality which is very damaging to the ordinary man's conception of Christianity. . . . 'Bible characters' are felt to be quite different from ordinary human beings."

Her way of breaking through this sense of unreality was to go back to the Greek Gospels and write a new translation that avoided the hoary ecclesiastical verbiage of the good old "Authorized Version" (KJV). "Nobody cares nowadays," she wrote to the BBC, "that Christ was 'scourged, railed upon, buffeted, mocked and crucified.'" Those were church words that meant little to the ordinary person. "But it does give people a slight shock to be shown that God was flogged, spat upon, called dirty names, slugged on the jaw, insulted with vulgar jokes, and spiked up on the gallows like an owl on a barn-door."

She wrote the play using colloquial language and cast actors who could speak with accents appropriate to the working-class status of the disciples. She insisted that the Roman soldiers "behave like common soldiers hanging a common criminal, or where is the point of the Story?" When such straight-laced groups as the Lord's Day Observance Society and the Protestant Truth Society heard about the play before its production, they campaigned against it, petitioning Winston Churchill and the Archbishop of Canterbury to ban these sacrilegious productions. A question was even put in the House of Commons, "whether the Ministry was going to revise the plays." The answer was no. The public, getting from this campaign only a skewed view of the planned plays, wrote in with outraged complaints. "A sinful man," fumed one such critic, must not presume to "impersonate the Sinless One." Exclaimed another, "Could anything be more distressful to reverent-minded Christians?"

The BBC defended Sayers throughout this storm of protest, and her series began airing in England and overseas on December 21, 1941. Now that the public could finally hear for themselves what she had done, the tide of response turned. "Rapturous letters poured in from listeners of all ages," grateful that Sayers had presented the story of Jesus in a realer and more powerful way than they had ever heard. C. S. Lewis was among those who loved *The Man Born to Be King;* for the rest of his life, as a devotional exercise, he read Sayers's play sequence each year during Holy Week.

The response gratified Sayers, but she became alarmed as people began to talk about her as an evangelist and to ask her to write "message plays" and evangelistic dramas. To do these things would have been, for Sayers, to compromise the nature of her work, destroying the integrity of storytelling in the service of religious propaganda. If a playwright "writes with his eye on the spiritual box-office," she warned, "he will at once cease to be a dramatist, and decline into a manufacturer of propagandist tracts. . . . He will lose his professional integrity, and with it all his power, including his power to preach the Gospel."

Certainly, though few in any age possess the combination of creative and intellectual gifts of a Dorothy Sayers, she embodies values that we can do well to "catch" today. Especially worthy of imitation are her passionate sense of the value of all "secular" work in the eyes of God, and her corresponding insistence that faithful folks maintain integrity in their work—whatever that work might be. Rising above the troubles and brokenness of her own life experience, she was driven by a desire to maintain *integrity* in her creative vocation. Today's characteristic evangelical pragmatism regularly justifies shoddy means by ultimate ends, resulting in both ministries and creative projects that, rushing to fulfill the evangelical mandate, end up looking tinny: forgettable, even dishonest. We can learn something from this passionately and intelligently Christian woman who refused half measures in her work, believing instead, as she said, that "the only Christian work is work well done."

A Divine Discovery

Sayers's final and arguably greatest work—her translation of Dante for the Penguin classics series—began in a bomb shelter. As the alarm sounded one day in the summer of 1944, indicating that the Germans had again dropped the hated V-1 rockets over London, Sayers grabbed a book on her way into the cellar shelter. It was her grandmother Sayers's copy of Dante's *Inferno*. She had been intending to read this since the year before when she had read her friend Charles Williams's *The Figure of Beatrice,* a study of Dante's key themes. But as she launched into the story in that cramped shelter, at the age of fifty-one, she little suspected how this "divine comedy" (the trilogy of *Inferno, Purgatorio* and *Paradiso*) would absorb the rest of her life. Writing to Williams afterward, she talked about this encounter with Dante as a sort of revelation: "I bolted my meals, neglected my sleep, work and correspondence, drove my friends crazy, and paid only a distracted attention to the doodlebugs [V-1s] which happened to be infesting the neighborhood at the time, until I had panted my way through the Three Realms of the Dead from top to bottom and from bottom to top." Then there was the deeper wisdom of Dante. "What Dante had to say about people and the state, as well as about the soul and God, seemed to Dorothy the answers the modern world was looking for."

She was captivated. And for the rest of her life, she labored—alongside other projects—to make Dante live again for a new generation. As *Inferno* and *Purgatorio* were published, the public read them avidly. Sayers's vibrant translation and clear, comprehensive notes caught up modern readers "brought up on science and psychiatry and television, but . . . illiterate in history and the classics" in that old Western tradition that C. S. Lewis had spoken about.

On December 17, 1957, Dorothy L. Sayers was halfway through her translation of *Paradiso*. She returned home from an exhausting Tuesday afternoon of Christmas shopping. What happened next is as much a mystery as any she wrote. Her handyman arrived on Wednesday morning to find the celebrated author, dead, at the foot of her stairs. The coroner diagnosed heart failure—perhaps brought on by her excessive weight, her smoking and the stress of her busy schedule. She was sixty-four years old. Her dear friend Barbara Reynolds, a distinguished Italianist and still alive at this writing, would complete the translation of the *Paradiso* and later write two biographical books that reveal, more than any other source, the character of this extraordinary woman.

Bishops, dignitaries and many friends attended the memorial service on January 14, 1958, at St. Margaret's Church, Westminster. There, a eulogy by C. S. Lewis was read and leather-bound copies of her essay "The Greatest Drama Ever Staged" were handed out to all. Then as now, Dorothy L. Sayers was recognized as one of England's most remarkable voices for the truth of faith.

Conclusion

A POSTMODERN CHALLENGE

FROM DANTE VIA SAYERS

We've lived vicariously, through this book, with ten varied characters from church history. So how can such stories help us today, individually and as the church? How can their unique translations (indeed, incarnations) of the gospel—from the midst of their particular experiences of brokenness and homelessness—help us figure out what translations we need to live out today, in our own, postmodern world? And how can the stories they told and the stories they lived help us "narrate ourselves back into" a living, active faith that will have real impact on our world?

Of all the people we've met here, I think it is Dante (through the perceptiveness of Sayers) who answers these questions best.

This may seem odd, since Dante is in some ways the least accessible figure in this book. Most folks today who encounter his *Inferno* never get any farther. Even such a sympathetic Christian reader as Geoffrey Nuttall warns us of the near-inevitable results of reading only the *Inferno:* "Many readers . . . find it so distasteful that they quickly abandon it, and never take up the *Comedy* again. . . . If the *Inferno* were the whole poem, one could hardly avoid the conclusion that Dante had a diseased mind, obsessed with sadistic and other sexual perversions." But Nuttall is careful to make the theological point that those who move on from the appearance of "Dante the sadist" to that of "God the sadist" miss. Dante's denizens of hell on some level *want* to be where they are. Their loves have become so disordered that they have arrived in hell of their own will. For Dante, says Sayers, "Hell is the state in which the will remains fixed eternally in that which it insisted on having; the torments it endures are simply the sin itself, experienced at last, without illusion, as that which it really is." She quotes Jacques Maritain, "It is a fearful thing to fall into the hands of the living God, for they give to every man that which he has desired."

Of course, the *Inferno* is not the whole poem. Dante's other two realms of the dead move much less in the closed circle of perverse human desire and much more in the divine dance of grace, led by the God of loving kindness who does not desire that any should perish. In *Purgatorio,* souls bound for heaven are lovingly cleansed of the sins that would keep them from standing before the Holy God. (Those who are uncomfortable with the doctrine of purgatory may wish to think of this part of the trilogy in allegorical terms—as an image of God's work in sanctification, here on earth; and this works to a great degree, not I think doing too much violence to Dante's story.) And *Paradiso* attains an even higher level of grace and love. It "pulsates with a passionate energy, a sheer, superabundant intellectual ecstasy."

All of this, however, would be nothing but an interesting antique unless it had something useful to say to us today. It is something more than sheer storytelling or poetic skill that has gotten modern fans of Dante—and we need to include here not only Sayers, but T. S. Eliot, Charles Williams and countless others—past the *Inferno* and under the spell of Dante's great poem. There is something more than aesthetic pleasure behind the fact that Dante is the ninth most written-about person in the catalog of the Library of Congress. And that "something more" comes to the heart of what I hope the lives recorded in this book can do for us today.

Sayers had found in Dante a surpassing storyteller and poet. He spoke directly to her imagination. All very well; he might do that for any of us. But why dedicate one's life to translating him? The answer is simple, and it's the same thing that made Sayers insist so categorically that stories and plays, whether they be about Jesus or an aristocratic detective with a monocle, must be *true to life*. What compelled Sayers about Dante was that he believed in the spiritual and theological importance of *images*—physical things that can be seen and touched. His great poem is full of landscapes, works of art and above all real, living, breathing people. He could have written a book of philosophy or a political tract—and in fact, he did both. But his magnum opus was one of the most vivid, image-rich epic poems the world has seen.

Why images? Why story? (And since this is a book of biography, why biography?) The answer to these questions seems to be: because, for Sayers, as for Dante, and Kempe, and Gregory, *the visible, physical world is loaded with spiritual meaning*. We see this in the horrible situations of the individual sinners in Dante's hell. They did not undergo punishments arbitrarily chosen by a sadistic God. Rather, these people's very bodies had become representations—*incarnations*—of the sins they had cultivated and indulged in their lifetimes.

Dante got the philosophical grounding for this move from the "virtue ethics" of Aristotle (via Aquinas). Virtue ethics expounds the simple idea that we develop our character—good or bad—by getting in the *habit* of doing certain sorts of things. In other words, what we call character is a set of dispositions to do certain things, based on the good or bad things we've habitually done in the past. We still *choose* to be virtuous— virtue is not an automatic reaction, however thoroughly we have been habituated to do good. But the dispositions that develop out of our habits do lead us naturally toward certain virtuous (or vicious) actions. Aristotle believed that our moral dispositions are in fact states of the "soul" or *"anima humana."* And this soul is not an airy, immaterial thing, but rather a *form,* which "structures and animates a material frame." In other words, what happens when a person develops a certain kind of moral character is that the person's very *body* becomes structured and animated by that character—their "gestures, facial expressions, and other 'outward looks that bear witness to the heart'" will show clearly what is in their heart.

We see this, again, most clearly in the twisted, grotesque forms of the damned in hell: each of them has in a sense *become* their sin. Their punishment is simply the natural outworking, in their very bodies, of their disordered loves. But we don't have to go back to Dante to see this remarkably physical way of talking about virtue and vice. It springs out at us in two modern authors, George MacDonald and C. S. Lewis, both of whom (it is no coincidence) were fans of Dante. In George MacDonald's children's story *The Princess and Curdie,* the young hero Curdie discovers that he can feel, when he takes a person's hand, the hoof, paw or claw of the animal that person is truly becoming based on the moral choices they are making. In C. S. Lewis's *Voyage of the Dawn Treader,* Eustace Scrubb turns into a dragon after he entertains "greedy, dragonish thoughts." Although we don't really view the soul in an Aristotelian way today, any more than Lewis or MacDonald, or Sayers, did, we *do* see all around us the inner character of people "bodied forth" in their faces, gestures and other "outward looks that bear witness to the heart." Can images have moral—even theological—value for us? Dante, following Aquinas and Aristotle, shows us that they can indeed.

Virtue ethics informed Dante's *Comedy* in another way too. For Aristotle, moral development is a thing involving imitation and models, and this (as we have seen) is a theme taken up with gusto by the early and medieval Christians. Athanasius exclaimed about his friend Antony: *"Simply by seeing his conduct, many aspired to become imitators of his way of life."* The many saints' lives that took their cue from his biography of Antony likewise put models before their readers. Gregory the Great, too, wrote a book of saints lives, the *Dialogues.* In this book Gregory sought to give the people of Italy a new group of "home-grown saints" to admire and imitate—"an alternative collection of *exempla* [that is, models] of sainthood," different from the martyrs of old, whose lives were relatable for those who lived close to the earth. "Compared with the martyrological literature," writes Markus, "Gregory's stories

are not of heroic deeds, nor are their actors heroes. The bulk of the stories are of the modest acts, in the kitchen garden and the monastic
farm—'delightful miracles'—of lowly men." Dante continued this tradition of writing biographical sketches for imitation—and, of course, for
warning. *Inferno* and the other two books show us people doing acts of
morality and immorality, justice and injustice.

The reason, then, that Sayers thinks modern people need to read
Dante—and need it badly enough that she dedicated years of painstaking work translating and annotating the *Comedy*—is just this: Dante
focused, via vivid images, on character and our responsibility for our
own character. Sayers came to call his *Comedy* "the drama of the soul's
choice"; this is simply a subjective way of expressing the objective idea
at the poem's center: justice. The reason Sayers devoted the last years of
her life to translating and annotating Dante's great poem was that she
found the great Florentine telling her world—a world far gone in moral
paralysis, irresponsibility and blame-shifting—what it most desperately
needed to hear: "that good and evil exist, that the will is free to choose
between them, that, consequently, the individual, even though in part
conditioned by heredity and environment . . . nevertheless remains
morally responsible; that damnation is self-willed; that, under grace,
repentance, contrition and reparation can liberate the soul to accept the
forgiveness of God."

"We must also be prepared, while we are reading Dante," Sayers continued, "to abandon any idea that we are the slaves of chance, or environment, or our subconscious; any vague notion that good and evil are
merely relative terms, or that conduct and opinion do not really matter;
any comfortable persuasion that, however shiftlessly we muddle through
life, it will somehow or other all come right." We must, in other words,
truly believe in God's gift to us of free will, for *"The Divine Comedy* is
precisely the drama of the soul's choice. It is not a fairy-story, but a great
Christian allegory, deriving its power from the terror and splendour of
the Christian revelation."

What Dante is doing, then, with his *Comedy,* is preaching an unsur-
passed sermon on human responsibility, and using some of the most

vivid images in human literature to do it. This addresses two problems in our own postmodern culture. First, we are inclined to avoid much talk about moral agency and moral responsibility (I will explain that claim in a moment). Second, and closely related, we are in danger of becoming effectively gnostics—spirit-flesh dualists for whom faith and spirituality are private matters with no real payoff in the visible, physical world. The *Comedy* is so valuable today, I think (as Sayers thought), precisely because it will not allow that dualism. Despite its topic and setting, the epic poem doesn't actually stay in the airy land of the otherworld for more than a line or two at a time in its entire fourteen thousand lines. Again and again Dante returns to the realm of human moral action and its impact in human lives.

This insistence on down-to-earth stories about real people, their actions and the consequences of those actions should not surprise us, even if we know nothing of virtue ethics, for Dante is a Christian. And neither Testament of the Christian Scriptures, despite their stunningly supernatural gospel message of God's transcendent love and grace, stays very long away from the theme of human moral action either. Though that gospel is so clearly *not* a teaching about a moral system, it clearly *does* revolutionize everything we thought we knew about human morality. Why? Because as Dante's story does, the gospel ties the personal, individual (and spiritual) realm of "my soul and its relation to God" securely to the horizontal (and thus messy and indeed physical) dimension of relationships with others—of justice, mercy and charity. The Bible and the *Comedy* alike insist that our spiritual lives have everything to do with that horizontal, social dimension. It is with Dante as with Matthew: sheep and goats are separated at the Judgment by these kinds of criteria: cups of cold water, clothing for the naked, visits to the imprisoned.

So Dante brings us repeatedly, as we follow him from the lowest hell to the highest heaven, back to face our own actions in the physical world and their consequences—not just earthly but eternal consequences. Even in paradise Dante's spokespeople, from humble contemplatives to emperors, join the resounding outcry over "What's wrong with the world?"—calling out that "things are not as they ought to be!" In this, they join the voices of all the "wrestling prophets" of this book: Antony against anger, Gregory against self-serving pastors, Comenius against international strife, Smith against racism, Sheldon against the oppression of the poor and on down the line.

I have said that today we are inclined to avoid much talk about moral agency and moral responsibility. Arguably we live today, as Sayers lived, in a time of moral torpor, when many have stopped *really* believing that we need to be careful of what we do as moral agents living among fellow humans made in the image of God. In our day, social aggregations have reached massive scale, and our political and economic systems deal more or less efficiently and impersonally with masses of people. (And as Hilaire Belloc, G. K. Chesterton and the Distributists insisted, isn't our economic system still totalitarian through its iron yoke of consumer capitalism and its all-powerful multinational corporations that concentrate wealth in a few hands? And our political system too, through the "servile state" with its well-meaning but dehumanizing social programs?) Living in this setting, it is so easy to stop behaving as if we in fact have any moral agency—easy to just ride with the flow of advertisements and fashions and sound-bite politics and the glow of the TV and movie screen, and presume that since we live in an enlightened nation with enlightened laws, all that "justice" stuff will just . . . be taken care of. Could it be that we, now, need to hear Dante's stringent moral-spiritual message more even than Sayers's readers did? After all, they had at least the bracing shock of war to keep them alert to moral and spiritual realities—as Lewis's Screwtape well knew. The wars in our world (the Western, developed world at least) are by and large comfortably distant and demand very little of ordinary citizens—the occasional terrorist act notwithstanding.

We Christians have ways of evading these responsibilities. And one of the worst is a theological way. "All that," some of us are inclined to say, "is God's business. The world is getting worse and worse, and trying to address it from a merely moral standpoint is putting a Band-Aid on a gaping wound. Let God handle the details of political and social life. We must simply preach the gospel, to save as many souls as we can before Jesus returns." Based on such faulty theology, even where we do confront the imperative to act morally in our world, our sense of moral agency is very narrow, so that only those things that touch us personally obsess our vision of moral responsibility. We can accept moral responsibility for abortion, for our sexuality, for perhaps our family. But that's about as far as it will usually go. What we do not tend to see is what Dante shows so clearly: our moral responsibility for the larger world around us—especially the moral responsibility of leaders.

As we have seen, Dante is not simply telling a tale of individual salvation, reflecting his own journey from inner brokenness to wholeness and holiness. Rather, his pilgrim progressively becomes aware of how salvation is not individual but global and cosmic. Hell, purgatory and paradise are all social experiences. In all three, at every juncture, Dante the pilgrim interacts with people. And many of those people are suffering for sins that have to do with their treatment of those around them—for failures of what we might call social justice, or for bad leadership and lack of responsibility for others. In the *Comedy,* then, postmodern Christians can find a concern for souls and for social salvation together in one place, in a vision that is uncompromisingly theological.

This is the challenge Dante, and I think each of the figures in this book, too, issues to us: Are we prepared to see the ways that our forebears in the faith cooperated with God's grace to shape and live exemplary lives, "bodying forth" what they believed? Are we willing to let those character witnesses speak to us about social as well as individual spirituality and morality? Will we take to heart their biographies, as well as the stories some of them wrote, and allow those narratives to begin to work in us and change us?

Athanasius's Antony, Dante's *Comedy,* Charles Sheldon's Henry Maxwell and Sayers's *Man Born to Be King*—the storytellers in this book have hoped the people they portrayed would get down into the hearts of their hearers and transform them. And in a humbler way, I hope the stories I have told here of all ten "patron saints for postmoderns" will challenge and change you. They certainly challenge me. And as I continue to "work out my salvation with fear and trembling," as "it is God who works in me to will and to act according to his good purpose," I hope that they will change me too (Phil 2:12-13).

Acknowledgments

I pull the thread of acknowledgments and find that it leads back to more people than I had imagined—thank you all!

First, my parents, Stanley and Barbara Armstrong. Aside from the obvious debt of existence, I owe them so much for raising me in both the nurture and admonition of the Lord and the curiosity and enthusiasm of the academy. From early on, I was encouraged to listen and join in as they talked about things that really matter. Later, I got to sit in a number of my father's undergraduate courses where he did likewise. Perhaps best of all, I benefited from both dad's and mom's painstaking editorial comments on my early efforts at scholarly writing (I knew every paper I gave to mom would return swimming in red ink!)

I owe two of my other professors at Saint Mary's University in Halifax, Nova Scotia, important debts of gratitude: Robert Bollini unveiled for me the glories *and* the discipline of history, never letting "good" alone in classroom discussion or written work, but pushing me toward "best" (as the best teachers do). Emero Stiegman showed me that the deepest things of the heart can be discussed fruitfully in an academic setting, and he convinced me at a critical juncture that the recovery of the church's memory is a noble and essential vocation.

I have also been formed by three of the best graduate mentors a student could ask for. The gifts they gave were many, but a few stand out above the others: Garth Rosell showed me the subtle art of presenting alien ideas with sympathetic power to a skeptical audience. Richard Lovelace connected history with spirituality at every step. And Grant Wacker showed me history as a moral undertaking, and storytelling as its great sacrament. I thank each of these and am even more amazed by what they did for me now that I, too, am living the hectic life of the professor. And I need to add a special appreciation to the Divinity School's Susan Keefe, who taught me to find worth in the early and medieval saints.

Ginger Kolbaba, Ed Gilbreath, Ted Olsen and other members of the Christianity Today International authors' group provided inspiration and information during the early stages of the planning for this book. Former *Campus Life* editor Chris Lutes suggested the final form of the book's title. My editor at InterVarsity Press, Cindy Bunch, believed in this project and wouldn't let it go even when major life changes delayed it well beyond its first deadline. She also answered with unfailing patience the countless detailed e-mails of this dysfunctionally perfectionist author.

My Bethel research fellow and friend Chris Brenna poured countless hours into the endnotes—they are his work entirely. Chris also provided incisive comments on the content and organization of the early chapters that have improved the end result greatly.

Oliver Nicholson of the University of Minnesota gave a Lenten course on Antony of Egypt at Minneapolis's Cathedral of St. Mark that was a high point of my first years here in the Twin Cities and gave me the nucleus of the Antony chapter. During a very busy time in his life, Bruce Hindmarsh shared liberally from his research on John Newton, acting as consulting editor for an issue of *Christian History & Biography* on Newton and making "Mr. Amazing Grace" a shoe-in for this book.

David Neff, Jennifer Trafton and Marshall Shelley allowed me to work out, in the pages of *Christian History & Biography,* <www.chris tianhistory.net>, and *Leadership Journal,* themes related to a number of the leaders in this book. Several classes full of Bethel Seminary students also engaged the saints in this book, finding countless points of contact in their own lives and ministries, and blessing me repeatedly with their insights on what these folks can mean to us today.

The Benedictines of St. John's Abbey in Collegeville, Minnesota, gave of their hospitality for a week spent wrestling with a couple of my chapters. The staff of the Marion E. Wade Center at Wheaton College, Wheaton, Illinois, provided the resources for a week of fruitful study at their facility and tracked down many bits of Sayersiana during a time when they were also hosting a meeting of the international Dorothy L. Sayers Society—to whom I also owe thanks for a stimulating conference. The staff of the Carl Lundquist Library at Bethel Seminary were unfailingly helpful and patient as I broke records (I am told) for most books checked out at one time. Greg and Meredith Nyberg graciously gave me the loan of their idyllic Minong, Wisconsin, vacation home on several occasions, including weekends during which the Smith and Sayers chapters were largely written.

My father- and mother-in-law, Allen and Joanne Creelman, have consistently given their love and support to me and our family throughout our odyssey of graduate education and academic life—far beyond our ability to repay. And of course my wife, Sharon, and children, Kate, Caleb, Grace, Anna Rose and John Allen, have had to put up with a husband and father struggling with the overwork, late hours, weekends away and rollercoaster moods that have come with the territory of writing a book. Somehow, in the midst of it all, they have still managed to love and encourage me—and Sharon is now saying I should consider writing another book. This is evidence indeed of the reality of grace.

Again, thank you all!

Notes

Introduction

page 13   "The first thing a principle does is kill somebody": from Dorothy L. Sayers, *Gaudy Night,* Lord Peter Wimsey Mystery Series (New York: HarperCollins, 1995), p. 363.

page 18   "a sharp image of what a life committed to God demands and promises": Robert C. Gregg, introduction to *The Life of Antony and the Letter to Marcellinus,* by Athanasius, trans. Robert C. Gregg (New York: Paulist Press, 1980), p. 13. All references to *The Life of Antony* are to this English edition.

Chapter One: Antony of Egypt

page 21   "lifted his feet, and as if seeing friends": Athanasius, *Life of Antony,* p. 98.

page 21   "Even his death has become something imitable!": Ibid., p. 89.

page 21   Antony had left one of his two sheepskin cloaks: Ibid., pp. 97-98.

page 22   "never succumbed, due to old age, to extravagance in food": Ibid., p. 98.

page 22   "Therefore, read these things now to the other brothers": Ibid., p. 99.

page 22   "Sell all you have, give to the poor": Ibid., p. 31.

page 23   Asceticism—in the Greek, *askesis*—meant "training": Oliver Nicholson, "St. Mark's Cathedral Lent Group on the Life of St. Anthony," lectures presented at St. Mark's Cathedral, Minneapolis, 2006.

page 23   fornication stood for not being a monk: Ibid. See also Peter Brown, *Society and the Holy Man in Late Antiquity* (Berkeley: University of California Press, 1982), p. 131.

page 24   nothing could live in those parts except demons: Nicholson, "St. Mark's."

page 24   he moved farther out to a ruined Roman fortress: *Life of Antony,* p. 40.

page 25   "He rendered service to the confessors": Ibid., p. 66.

page 25   "washed his upper garment": Ibid.

page 25   "The Lord was protecting him to benefit us": Ibid (emphasis is mine).

page 25   The root of the term "monastic" is *monos,* meaning "sole": Arthur G. Holder, "Making True Disciples: Models of Theological Education from the Early Church," *The Saint Luke's Journal of Theology* 34, no. 3 (1991): 21; cf. p. 25.

page 26   vision of a silver plate . . . and then a real pile of gold: *Life of Antony,* p. 40. This way of framing dependence/independence, and the use of these temptations to illustrate the point, come from Nicholson, "St. Mark's."

page 26   monks eked out a living by simple handiwork: Nicholson, "St. Mark's."

page 26   The monks did engage in inward contemplation: See Douglas Burton-Christie, "Words and Praxis," in *The Word in the Desert: Scripture and the Quest for Holiness in Early Christian Monasticism* (Oxford: Oxford University Press, 1993), pp. 134-80.

page 26   he went with a caravan of Arabs several days' journey: *Life of Antony,* pp. 67-69.

page 27   the monks he had left behind traveled to see the holy man: Ibid., pp. 71-72.

page 27   *"Do not let the sun go down on your anger":* Ibid., p. 72.

page 27   Many tracts and passages of ancient writing deal with this subject: See for example Galen, "On the Affections and Errors of the Soul," in *Galen: Selected Works,* trans. Peter Singer (Oxford: Oxford University Press, 2002); cf. Michel Rene Barnes, "Galen and Antony: Anger and Disclosure," in *Studia Patristica,* vol. 30, ed. Elizabeth A. Livingstone (Leuven: Peeters, 1997), pp. 136-43.

page 27   "recount to himself his actions of the day and night": *Life of Antony,* p. 72.

page 28   "He was disconsolate at being annoyed": Ibid., pp. 84-85.

page 28   "His arrival worked to the advantage": Ibid., p. 94.

page 28   "I had many . . . invitations to conduct law suits": Charles Finney, *The Memoirs of Charles Finney,* ed. Garth M. Rosell and Richard A. G. Dupuis (Grand Rapids: Academie Books, 1989), p. 40.

page 29   "all is seared with trade; bleared, smeared with toil": from "God's Grandeur," by Gerard Manley Hopkins.

page 29   "For who went to him grieving and did not return rejoicing?": *Life of Antony,* p. 94.

page 30   "the experience of holiness": Lucius C. Matlack, "Holiness in the Family," *Advocate of Christian Holiness* (Boston: National Camp-Meeting Association, 1873)

page 31	the famous "garden conversion" of the father of Western theology, Augustine of Hippo: For the entire story that follows, see *Confessions of St. Augustine* 8.6-12.
page 31	"What is the matter with us? Didn't you hear?": *Confessions* 8.8.
page 32	"Take up and read": *Confessions* 8.12.
page 32	"the first great manifesto of the monastic ideal": Derwas Chitty, *The Desert a City: An Introduction to the Study of Egyptian and Palestinian Monasticism Under the Christian Empire* (Crestwood, N.Y.: St. Vladimir's Press, 1966), p. 2.
page 33	"The name of the monks carries public weight": *Life of Antony,* p. 29.
page 33	"the desert was made a city": Ibid., p. 42.
page 33	The Emperor Constantine and his two sons Constantius and Constans: Ibid., p. 89.
page 34	"It was as if he were a physician given to Egypt by God": Ibid., p. 94.
page 34	"open the gates of heaven": Peter Brown, "The Rise and Function of the Holy Man in Late Antiquity," in *Society and the Holy in Late Antiquity* (Berkeley: University of California Press, 1982), p. 106.
page 34	"The rise of monasticism was, after Christ's commission to his disciples": Mark A. Noll, *Turning Points: Decisive Moments in the History of Christianity,* 2nd ed. (Grand Rapids: Baker Academic, 2000), p. 85.
page 35	"men of concern, and to give attention to justice and to the poor": *Life of Antony,* p. 90.
page 35	"not to escape neighbors but to grasp more fully what the neighbor is": Rowan Williams, *Where God Happens* (Boston: Shambhala/New Seeds, 2007), pp. 32-33.
page 35	counseled moderation in bodily asceticism: *Life of Antony,* p. 50.
page 36	*The Sayings of the Desert Fathers:* Benedicta Ward, ed., *The Sayings of the Desert Fathers,* rev. ed., Cistercian Studies 59 (Kalamazoo, Mich.: Cistercian, 1987).
page 36	"The essence of the spirituality of the desert": Benedicta Ward, foreword to *The Desert Christian: Sayings of the Desert Fathers—The Alphabetical Collection,* trans. Benedicta Ward (New York: Macmillan, 1980), p. xix.
page 36	"a living text, a means of formation of a monastic life": Jean Leclercq, *The Love of Learning and the Desire for God* (New York: Fordham University Press, 1982), p. 99.
page 36	"The testings and miracles of Antony fixed themselves": Introduction to *Life of Antony,* p. 13.

Chapter Two: Gregory the Great

page 38   True spirituality always engages: Carl Trueman, "Minority Report: Why Should Thoughtful Evangelicals Read the Medieval Mystics?" *Themelios* 33, no. 1 (2008), <http://www.thegospelcoalition.org/publications/33-1/minority-report-why-should-thoughtful-evangelicals-read-the-medieval-mystics>.

page 38   Gregory lived at a point of transition in Western history: For much in the following few paragraphs, I am indebted to the outstanding lectures of medievalist Susan Keefe, Duke Divinity School.

page 38   estate loomed across from the Circus Maximus: John Moorhead, *Gregory the Great,* Early Church Fathers, ed. Carol Harrison (New York: Routledge, 2005), p. 1.

page 38   almost two decades of ravaging wars across Italy: Carole Straw, *Gregory the Great: Perfection in Imperfection* (Berkeley: University of California Press, 1988), pp. 2-3.

page 39   "Large areas of Rome became deserted": Judith Herrin, *The Formation of Christendom* (Princeton, N.J.: Princeton University Press, 1989), p. 148.

page 40   Gregory's education had probably been quite good: Straw, *Gregory the Great,* p. 5.

page 40   Both this education and his aristocratic background: Thomas C. Oden, *Care of Souls in the Classic Tradition,* Theology and Pastoral Care Series, ed. Don Browning (Philadelphia: Fortress, 1984), p. 45.

page 40   He had been raised in a pious family: Straw, *Gregory the Great,* p. 5.

page 40   "While my mind obliged me to serve": The dedicatory letter to Leander at the beginning of his massive commentary on Job, the *Moralia;* quoted in R. A. Markus, *Gregory the Great and His World* (New York: Cambridge University Press, 1997), p. 9.

page 41   "I fled all this with anxiety": Bernard McGinn, *The Growth of Mysticism: Gregory the Great Through the 12th century,* vol. 2 of *The Presence of God: A History of Western Christian Mysticism* (New York: Crossroad, 1994), pp. 34-35.

page 41   "from which so much of the seventh-century leadership of the church": Oden, *Care of Souls in the Classic Tradition,* p. 46.

page 41   the world culture that would soon emerge: The classic sources on these changes are R. A. Markus, *The End of Ancient Christianity* (New York: Cambridge University Press, 1990), and Herrin, *Formation of Christendom.*

page 42   "the soul's effort in entering into itself": Markus, *Gregory the Great and His World,* p. 22.

page 42	"to enjoy the light within is": McGinn, *The Growth of Mysticism*, p. 56.
page 42	Gregory followed Benedict's more moderate way: Straw, *Gregory the Great*, p. 18.
page 43	Then during the bitter winter of 589–590: Oden, *Care of Souls in the Classic Tradition*, p. 49.
page 44	"I am being smashed by many waves of affairs": Moorhead, *Gregory the Great*, p. 3.
page 44	"My sad mind, labouring under the soreness of its engagements": Gregory, preface to *Dialogues*.
page 44	part of him loved the prominence and importance: Straw, *Gregory the Great*, p. 25.
page 44	the new pope felt obliged to pour himself out in labor for his people: Herrin, *Formation of Christendom*, p. 160.
page 45	the city's wealthy senatorial class had fled with their goods: Ibid., pp. 146-47.
page 46	the Latin *saeculum:* "saeculum or saeclum," *An Elementary Latin Dictionary* (New York: Oxford University Press, 1999), pp. 744-45.
page 46	it seemed that the active and contemplative lives could not be reconciled: "His whole experience before becoming pope pointed toward a way of defining the two lives as alternative forms of living here, in this world." Markus, *Gregory the Great*, p. 19.
page 46	"the most widely read single text in the history of pastoral care": Oden, *Care of Souls in the Classic Tradition*, p. 54.
page 46	the *Rule of Pastoral Care:* Markus, *Gregory the Great*, p. 14. There are two modern editions of this book—both of them somewhat stilted and problematic in various ways (see Oden, *Care of Souls in the Classic Tradition*, p. 55 on the limitations of these translations). The one I recommend appears in The Ancient Christian Writers series, under the title *Pastoral Care*, trans. Henry Davis (New York: Paulist Press, 1950/1978). All quotations are from this edition.
page 46	"joined in the night . . . to the fertile Leah": Markus, *Gregory the Great*, p. 20.
page 46	"Jacob begins with Leah, attains Rachel, and returns to Leah": Straw, *Gregory the Great*, p. 20.
page 47	these two modes of life were not as mutually exclusive as he and the church had taught: Markus, *Gregory the Great*, p. 18.
page 47	he ate and drank with sinners by day: McGinn, *Growth of Mysticism*, p. 78.
page 47	"turn away from the distractions of knowing about *things*": Ibid., p. 57.

page 48   "worldly asceticism": See Max Weber, *The Protestant Ethic and the Spirit of Capitalism,* trans. Talcott Parsons (Mineola, N.Y.: Dover Publications, 2003). It refers to a kind of discipline in the midst of one's everyday work that is treated as having a spiritual value as high as any ancient ascetic practice.

page 49   "God's involvement with creation": Straw, *Gregory the Great,* pp. 49-50.

page 49   the new, sacred world of the medievals: Probably the best modern account of this world-affirming medieval spirituality is to be found in C. S. Lewis's late work, based on decades of lectures, *The Discarded Image* (Cambridge: Cambridge University Press, 1994).

page 49   Gregory felt the average person heard most clearly from God: McGinn, *Growth of Mysticism,* p. 36.

page 49   "an underlying sense of the triumph of joy and peace": Ibid., pp. 44-46.

page 50   by integrating the active life, with all its brokenness: Straw, *Gregory the Great,* p. 25.

page 50   "no part of life remains untouched by the sacred": Ibid.

page 50   "deeply felt sense of the radical insufficiency of all terrestrial goods": McGinn, *Growth of Mysticism,* p. 48.

page 51   "were not above usurping funds or land": Straw, *Gregory the Great,* p. 82.

page 51   "only they who despised power could be trusted": Ibid., p. 5.

page 52   "from the servant of the servants of God": Ibid.

page 52   "how one should come to government": Moorhead, *Gregory the Great,* p. 13.

page 52   to turn one's back on glory and keep oneself humble: Ibid., p. 41.

page 52   "gentle hissing that calms horses, excites young puppies": Gregory I, *Pastoral Care,* part 3, prologue, in *St. Gregory the Great: Pastoral Care,* trans. Henry Davis, Ancient Christian Writers: The Works of the Fathers in Translation 11, ed. Johannes Quasten and Joseph Plumpe (New York: Newman, 1978), p. 89.

page 52   "men and women; the young and the old": Ibid., pp. 90-91.

page 52   The pastor must be all things to all people: Markus, *Gregory the Great,* p. 29.

page 52   Not surprisingly, as Gregory's "rule" seems to have been modeled: McGinn, *Growth of Mysticism,* p. 37.

page 53   "Wherever you go, let the *Pastoral Book* of St. Gregory go with you": Ibid., pp. 37-38.

page 53   *The Ecclesiastical History of the English People:* A Penguin edition is available that won't break the bank: Venerable Bede, *Ecclesiasti-*

cal *History of the English People,* trans. Leo Sherley-Price (New York: Penguin, 1990).

page 53   "Since we hold the same faith": Ibid., pp. 78-79.

page 54   "not on that account to be deprived of communion": Ibid., p. 80.

page 54   "The temples of the idols among that people": Ibid., p. 92.

page 54   the principle of "translatability": See Lamin Sanneh, *Translating the Message: The Missionary Impact on Culture* (Maryknoll, N.Y.: Orbis, 1989).

page 55   "In the church, because united in one faith": Markus, *Gregory the Great,* p. 74.

Chapter Three: Dante Alighieri

page 57   "marked with our image": Dorothy Sayers, introduction to *The Comedy of Dante Alighieri, the Florentine, Cantica I: Hell* (New York: Penguin Books, 1979), p. 9.

page 57   "my heart and will were wheeled by love": Ibid., p. 9, quoting Dante.

page 57   "perambulating labels": The term comes from the *Comedy's* most widely read modern translator, Dorothy Sayers, from "And Telling You a Story: A Note on *The Divine Comedy,*" in *Essays Presented to Charles Williams,* ed. C. S. Lewis (Grand Rapids: Eerdmans, 1966), p. 15.

page 57   "drama of the soul's choice": This, again, is Sayers's term, in her introduction to *The Comedy,* p. 11.

page 58   Dante's early education took place: Arnoldo Mondadori, ed., *Dante: His Life, His Times, His Works* (New York: American Heritage Press, 1970), p. 9; Giuseppe Mazzotta, "Life of Dante," in *The Cambridge Companion to Dante,* ed. Rachel Jacoff (Cambridge: Cambridge University Press, 1993), p. 5.

page 58   At the age of nine, Dante was attending one of the parties: Mondadori, *Dante,* p. 10.

page 59   "her stride; her eyes; her silence; her smile; her aura": Mazzotta, "Life of Dante," p. 6.

page 59   Beatrice's luminous person set Dante on "the path of self-discovery": Ibid.

page 59   God uses romantic love as a sort of mediating influence: See Charles Williams, *Outlines of Romantic Theology,* reprinted in *Religion and Love in Dante: The Theology of Romantic Love,* ed. Alice Mary Hadfield (Grand Rapids: Eerdmans, 1990).

page 59   "first found entry to that faith": Dante Alighieri, *Paradiso,* trans. Allen Mandelbaum (New York: Bantam Books, 1982), 25.10-11, cited in Peter S. Hawkins, *Dante: A Brief History* (Malden, Mass.: Blackwell, 2006), p. 106.

page 60 "A miraculous vision appeared to me": Dante Alighieri, *La Vita Nuova (The New Life),* sec. 42, trans. A. S. Kline (2001) <www.ad kline.freeuk.com/TheNewLifeIV.htm#_Toc88710693>.

page 60 Then in the *Purgatorio* and *Paradiso:* Hawkins, *Dante: A Brief History,* p. 82.

page 61 "Now turn around and listen well": Dante Alighieri, *The Divine Comedy,* vol. 3, *Paradise,* trans. Mark Musa (New York: Penguin Books, 1984), p. 214.

page 61 "the complete reversal of the love affair": Hawkins, *Dante: A Brief History,* p. 82.

page 61 "the lady turns to God": Ibid.

page 61 the young man grew intellectually under two mentors: Mondadori, *Dante,* pp. 11-12.

page 61 In 1285, while the true apple of his eye had still been alive: Mazzotta, "Life of Dante," p. 6.

page 62 Dante had fought in two of the endless skirmishes: As a cavalryman, he served at the battle of Campaldino, between Florence and Arezzo. Then he helped take the Castle of Caprona from Pisa. Mondadori, *Dante,* p. 12.

page 62 "gay parties [and] lavish banquets": Ibid.

page 62 "a sort of battle of insults": Ibid., pp. 12, 14.

page 62 "Much doth it grieve me that thy noble mind": Guido Cavalcanti, Sonnet 23, "To Dante, rebuking him for his way of life after the death of Beatrice," from *The Sonnets and Ballate of Guido Cavalcanti,* trans. Ezra Pound (Boston: Small, Maynard and Company, 1912).

page 63 period of intense study in the Franciscan and Dominican schools: This was during 1291-1294. Dante probably studied at two *scuole de li religiosi:* with the Dominicans at Santa Maria Novella and with the Franciscans at Santa Croce (Robert Hollander, "Chronology of Dante's Life" [based on a chronology by Giorgio Petrocchi], *Dante: A Life in Works* [New Haven: Yale University Press, 2001], p. xi).

page 63 "hard at first to penetrate their meaning": Dante Alighieri *Convivio* 2.12. 2-7, quoted in Kenelm Foster, O.P., "The Mind in Love: Dante's Philosophy," in *Dante: A Collection of Critical Essays,* ed. John Freccero (Englewood Cliffs, N.J.: Prentice-Hall, 1965), p. 45.

page 63 "a man looking for silver accidentally hits on gold": Ibid.

page 63 the beloved Lady Poverty of Francis of Assisi: See *Paradiso* 11.

page 63 "O how many nights there were": *Convivio* 3.1.3, in Foster, "Mind in Love," p. 46.

page 64 "Through the joy of sheer knowing": Foster, "Mind in Love," p. 50.

page 64 "love the universe as a man can love his own city": C. S. Lewis, *Discarded Image* (Cambridge: Cambridge University Press, 1994), p. 203.

page 64 "'theomorphic,' or God-shaped": Timothy B. Shutt, *Dante and His Divine Comedy: Course Guide* (Prince Frederick, Md.: Recorded Books, LLC, 2005), p. 16.

page 64 "The glory of Him who moves all things": *Paradiso* 1.1-5, in Foster, "Mind in Love," p. 50.

page 64 "'But your life . . . is breathed in directly by the supreme Good": *Paradiso* 7, in Foster, "Mind in Love," p. 57.

page 65 "the natural thirst which nothing slakes": *Purgatorio* 21.103, in Foster, "Mind in Love," p. 57.

page 65 perhaps even the transporting joy of mystical experience: In the last few cantos of *Paradiso,* Dante's pilgrim visits the highest ethereal heaven, which "in effect is the divine mind." William R. Cook and Ronald B. Herzman, "Dante's *Divine Comedy:* Part 1," *The Great Courses: Literature & English Language Course Guidebook* [printed material offered with recorded lectures by The Teaching Company, Course no. 287, 24 lectures, 30 min. lecture], p. 83. Find at <www.teach12.com/ttcx/CourseDescLong2.aspx?cid=287>.

page 66 "the good of the intellect": *Convivio* 2.13.6, in Foster, "Mind in Love," p. 53.

page 66 In 1295 these loyalties began to play a key role: Mondadori, *Dante,* pp. 12, 14.

page 66 "a persistent danger zone": Mazzotta, "Life of Dante," p. 5.

page 66 Conflict arose not only from class difference: Ibid., pp. 14-15.

page 67 Layers of tension piled up: Ibid., p. 14.

page 67 The most pervasive struggle: Shutt, *Dante and His Divine Comedy,* p. 8.

page 67 "God had chosen, after all, to submit himself": Ibid.

page 67 "Wasn't the pope, after all, the Vicar of Christ?": Ibid.

page 67 in 1300 Dante, serving in Florence's highest leadership: Mondadori, *Dante,* p. 17.

page 67 "destroyed their houses, and condemned by default": Ibid., p. 18.

page 68 "as a ship without sails and without rudder": *Convivio* 1.3.4-5.

page 68 "how salt the bread of strangers is": *Paradiso* 27, pp. 59-60.

page 68 "retreated from the grim squalid quarters": Mazzotta, "Life of Dante," pp. 8-9.

page 68 "he must have longed during this time": Ibid., pp. 9-10.

page 68 "the root and bark of the politics": Cook and Herzman, "Dante's *Di-*

vine Comedy," p. 37.

page 69   "he was honorably received by the lord of that city": Bonnie C. Harvey, "A Poet Without Honor," *Christian History* 70, no. 2 (2001): 25; quoting Giovanni Boccaccio, *Trattatello in laude di Dante.*

page 69   "dense woods of pine trees near the city": Mazzotta, "Life of Dante," p. 11.

page 69   the contemplative theology of such men as Benedict: Ibid.

page 70   "the way out of the darkness": Ibid., p. 9.

page 70   "Aquinas the Dominican extols the holiness of Francis of Assisi": Dorothy Sayers, "Divine Poet and the Angelic Doctor," *Further Papers on Dante* (London: Methuen, 1957), p. 51.

page 71   "probably amused as well as delighted himself": Ibid.

page 71   "Once upon a time he had known the right way": Nuttall, *Faith of Dante,* p. 3.

page 72   Ulysses, in an imagined dialogue with Dante: Cook and Herzman, "Dante's *Divine Comedy*," p. 37.

Chapter Four: Margery Kempe

page 74   In 1373 was born a remarkable person: Barry Windeatt, introduction to *The Book of Margery Kempe,* by Margery Kempe (New York: Penguin, 1994), p. 10.

page 75   many modern Christians . . . have become fascinated with her: see online resources at <http://www.luminarium.org/medlit/margery .htm>, <http://www.holycross.edu/departments/visarts/projects/ kempe> and especially <http://www.holycross.edu/departments/ visarts/projects/kempe/text/main.htm>, which provides links to a timeline of Kempe's life, summaries of the chapters of her book and a comprehensive glossary of terms in her book that may be unfamiliar to modern readers.

page 75   Its merchants traded profitably with other North European ports: Barry Windeatt introduction to *The Book of Margery Kempe,* by Margery Kempe (Cambridge: D. S. Brewer, 2004), p. 3.

page 75   though most folks were still illiterate, reading and writing were on the rise: John Nelson Miner, "Schools and Literacy in Later Medieval England," *British Journal of Educational Studies* 11, no. 1 (1962): 16-27.

page 76   many people avoided the heavy pre-Communion penitential requirements by receiving: see Joseph Lynch, "Religion with a Human Face," *Christian History* 15, no. 1 (1996): 16.

page 76   Sunday after Sunday, the Mass was presented to passive audiences: Bernard McGinn, *The Growth of Mysticism: Gregory the Great*

Through the 12th Century, vol. 2 of *The Presence of God: A History of Western Christian Mysticism* (New York: Crossroad, 1994), p. 23.

page 76   In the face of these changes, the English layfolk of 1373 were seeking other ways to an experience of union with God in Christ: On the distinctively English medieval tradition of affective (emotional) piety, see Clarissa W. Atkinson, *Mystic and Pilgrim: The Book and the World of Margery Kempe* (Ithaca, N.Y.: Cornell University Press, 1983), pp. 129-56.

page 77   "for not having kissed the place of the wounds where the nails pierced": From *Prayer to Christ,* available in *The Prayers and Meditations of St. Anselm: With the Proslogion,* trans. by Benedicta Ward (New York: Penguin, 1973), p. 97.

page 77   Bernard had contributed an intense Marian devotion: Joan M. Nuth, *God's Lovers in an Age of Anxiety: The Medieval English Mystics* (Maryknoll, N.Y.: Orbis, 2001), p. 21.

page 77   And Francis and his followers had spread a Christ-centered devotion: see Lynch, "Religion with a Human Face," p. 12.

page 77   "an intense, intimate relationship to Christ": Nuth, *God's Lovers in an Age of Anxiety.*

page 77   monks, nuns and layfolk alike tried to imitate Jesus' passion or to experience something of the same extreme suffering as had their Lord: Take, for example, Julian of Norwich's request to God that she experience "three wounds."

page 78   "in a mantle of purple silk . . . upon her bedside": Margery Kempe, *The Book of Margery Kempe* (New York: Penguin, 1994), p. 42.

page 78   "She was enormously envious of her neighbors": Ibid., p. 44.

page 78   She resolved to live in celibacy, in imitation of the holy nuns and monks: This desire for chastity on the part of a lay Christian, with the goal of becoming "espoused to Christ," was no innovation of Margery's. Bernard McGinn, in his *Growth of Mysticism,* tells us, for example, that Caesarius of Arles (c. 470/1–543) had used spousal language to describe the union of Christ with the individual soul (not just the church), and that he felt this privilege was accessible not only to celibate monastics, but also to laypeople. See McGinn, *Growth of Mysticism,* pp. 31ff., on how this theme continued to be developed throughout the medieval period.

page 78   when she tried to get her long-suffering husband: *Book of Margery Kempe,* pp. 46-47.

pages 78-79   "She hated the joys of the world": Ibid., p. 48.

page 79   "A man whom she liked said to her": Ibid. For narration of the entire episode, see pp. 48-51.

page 79   she prevailed on John to take a vow: Ibid., pp. 58-60.

page 79   Most late-medieval adults went on pilgrimage: Richard Kieckhefer, "Major Currents in Late Medieval Devotion," in *Christian Spirituality: High Middle Ages and Reformation,* ed. Jill Raitt (New York: Crossroad, 1987), p. 85. Kieckhefer continues, "A pilgrim from Nuremberg named Martin Ketzel, on returning home, engaged a sculptor to carve a series of stations representing the 'seven falls,' or the points in his passion when Christ fell to the ground. Late fifteenth- and early sixteenth-c. authors wrote reflections on [such] stations, to be used for meditation as a person proceeded from one image to another. Among the most important of these authors was a Belgian Carmelite, John Pascha, who in the early sixteenth-c. devised a list of fourteen stations identical to those used in modern devotion."

page 80   "wept and sobbed as plenteously": *Book of Margery Kempe,* p. 104.

page 80   transformed into Christ's body and blood: For a discussion of the importance of the doctrine of transubstantiation in medieval Christian practice, see Lynch, "Religion with a Human Face," p. 16.

page 80   "preachers generally tolerated her loud sobbing": Ibid., p. 11.

page 81   "explosive reactions of repentance and religious exaltation": Ibid., p. 12.

page 81   "saw Christ, not as an ancient historical figure": Martin Thornton, *Margery Kempe: An Example in the English Pastoral Tradition* (London: SPCK, 1960), p. 35. I believe many medieval folks shared this sense of the vivid presence of Christ—though most not as intensely as Margery, perhaps. In his masterly *The Discarded Image,* C. S. Lewis describes how vibrant and full of life and meaning the whole universe was to many medieval folk. It would not be much of a stretch, then, to experience Christ as vibrantly present in the ordinary streets and events of this world.

page 81   her confessor came to her and, finding her weeping: *Book of Margery Kempe,* p. 187.

page 81   I imagine this to be something like what Margery: Thornton, *Margery Kempe,* p. 35. Keep this in your memory for the chapter on the twentieth-century writer and lay theologian Dorothy Sayers, because Thornton goes on to link Margery with Sayers, saying, "To Margery, Miss Dorothy Sayers' *The Man Born To Be King* would be no daring experiment but the only sensible way in which such a play could be written."

page 82   "the rich freedom, the perfect understanding": Ibid., p. 27.

page 82	This, too, was part of the spiritual tradition: see Atkinson, *Mystic and Pilgrim*, pp. 129-56.
page 82	"the Mother of God . . . amiable lady, humble lady, loving lady": *Book of Margery Kempe* 2.10. "Marian Christians" account for a greater percentage of the world church than those who are not engaged in Marian devotion. Though this doesn't prove the orthodoxy of some Marian beliefs and practices, it certainly should give non-Marian Christians pause, encouraging them to dig more deeply in this stream of Christian spirituality.
page 83	"As a prophet," Thornton concludes: Thornton, *Margery Kempe*, p. 22.
page 84	They have become convinced that everything in the church: This opinion, by the way, owes much to the still-powerful influence of nineteenth-century romantic individualism; see Charles Taylor, *Sources of the Self* (Cambridge: Cambridge University Press, 1992), on modern "expressivism."
page 84	seeking first purgation from sin, then spiritual illumination: This Pseudo-Dionysian sequence is quite correctly worrisome to Protestants today. Believing as we do in salvation by grace, we assume we have real union with God from our conversion onward; we don't have to "earn" it through a long effortful climb.
page 85	Thornton concludes that Margery's book: see Thornton, *Margery Kempe*, pp. 19-21, 32-33, 43-44; see also Thorton's appendix cataloging the many forms of prayer Kempe practiced.
page 86	"Woman, give up this life that you lead": *Book of Margery Kempe*, p. 168.
page 86	"There was a dinner of great joy and gladness": Ibid., p. 210.
page 87	Though she was emotionally focused, she was not individualistic: Thornton, *Margery Kempe*, p. 65.
page 87	After her many pilgrimages, Margery settled: See *Book of Margery Kempe*, pp. 216-21.
page 87	The last few chapters of Margery's autobiography: See ibid., pp. 265-97.
page 89	"the believers' alliance of compassion": Ellen M. Ross, *The Grief of God: Images of the Suffering Jesus in Late Medieval England* (Oxford: Oxford University Press, 1997), p. 7.
page 89	"amusing ourselves to death": In the immortal words of Neil Postman, *Amusing Ourselves to Death: Public Discourse in the Age of Show Business* (New York: Penguin, 1985).
page 89	But our modern malaise—termed by philosophers *anomie:* For an incisive diagnosis, see Charles Taylor, *The Malaise of Modernity*

(Concord, Ont.: Anansi, 1996).

page 89   "Why do you weep so, woman?": *Book of Margery Kempe,* p. 163.

page 91   the vision of Gibson's *Passion of the Christ* lies in the same medieval tradition of piety: Chris Armstrong, "The Fountain Fill'd with Blood," *Christianity Today,* March 2004.

Chapter Five: John Amos Comenius

page 92   In the best surviving portrait of John Amos Comenius: Ca. 1660, by J. Ovens, held today in the Museum Catharijneconvent in Utrecht. The portrait adorns the cover of the best modern edition of Comenius's *Labyrinth of the World and the Paradise of the Heart,* ed. Howard Louthan and Andrea Sterk (Mahwah, N.J.: Paulist Press, 1998). To get a good look, find that title on Amazon.com and click on the cover to enlarge it.

page 93   the new empiricism of Francis Bacon: See Ed Robinson, "John Amos Comenius: Exemplar of Integration," *Christian Education Journal* 2, no. 2 (1998): 49-51.

page 93   John Amos Comenius: "Comenius" is a Latinized form of "Komensky," his surname in the Czech language of his homeland; J. Philip Arthur, "Comenius: That Incomparable Moravian," in *Fulfilling the Great Commission: Papers Read at the 1992 Westminster Conference* (London: The Westminster Conference, 1992), p. 130.

page 93   part of what is now the Czech Republic: The present-day Czech Republic comprises the former nations of Moravia and Bohemia, along with other territories.

page 93   Nivnice, lay on a rolling plain near a low mountain range: Matthew Spinka, *John Amos Comenius: That Incomparable Moravian* (New York: Russell and Russell, 1967), p. 24.

page 93   preacher of nonresistance and church-state separation named Peter Chelcicky: Arthur, "Comenius," p. 131; Spinka, *John Amos Comenius,* p. 9.

page 94   "tender Epistles of St. John": J. E. Hutton, *History of the Moravians,* 2nd ed. (London: Moravian Publication Office, 1909; online repr., Grand Rapids: Christian Classics Ethereal Library, 2007), <http://www.ccel.org/h/hutton/moravian>, chapter VII, "The Brethren at Home," esp. p. 46.

page 94   the Unity numbered some hundred thousand members: Spinka, *John Amos Comenius,* p. 11.

page 94   in 1604, when he was just twelve, John lost both of his parents: Arthur, "Comenius," pp. 130-31; Eva Chybova Bock, "John Amos Comenius: Pioneer of Church Unity and Teacher of Nations," *Reli-*

gion in Life 22, no. 3 (1953): 381.

page 94   to live with his aunt in the nearby town of Straznice: Howard Louthan and Andrea Sterk, introduction to *John Comenius: The Labyrinth of the World and the Paradise of the Heart,* Classics of Western Spirituality, ed. Bernard McGinn (New York: Paulist Press,
1998), p. 10.

page 95   "slaughter-houses of minds": S. S. Laurie, *John Amos Comenius:
His Life and Educational Works,* 6th ed. (Cambridge: Cambridge
University Press, 1899), p. 55.

page 95   "seemed to have been the invention of some wicked spirit": Laurie,
John Amos Comenius, p. 55, citing a professor named Lubinus at
Rostock.

page 95   Comenius's elementary school experience, though excruciating:
Spinka, *John Amos Comenius,* p. 25.

page 95   "diligence, industry, and genuine love of learning": Ibid., pp. 26-27.

page 95   John Lanecky, later a bishop of the Brethren: Ibid., p. 27.

page 95   "for Charles of Zerotin himself, having been educated abroad": Ibid.,
p. 26.

page 96   Comenius began studies at a well-known college at Herborn: Ibid.,
p. 27.

page 96   the house of Comenius's Heidelberg professor David Pareus: Ibid.,
pp. 30-31.

page 96   "the colossal task of writing, single-handed, a sixteen-volume encyclopedia": Ibid., p. 31.

page 97   he took on a teaching position at the Latin school: Bock, "John Amos
Comenius," p. 381.

page 97   Comenius was ordained a minister in the Unity of the Brethren
Church: Ibid. Silesia was a central European country whose old borders now fall mostly within Poland, with bits in the Czech Republic
and Germany—in Comenius's time, the town of Fulnek was, because
of this proximity, mostly German-speaking and Catholic.

page 97   Leading local Catholics "bullied and badgered him": Spinka, *John
Amos Comenius,* p. 33.

page 97   "the only period of tranquility in his native country": Laurie, *John
Amos Comenius,* p. 57.

page 97   *cuius regio eius religio*—"Whose reign, his religion": Spinka, *John
Amos Comenius,* p. 1.

page 98   When two Catholic councilors were sent to Prague: Arthur, "Comenius," pp. 132-33. Historians estimate that half of Germany's population was lost in the fighting; Randy Peterson, "The Thirty Years'
War," *Christian History* 6, no. 1 (1987): 17.

page 98   After the defenestration in 1618, the Bohemians raised an army: Ibid.

page 98   "the weapons for stabbing, for chopping, for cutting": Hutton, *History,* p. 90.

page 98   "Not a few (of whose number I, unhappy, am one)": John Comenius, *The Sorrowful,* quoted in Spinka, *John Amos Comenius,* p. 38.

page 98   John Comenius was never to see Fulneck: Bock, "John Amos Comenius," p. 383.

page 98   With the Hapsburgs now in power: Josef Smolik, "Comenius: A Man of Hope in a Time of Turmoil," *Christian History* 6, no. 1 (1987): 15.

page 99   stayed at a town called Brandeis, in Bohemia's far northeast: Arthur, "Comenius," p. 133.

page 99   across the river from the town sat Comenius's hut: Frantisek Lützow, introduction to *The Labyrinth of the World and the Paradise of the Heart,* by John Amos Comenius, ed. Frantisek Lützow (New York: E. P. Dutton, 1901), p. 36.

page 99   the *Labyrinth* is a "philosophical work" and "a book of adventure": Ibid., p. 29.

page 99   "human mind begins to understand the difference between good and evil": Ibid., p. 19.

page 100   "did nothing but change clothes, putting on one costume after another": Comenius, *Labyrinth* 7.9, in Louthan and Sterk, *John Comenius,* p. 74.

page 100   "had become accustomed to stuffing": Comenius, *Labyrinth* 9.7, in ibid., p. 86.

page 100   "They took up one task": Comenius, *Labyrinth* 7.9, in ibid., p. 74.

page 100   "screamed, shrieked, stank, quarreled": Comenius, *Labyrinth* 8.5, in ibid., p. 81.

page 100   "as many poisons as medicines": Comenius, *Labyrinth* 10.9, in ibid., p. 99.

page 100   "came out of them again undigested": Comenius, *Labyrinth* 10.7, in ibid., pp. 96-97.

page 100   "The more learned one considered himself or was esteemed by others": Comenius, *Labyrinth* 10.9-10, in ibid., pp. 98-100.

page 100   "These people are like peasants in a tavern": Comenius, *Labyrinth* 11.1, in ibid., p. 102.

page 101   Sick at heart and thinking of ending it all: Comenius, *Labyrinth* 39.1-2, in ibid., pp. 189-90.

page 101   "the Paradise of the heart!": Transparently, this is the Brethren community, though Comenius admits in an introductory "note to the reader" that his portrayal is intended to reflect their ideals—which (it is implied) are not always practiced. See Paul Heidebrecht, "The Labyrinth of the World and the Paradise of the Heart," *Christian History* 6, no. 1 (1987): 25.

page 101   By 1624 the persecution against the Brethren: Laurie, *John Amos Comenius,* p. 58.

page 102   "Nothing have we taken with us": Hutton, *History,* p. 91.

page 102   "buried their Bibles in their gardens": Ibid., p. 92.

page 102   The Brethren's hopes peaked after 1630: Arthur, "Comenius," pp. 138-39.

page 102   teaching at a gymnasium there: Hutton, *History,* p. 92.

page 102   "They must begin, he said, by teaching the children": Ibid.

page 102   he wrote the *Janua Linguarum:* Ibid., p. 95.

page 103   "not only willed to become as a little child": John Comenius, *The School of Infancy,* chap. 1, in *Comenius: Servant of Man and Father of Modern Education,* ed. Ernest M. Eller (Chapel Hill: University of North Carolina Press, 2003), p. 59.

page 103   "the age, interests and mental ability of the pupil": It was perhaps this insight more than any other that led the twentieth-century Swiss developmental psychologist and educationist Jean Piaget to say that Comenius's educational theory *needs no correction* today. (Jean Piaget, "The Significance of John Amos Comenius at the Present Time," introduction to *John Amos Comenius, 1592-1670: Selections* [Paris: UNESCO, 1957].)

page 103   Cardinal Richelieu sought his services for France: Louthan and Sterk, *John Comenius,* p. 14.

page 104   "Why," asks Comenius, "should we need other teachers": Laurie, *John Amos Comenius,* p. 69.

page 104   "pansophism": See Matthew Spinka, "Comenian Pansophic Principles," *Church History* 22 (1953): 155-65.

page 104   Comenius worked toward the goal: Paul Heidebrecht, "Learning from Nature: The Educational Legacy of Jan Amos Comenius," *Christian History* 6, no. 1 (1987): 22-23, 35.

page 105   He and others brought Comenius to England: Spinka, *John Amos Comenius,* p. 77.

page 105   by the civil war then brewing: Ibid., p. 78.

page 105   it did inspire England's great Royal Society: Ibid., p. 78.

page 105   "fathers of modern science": Chris Armstrong, "The *Christian* Face of the Scientific Revolution," *Christian History* 76 (2002): 47.

page 105   "as the remedy of the chief problems confronting Europe": Spinka, *John Amos Comenius,* p. 79.

page 105   failure to know things accurately and experientially: Robert Fitzgibbon Young, *Comenius in England* (London: Humphrey Milford, 1932), pp. 30-31.

page 106   "All were speaking their own language": Comenius *Labyrinth* 7.4-6, in Louthan and Sterk, *John Comenius,* pp. 72-73.

page 107   "joining a communion in which ye find the truth": John Comenius, *The Bequest of the Unity of Brethren,* trans. Matthew Spinka (Chicago: National Union of Czechkoslovak Protestants in America, 1940), pp. 22-23.

page 107   "lively desire for unanimity of opinion": Comenius, *Bequest,* pp. 29-31.

page 108   "reforms intended to lead others out of the labyrinth": Louthan and Sterk, *John Comenius,* p. 26.

page 108   "insatiability of Mind, which pries into everything": Ibid., p. 19.

page 108   "The bridle is Vanity": Comenius, *Labyrinth* 4.3-5, in ibid., p. 66-67.

page 108   "the process by which people could be trained to see beyond": Ibid., p. 26.

page 109   "If all men understand each other": Spinka, *John Amos Comenius,* p. 83.

page 110   "In essentials, unity; in non-essentials, liberty; in all things, charity": Comenius quoted this in his *Unum Necessarium,* and though commonly attributed to Augustine, the phrase originated with a seventeenth-century Lutheran Pietist named Peter Meiderlin. For more on the phrase's origin, see Hans Rollmann, "'In Essentials Unity': The Pre-History and History of a Restoration Movement Slogan" (adapted from a lecture given at the Christian Scholars Conference, David Lipscomb University, Nashville, July, 1996), <http://www.mun.ca/rels/restmov/texts/unitas/essrev.html#N_5_>.

page 111   equal opportunity for all students: See <http://ec.europa.eu/education/lifelong-learning-programme/doc84_en.htm>. The brief video on this page features schoolchildren speaking in several European languages about cooperative projects designed (says the voiceover) "to bring Europe's pupils and teachers together, across borders."

Chapter Six: John Newton

page 113   "designed by divine providence for an healer of breaches": Steve Turner, *Amazing Grace: The Story of America's Most Beloved Song* (New York: HarperCollins, 2002), p. 109.

page 114   "old African blasphemer": Ibid., p. 107.

page 114   He was born in London, an only child, in 1725: John Pollock, *Amazing Grace: The Dramatic Life Story of John Newton* (San Francisco:

Harper & Row, 1981), pp. 17-20; D. Bruce Hindmarsh, *John Newton and the English Evangelical Tradition* (Oxford: Clarendon, 1996), p. 16.

page 114   From age eleven to seventeen John accompanied his father: Pollock, *Amazing Grace,* pp. 20-22.

page 114   After each fall he would rise again, resolving: Hindmarsh, *John Newton,* p. 17.

page 114   In 1742, soon after John's father retired from the sea: Ibid.

page 115   When John could no longer put off his return home: Pollock, *Amazing Grace,* pp. 26-30.

page 115   In the company of the rough crew: Hindmarsh, *John Newton,* p. 17.

page 115   On the way back from Venice, Newton: Pollock, *Amazing Grace,* pp. 30-32.

page 116   In the following months Newton missed a second voyage: Ibid., pp. 33-36.

page 116   As bad as the physical privations aboard this ship were: Ibid., pp. 37-38.

page 116   Enjoying the heady release of his new creed: Ibid., p. 39.

page 117   At Christmas 1744 the Harwich moored north of the straits of Dover: Hindmarsh, *John Newton,* p. 18; Pollock, *Amazing Grace,* pp. 44-47.

page 117   Newton was soon able to secure a transfer: Hindmarsh, *John Newton,* p. 18; Pollock, *Amazing Grace,* p. 49.

page 117   "During the next two years": Hindmarsh, *John Newton,* p. 18.

page 117   Newton became lower than a slave: Pollock, *Amazing Grace,* pp. 56-57, 61-62.

page 118   a captain deputized by his father did actually find Newton: Ibid., pp. 66-68.

page 118   the younger Newton had found a new master: Hindmarsh, *John Newton,* p. 18; Pollock, *Amazing Grace,* p. 67.

page 118   On this voyage, Newton surpassed his earlier immorality: Pollock, *Amazing Grace,* p. 77.

page 118   Just as Newton seemed irrevocably lost to the faith: Hindmarsh, *John Newton,* pp. 18-19; Pollock, *Amazing Grace,* pp. 69-72.

page 118   The *Greyhound*'s voyage from Brazil to Newfoundland: Hindmarsh, *John Newton,* p. 19; Pollock, *Amazing Grace,* pp. 76-81.

page 118   "Tied to the ship to prevent being washed away": Hindmarsh, *John Newton,* p. 19.

page 118   Newton was convinced that he had sinned too much: Pollock, *Amazing Grace,* pp. 74, 76-77.

page 119   Newton's new faith would not find a solid footing for some months:

Ibid., pp. 94-96.

page 119   "crucified the Son of God afresh": Ibid., p. 96.

page 119   "What a poor creature I am in myself": Ibid., p. 97.

page 119   On the matter of slavery, Newton's progress was slow: Hindmarsh, *John Newton*, pp. 22, 44; Pollock, *Amazing Grace*, p. 131.

page 119   Just before he received his first command: Hindmarsh, *John Newton*, p. 20; Pollock, *Amazing Grace*, pp. 100-103.

page 120   As Newton prepared for his second voyage: Pollock, *Amazing Grace*, pp. 122-23.

page 120   When in January, having reached the Guinea Coast: Ibid., pp. 123-24.

page 120   But nearly as soon as he left Newton, Lewis began indulging: Hindmarsh, *John Newton*, p. 21; Pollock, *Amazing Grace*, pp. 124-25.

page 120   Newton himself contracted a similar fever: Pollock, *Amazing Grace*, p. 125.

page 121   "I was all ears": Ibid., p. 126.

page 121   "Newton had thought of God as a distant potentate": Ibid., p. 127.

page 121   Newton's prayers as he recovered: Ibid., p. 135.

page 121   When in 1756 the Seven Years' War broke out: Ibid., pp. 142-43.

page 121   Newton himself became known as "Young Whitefield": Ibid., p. 137.

page 122   he began teaching himself the biblical languages: Ibid., pp. 143-44.

page 122   Slowly there dawned on Newton the knowledge: Hindmarsh, *John Newton*, pp. 83-105; Pollock, *Amazing Grace*, pp. 144-52.

page 122   They had exiled him to England's Siberia: Hindmarsh, *John Newton*, p. 171.

page 123   The lace trade, the area's main industry: Pollock, *Amazing Grace*, p. 154.

page 123   And not all the local clergy appreciated Newton: Hindmarsh, *John Newton*, pp. 206-7.

page 123   "I get more warmth and light": Ibid., p. 75.

page 123   He especially labored for the children of Olney parish: Ibid., pp. 191-92, 196-97.

page 123   "The Lord . . . proclaims a free pardon": Ibid., p. 190, quoting MS Sermon notebook 4, Cowper and Newton Museum, Olney, Buckinghamshire.

page 123   "Let us chide our cold unfeeling hearts": Ibid.

page 124   More than just a personal habit: Turner, *Amazing Grace*, p. 109.

page 124   the key moment of Newton's long career: Hindmarsh, *John Newton*, p. 15; Pollock, *Amazing Grace*, pp. 155-56. The book is available today in a reprint of the 1841 edition titled *The Life & Spirituality of John Newton* (Vancouver: Regent College Publishing, 1998).

page 125   "firm discipline, warm fellowship, and apostolic zeal for missions": David Bebbington, *Evangelicalism in Modern Britain: A History from the 1730s to the 1980s* (New York: Routledge, 1989), p. 40.

page 125   Newton also penned many hymns: Hindmarsh, *John Newton,* pp. 258-62.

page 125   the brilliant but mentally unstable poet William Cowper: Pollock, *Amazing Grace,* p. 156.

page 125   as a testament to their friendship: Hindmarsh, *John Newton,* p. 257.

page 125   which included "Amazing Grace": Turner, *Amazing Grace,* p. 88.

page 126   a 1990 documentary: Bill Moyers, *Amazing Grace with Bill Moyers,* videocassette, prod. and dir. Elene Mannes, 80 min. (Alexandria, Va.: PBS Home Video, 1990).

page 126   I like to think that he would have had great sympathy for this musical setting: See Turner, *Amazing Grace,* for a full account of the matching of Newton's words to the new American melody.

page 126   He established a variety of "social meetings": Hindmarsh, *John Newton,* pp. 195-202.

page 126   "nothing has been more visibly useful": Ibid., p. 200, quoting Newton's *Letters.*

page 126   the reckless behavior typical of Guy Fawkes Day: Pollock, *Amazing Grace,* pp. 167-68.

page 126   the townspeople were increasingly afflicted by spiritual deadness: Ibid., p. 169.

page 126   "I am more of a Calvinist than anything else": Hindmarsh, *John Newton,* pp. 167-68.

page 127   Newton was something of a spiritual eclectic: Ibid., pp. 328-29.

page 127   Newton founded the Eclectic Society: Ibid., pp. 312-14.

page 127   "the society that bears no name, and espouses no party": Ibid., p. 313.

page 127   "If we stretch our authority, we lose it": The quotation is from the notes of the Eclectic Society meeting of December 10, 1787. The question for that day was "What is the nature and obligation of conjugal duties?" In response to the question the members recommended a "softening" of male headship. "Authority as the remedy" may prove to be the "disease" itself; instead, it is best to "leave some things to the Woman." "If we stretch our authority," Newton concluded, "we lose it." Aaron Belz, "Not a Synod but a Salon," *Christian History & Biography* 81 (Winter 2004).

page 127   the Eclectic Society became the model: Ibid., pp. 312-14.

page 128   the author and philanthropist Hannah More: Pollock, *Amazing Grace,* p. 176.

page 129   Over the fireplace in his vicarage study at Olney: Ibid., p. 153.

page 129   "John Newton, clerk, once an infidel and libertine, a servant of slaves in Africa": Hindmarsh, *John Newton*, p. 14.

page 129   "Whatever I may doubt on other points": Ibid., p. 48.

Chapter Seven: Charles Simeon

page 130   "proud, imperious, fiery-tempered; a solitary individual": Michael Hennell, "Simeon and the Ministry," in *Charles Simeon (1759–1836): Essays Written in Commemoration of His Bi-Centenary by Members of the Evangelical Fellowship for Theological Literature*, ed. Arthur Pollard and Michael Hennell (London: SPCK, 1959), p. 152.

page 130   Simeon would mentor some 30 percent of the Anglican ministers: Gordon MacDonald, "Charles Simeon: An Expositor Who Touched the World," *Expositapes* (Denver: Denver Seminary, n.d.), audiocassette, 2.4.

page 130   send countless chaplains to India: Marcus L. Loane, *Cambridge and the Evangelical Succession* (London: Lutterworth, 1952), pp. 196-97.

page 130   hugely influential Church Missionary Society: Hugh Evans Hopkins, *Charles Simeon of Cambridge* (Grand Rapids: Eerdman, 1977), p. 151.

page 131   Simeon was born into a family of means and privilege: Handley C. G. Moule, *Charles Simeon,* 2nd ed. (Chicago: InterVarsity Press, 1956), p. 17.

page 131   Known as "'Chin Simeon'": G. B. C. Davies, "Simeon in the Setting of the Evangelical Revival," in *Charles Simeon (1759–1836): Essays Written in Commemoration of His Bi-Centenary by Members of the Evangelical Fellowship for Theological Literature,* ed. Arthur Pollard and Michael Hennell (London: SPCK, 1959), pp. 22-23.

page 131   Simeon also lacked any notable intellectual talent: Hopkins, *Charles Simeon of Cambridge,* p. 13.

page 131   His college's chapel was well attended: Ibid., p. 24.

page 131   "a state of spiritual panic": Ibid., p. 28.

page 131-32   "Satan himself was as fit to attend [the sacrament] as I": Charles Simeon, *Memoirs of the Rev. Charles Simeon,* ed. William Carus (London: J. Hatchard, 1847), p. 4.

page 132   "it has been a comfort to me even to this very hour": Ibid., p. 5.

page 132   "to this effect—'That the Jews knew what they did'": Ibid., p. 6.

page 132   "What, may I transfer all my guilt to another?": Ibid.

page 132   "began to have a hope of mercy": Ibid.

page 132   "on the Sunday morning, Easter-day, April 4": Ibid.

page 133   "From that hour peace flowed in rich abundance": Ibid.

page 133   he instituted family prayers for the servants: Davies, "Simeon in the
                  Setting of the Evangelical Revival," p. 25.

page 133   "felt himself an undone sinner": Simeon, *Memoirs*, p. 22.

page 133-34   "I am come to enquire after your welfare": Hopkins, *Charles Simeon
                  of Cambridge*, p. 35; cf. H. Venn, *Life and Letters of the Rev. H.
                  Venn*, quoted in Moule, *Charles Simeon*, p. 35.

page 134   "solemnly appealed to them, and then knelt down to pray": Moule,
                  Charles Simeon, p. 36.

page 134   "a thing unknown there for near a century": Hopkins, *Charles Sim-
                  eon of Cambridge*, p. 35.

page 134   "St. Edward's is crowded like a theatre on the first night": Ibid.

page 134   "Oh sir, I am so glad you are come": Moule, *Charles Simeon*, pp. 35-36.

page 134   "much necessary wisdom and balance": Davies, "Simeon in the Set-
                  ting of the Evangelical Revival," p. 25.

page 135   "painful to the feelings of others": Charles Jerram, *Memoirs of Charles
                  Jerram (1855)*, quoted in Arthur Pollard, "The Influence and Signifi-
                  cance of Simeon's Work," in *Charles Simeon (1759–1836): Essays
                  Written in Commemoration of His Bi-Centenary by Members of the
                  Evangelical Fellowship for Theological Literature*, ed. Arthur Pol-
                  lard and Michael Hennell (London: SPCK, 1959), pp. 159-60.

page 135   "Chas. Proud and Irritable": Pollard, "Influence and Significance of
                  Simeon's Work," p. 160.

page 135   "for your kind observations respecting misguided zeal": Jerram,
                  Memoirs, in Pollard, "The Influence and Significance of Simeon's
                  Work," p. 160.

page 135   "Well, it's green now, and we must wait": J. Venn, *Annals of a Cleri-
                  cal Family (1904)*, 119n., quoted in Hopkins, *Charles Simeon of
                  Cambridge*, pp. 101-2; cf. Moule, *Charles Simeon*, p. 45.

page 136   "I was particularly struck with the humiliation": Moule, *Charles
                  Simeon*, pp. 34-35.

page 136   "Mr. Simeon's character shines brightly": Edwin Sidney, *The Life of
                  the Rev. Rowland Hill, A.M.* (London: Wertheim, Mackintosh, and
                  Hunt, 1844), p. 174.

page 136   "my affectionate friend Simeon": Simeon, *Memoirs*, p. 50.

page 136   "calls me his father; he pours out his prayer for me": Henry Venn,
                  The Life and a Selection of Letters of the Late Henry Venn, M.A., ed.
                  Henry Venn, B.D. (London: John Hatchard and Son, 1834), p. 481.

page 136   "very poor church folks": Hopkins, *Charles Simeon of Cambridge*, p.
                  39.

page 137   "short black coat, breeches and gaiters, black gloves": Ibid., p. 55.

page 137   "destined to wage irreconcilable war": Ibid.

page 138   When Simeon did reach the pulpit and begin his sermon: MacDonald, "Charles Simeon."

page 138   they slandered him and excluded him from their circle: John Stott, introduction to *Evangelical Preaching: An Anthology of Sermons by Charles Simeon,* ed. James M. Houston (Vancouver: Regent College Publishing, 1986), p. xxxi.

page 138   "was so touched that he had to hurry back": Hopkins, *Charles Simeon of Cambridge,* p. 79.

page 138   "In this state of affairs, I saw no remedy but faith and patience": Simeon, *Memoirs,* p. 26.

page 138   "went for a walk with his Greek Testament in his hand": Ibid., p. 395.

page 138   "When I read that, I said, 'Lord, lay it on me' ": Ibid.

page 138   "I have wished rather to suffer than to act": Ibid., p. 52.

page 139   his changing reputation among Cambridge undergraduates: Hopkins, *Charles Simeon of Cambridge,* p. 86.

page 139   "idle undergraduates who rejoiced": Ibid., pp. 80-81.

page 139   At a particular Eclectic Society meeting: Josiah Pratt, ed., *Eclectic Notes* (Oxford: J. Nesbit, 1865), p. 211, quoted in Hopkins, *Charles Simeon of Cambridge,* p. 121.

page 139   "earnest and impassioned to no ordinary degree": Simeon, *Memoirs,* p. 38.

page 140   Theological and biblical language courses were sketchy at best: Richard H. Schmidt, *Glorious Companions: Five Centuries of Anglican Spirituality* (Grand Rapids: Eerdmans, 2002), p. 165.

page 140   "The ordination examination consisted merely": Hopkins, *Charles Simeon of Cambridge,* p. 85.

page 140   "one can see the rows of old-fashioned hat and coat pegs": Ibid., p. 70.

page 141   "Don't let Satan make you overwork": Hennell, "Simeon and the Ministry," p. 153.

page 141   "It requires more deeply-rooted zeal": Ibid.

page 141   "Never weary your hearers by long preaching": Ibid., pp. 87-88.

page 141   "suggested that they might try rehearsing their sermons": Ibid.

page 141   "Scope out the biblical text and analyze it": Schmidt, *Glorious Companions,* p. 165.

page 142   "Does it uniformly tend to *humble the sinner?*": Ibid., p. 169.

page 142   "If a man's heart is full of love, he will rarely ever offend": MacDonald, "Charles Simeon."

page 142   "the presence of God the Holy Spirit" be invited into each service": Hopkins, *Charles Simeon of Cambridge,* pp. 88-89.

page 142   "encourage us to propose our doubts": Simeon, *Memoirs,* p. 380.

page 143   Cambridge University Prayer Union: See <www.ivcf.ca/public/philosophy/History2.html>.

page 143   "Bible Christians, not system Christians": W. R. Ward, *Early Evangelicalism: A Global Intellectual History, 1670-1789* (Cambridge: Cambridge University Press, 2006), p. 188.

page 143   "I have read Paul, and caught something of his strange notions": Simeon, *Memoirs,* p. 352.

page 143   it was Simeon more than anyone else whose therapeutic influence: Moule, cited in Pollard, "The Influence and Significance of Simeon's Work," p. 164.

page 143   By 1811 Simeon was spending two-thirds of his time: Hopkins, *Charles Simeon of Cambridge,* p. 84.

page 144   "a seat in the saddle so triumphant": James Stephen, *Essays in Ecclesiastical Biography* (New York: Longmans, Green, 1907), p. 239.

page 144   Hopkins, called him "his own worst enemy": Hugh Evans Hopkins, quoted by Gordon MacDonald in "Stepping off the Treadmill," online: <www.christianitytoday.um/le/199/call/914035.html>.

page 144   He called the conversation parties "a foretaste of heaven": Hopkins, *Charles Simeon of Cambridge,* p. 89.

page 145   "Mr. Simeon watches over us as a shepherd over his sheep": Simeon, *Memoirs,* p. 58.

page 145   "spiritual affections" from its workers: Hennell, "Simeon and the Ministry," p. 148.

page 145   "many mistake their calling and with devoted hearts": Hopkins, *Charles Simeon of Cambridge,* p. 85.

page 145   "partly from a sense of obligation to [God] for his redeeming love": Hennell, "Simeon and the Ministry," p. 148.

page 145   By 1829 he had copies of more than seven thousand letters: Hopkins, *Charles Simeon of Cambridge,* p. 122.

page 145   "as soon as he was convinced": Ibid., p. 85.

page 146   Simeon founded a trust drawing on other sources: Ibid., p. 87.

page 146   "I spent this day . . . "TALK NOT ABOUT MYSELF": Ibid., p. 155.

page 147   "Now I see *why* I have been laid aside": Ibid., p. 111

page 147   like the peach in Henry Venn's parable: J. Venn, *Annals of a Clerical Family* (1904), in Hopkins, *Charles Simeon of Cambridge,* pp. 101-2; cf. Moule, *Charles Simeon,* p. 45.

page 147   "As he grew older": Hennell, "Simeon and the Ministry," p. 152.

Chapter Eight: Amanda Berry Smith

page 148   At various times an evangelist: Adrienne M. Israel, *Amanda Berry*

Smith: From Washerwoman to Evangelist, Studies in Evangelicalism 16 (Lanham, Md.: Scarecrow Press, 1998), p. 2.

page 149   Born Amanda Berry in Long Green, Maryland: Ibid., p. 11.

page 149   "They were getting me ready for market": Amanda Berry Smith, *An Autobiography: The Story of the Lord's Dealings with Mrs. Amanda Smith the Colored Evangelist: Containing an Account of Her Life Work of Faith, and Her Travels in America, England, Ireland, Scotland, India, and Africa, as an Independent Missionary* (Chicago: Meyer and Brother, 1893), p. 22. From the first electronic edition provided by the University of North Carolina at Chapel Hill at <http://docsouth.unc.edu/neh/smitham/smith.html>.

page 149   her mother, Mariam, had been instrumental in the conversion: Ibid., pp. 19-22.

page 150   "would allow my father to do what he could": Ibid., p. 31.

page 150   "good white people all over the neighborhood": Ibid., p. 33.

page 150   "All the rich respectable people . . . backed her up": Ibid., p. 34.

page 150   "she came to me, a poor colored girl sitting away back by the door": Ibid., p. 28.

page 150   "arranged to keep a boarding house during the camp meeting": Ibid., pp. 32-33.

page 151   many pre-Civil War blacks received their salvation: See John B. Boles, *Religion in Antebellum Kentucky* (Lexington: University Press of Kentucky, 1976).

page 151   she attended a largely white Bible study: Smith, *Autobiography,* pp. 28-29.

page 151   Smith's experiences continued to teach her: Kelly Willis Mendiola, "The Hand of a Woman: Four Holiness-Pentecostal Evangelists and American Culture, 1840-1930" (Ph.D. diss., University of Texas at Austin, 2002), pp. 148-49.

page 152   She was married to two difficult husbands: Smith, *Autobiography,* pp. 57-58.

page 152   "I was on this platform with a large Bible opened": Ibid., pp. 42-43, 45.

page 152   "Hallelujah!" she cried out, "I have got religion": Ibid., p. 42; Mendiola, "Hand of a Woman," pp. 152-53.

page 153   Having (as she said) "high-toned" aspirations at that point in her life: Smith, *Autobiography,* p. 61.

page 153   Smith moved to a damp basement apartment advertised as furnished: Ibid., p. 67; cf. Israel, *Amanda Berry Smith,* pp. 37-40.

page 153   Sometimes she worked twenty-four hours at a stretch: Smith, *Autobiography,* p. 68.

page 153   began to seek entire sanctification: Ibid., pp. 84-85.

page 154   "[My] hunger [for sanctification] went on": Amanda Berry Smith, "The Experience of Mrs. Amanda Smith," in *Holiness Readings: A Selection of Papers on the Doctrine, Experience and Practice of Holiness* (Brooklyn: Lyceum, 1883), p. 84. Online at <http://books. google.com/books/pdf/Holiness_readings.pdf?id=t58HAAAAQA AJ&output=pdf&sig=ACfU3Uo2gMYAp_D5QnSa8fxZYRd CROyrQ>.

page 155   Smith felt Inskip was "preaching right to me": Smith, *Autobiography*, p. 75.

page 155   "The vacuum in my soul began to fill up": Mendiola, "Hand of a Woman," pp. 162-63; Smith, *Autobiography*, p. 76.

page 155   "just as I went to say 'Glory to Jesus!'": Smith, *Autobiography*, p. 78.

page 155   "Brother Inskip answered, 'Amen, Glory to God": Ibid., p. 79.

page 155   "I always had a fear of white people": Ibid., p. 80.

page 156   "they looked so small. The great mountain had become a mole-hill": Ibid., p. 80.

page 156   "I had become a speckled bird among my own people": Ibid., p. 108.

page 156   "we poor souls who dared to testify": Ibid., p. 109.

page 157   "there was not a member . . . that believed in the doctrine of holiness": Ibid., pp. 108-12.

page 157   Mr. Mackey, was "a good friend to the colored people": Ibid., pp. 112-13.

page 158   In October 1870 she began traveling as an evangelist: Ibid., p. 152.

page 158   "'There is a lady here, Mrs. Amanda Smith'": Ibid., p. 156.

page 158   "from the colored people to the white people": Ibid., pp. 156-58.

page 158   The meeting that summer was in Harford County: Israel, *Amanda Berry Smith*, p. 51.

page 158   They were very different from the wild, emotional camp meetings of the frontier period: Ibid., pp. 51-52.

page 158-59   "packed with emotion, Methodist enthusiasm, and spiritual expectancy": Melvin Easterday Dieter, *The Holiness Revival of the Nineteenth Century*, 2nd ed., Studies in Evangelicalism 1 (Lanham, Md.: Scarecrow Press, 1996), p. 90.

page 159   "as sudden as if a flash of lightning from the heavens": William McDonald and John Searles, *The Life of Rev. John S. Inskip: President of the National Association for the Promotion of Holiness* (Boston: McDonald & Gill, 1885), pp. 200-201.

page 159   "four clergymen and a tall black woman in Quaker dress": Mendiola, "Hand of a Woman," pp. 138-39.

page 159   She was indeed a commanding presence: Israel, *Amanda Berry*

Smith, p. 1.

page 160   "I lifted my head, and at a short distance": James M. Thoburn, introduction to Smith, *Autobiography,* pp. v-vi.

page 160   "The people followed me about": Smith, *Autobiography,* pp. 183-84.

page 161   found an orphanage and "industrial school" for abandoned children: John H. Bracey, "Smith, Amanda Berry," in *Notable American Women: 1607-1950. A Biographical Dictionary,* vol. 3, P-Z, ed. Edward T. James et al. (Cambridge, Mass.: Belknap Press, 1971), pp. 304-5.

page 161   "No," she wrote, "we who are the royal black are very well satisfied": Smith, *Autobiography,* p. 117 (emphasis mine).

page 161   "No, no, . . . as the Lord lives, I would rather be black": Ibid., p. 118 (emphasis mine).

page 162   "If you want to know and understand properly": Ibid., pp. 116-17.

page 162   "ministerial biography, travel narrative and success story": Mendiola, "Hand of a Woman," p. 276.

page 163   "It was a wonderful meeting that afternoon": Smith, *Autobiography,* pp. 184-85.

Chapter Nine: Charles M. Sheldon

page 165   "What I feel puzzled about is, what is meant by following Jesus": Charles Sheldon, *In His Steps* (New York: Jeremy P. Tarcher/Penguin, 2006), pp. 8-10. The edition cited here is by no means the only one, as there are numerous hardcover and paperback reprints.

page 166   The tramp's question echoes: *In His Steps,* pp. 12-19.

page 166-67   few have confused Sheldon's novel with great literature: Gary Scott Smith, "Charles M. Sheldon's *In His Steps* in the Context of Religion and Culture in Late Nineteenth Century America," *Fides et Historia* 22, no. 2 (1990): 47.

page 167   Sheldon was born February 26, 1857, in Wellsville, New York: Timothy Miller, *Following in His Steps: A Biography of Charles M. Sheldon* (Knoxville: University of Tennessee Press, 1987), p. 1.

page 167   Sheldon's father. . . served as that denomination's first home missions superintendent: Ibid., pp. 5, 7.

page 167   "the stupidity of those who regard physical toil": Ibid., p. 7.

page 167   "hunted with the Dakota [Indians]": Ibid., p. 5.

page 167   "Each morning, the family would sit together": Ibid., p. 7; Susan Wharton Gates, "Rediscovering the Heart of Public Administration: The Normative Theory of *In His Steps,*" (Ph.D. diss., Virginia Polytechnic Institute and State University, 1998), p. 57.

page 167-68   his conversion as a teenager was unemotional: Miller, *Following in*

His Steps, p. 8.

page 168   Sheldon went on to receive his education: Ibid., pp. 12-14.

page 168   "controversy between old-line Calvinists and new moderates": Ibid., p. 14.

page 168   "accepting modern biblical criticism": Ibid., p. 14.

page 168   "a theology which is not Christocentric is like a Ptolemaic astronomy": Ibid., p. 15.

page 168   "New England classic, with about 175 members and a white frame building": Ibid., p. 16.

page 168   Sheldon launched into his new ministry by "boarding around": Ibid., p. 17; Gates, "Rediscovering," p. 59.

page 169   to meet the practical as well as the spiritual needs in his community: Miller, *Following in His Steps,* pp. 16-18.

page 169   when more than two dozen townspeople died of typhoid: Ibid., p. 17.

page 169   He immediately moved west to accept the founding pastorate: Smith, "Charles M. Sheldon's *In His Steps,*" p. 48; Miller, *Following in His Steps,* p. 21.

page 170   "a Christ for the common people": Miller, *Following in His Steps,* p. 23.

page 172   In the 1890s all of this worsened as economic depression returned: Wayne Elzey, "'What Would Jesus Do?' *In His Steps* and the Moral Codes of the Middle Class," *Soundings* 58, no. 4 (1975): 472-73.

page 172   "the horrible blunder and stupidity," as he called it: Gates, "Rediscovering," p. 65.

page 172   he left the pulpit, put on his oldest clothes and set out: Miller, *Following in His Steps,* pp. 24-25.

page 173   his time in the black community at Tennesseetown: Ibid., pp. 46-65; Gates, "Rediscovering," p. 66.

page 173   Sheldon stayed several weeks here: Miller, *Following in His Steps,* pp. 46-65.

page 173-74   Sheldon was the first local white to point the finger: Ibid., p. 49; Gates, "Rediscovering," pp. 66-67.

page 174   Sheldon talked the owner of a local speakeasy: Gates, "Rediscovering," p. 67.

page 174   "Everybody loved him, everybody": Ibid., p. 68.

page 174   he became an early civil rights advocate: Miller, *Following in His Steps,* p. 157.

page 174   "One had better stay in an environment to which he is accustomed": Ibid., p. 203.

page 174   his daily regimen included: Ibid., p. 197-98.

page 175   "to inspire church members to love and good works": Gates, "Redis-
                covering," p. 70.

page 175   By the time he retired in 1919 he had written over thirty such stories,
                including *In His Steps:* Miller, *Following in His Steps,* p. 50.

page 175   "white middle-class characters come face to face": Gates, "Rediscov-
                ering," p. 71.

page 175   Sheldon particularly dedicated himself to the youth and children of
                Central Church: Miller, *Following in His Steps,* pp. 199-201.

page 175-76   "The Young People's Good Citizenship Federation of Topeka": Ibid.,
                p. 201.

page 176   "the Altruist Club . . . high school and college girls and women":
                Ibid., pp. 35, 201.

page 176   "more missionaries than any other church in America": Ibid., p.
                194.

page 176   Other innovative Central Church programs included: Ibid., p. 188.

page 176   his wife was eventually forced to give him an allowance: Ibid., p.
                204.

page 176   "Open Door" program: Ibid., p. 190.

page 176   he spent much effort fighting Sunday labor: James H. Smylie, "Shel-
                don's *In His Steps:* Conscience and Discipleship," *Theology Today*
                32 (April 1975): 37.

page 177   "The policeman . . . is in a position to be the greatest human 'mixer'":
                Charles M. Sheldon, "The New Police," *Colliers,* July 5, 1913, quoted
                in Gates, "Rediscovering," p. 74.

page 177   "veto every war budget": Charles M. Sheldon, "If I Were President,"
                The Christian Herald, May 1936, quoted in Gates, "Rediscovering,"
                p. 74.

page 177   Walter Rauschenbusch: Gates, "Rediscovering," pp. 87-88; See for
                example Rauschenbusch's *A Theology for the Social Gospel* or
                Christianizing the Social Order.

page 178   ecclesiastical categories of that wise Jesuit, Avery Dulles: Avery
                Dulles, *Models of the Church* (Garden City, N.Y.: Doubleday, 1974),
                chaps. 5-6.

page 178   Nazarene historian Timothy L. Smith has argued: Timothy L. Smith,
                "The Evangelical Origins of Social Christianity," in *Revivalism and
                Social Reform in Mid-Nineteenth-Century America* (Nashville:
                Abingdon, 1957), pp. 148-62.

page 179   that sympathetic minister was preaching a sermon: *In His Steps,* p.
                3.

page 179   only through a change in individual sinners' hearts: Smith, "The
                Evangelical Origins," pp. 65-66.

page 179-80   Sheldon simply refused to become drawn into theological controversy: Miller, *Following in His Steps,* p. 183.

page 180   "It is not death but life I greet . . . when he who loves me calls me
home": Ibid., p. 219.

Chapter Ten: Dorothy L. Sayers

page 181   C. S. Lewis once divided all of Western history: C. S. Lewis, *De De-
scriptione Temporum* (Cambridge: Cambridge University Press,
1955).

page 182   "a beautiful little medieval city": Alzina Stone Dale, *Maker and
Craftsman: The Story of Dorothy L. Sayers* (Grand Rapids: Eerdmans, 1985), p. 2.

page 182   "It might be an old-fashioned city": Quoted in ibid., p. 3.

page 183   "about Boadicea, the Briton Queen who defied the Roman legions":
Ibid., p. 5.

page 183   Even the rectory itself seemed a thing of the legendary past: Ibid.

page 183   The Fens did not offer many companions of her age: Ibid., p. 11.

page 183   She was certainly precociously bright: Ibid., pp. 11, 13.

page 183   "a cheerful little tomboy, ruler of her own small world": Ibid., p. 7.

page 183   When she wasn't learning Latin from her father: "Her relationship
with her father had been loving and secure. He was a figure of authority, as a priest as well as a father, but an authority of 'mild state-
liness,' the phrase she said best described him." Barbara Reynolds,
Dorothy L. Sayers: Her Life and Soul (New York: St. Martin's Grif-
fin, 1993), p. 206.

page 183   This early passion for swashbuckling tales: Ibid., p. 41.

page 184   Sayers's romantic streak seems to have emerged: For Lewis's own
account of similar experiences, see C. S. Lewis, *Surprised by Joy:
The Shape of My Early Life* (Orlando: Harcourt, Inc., 1966).

page 184   "it was as though the whole scent of summer": The unfinished novel
is called *Cat o' Mary.*

page 184   Dorothy L. Sayers never stopped being that young lady intoxicated:
Reynolds, *Dorothy L. Sayers,* p. 43.

page 184   "Except ye become as little children": Nancy M. Tischler, *Dorothy
Sayers: A Pilgrim Soul* (Atlanta: John Knox Press, 1980), p. 139.

page 184   The two frameworks that shaped and directed this passionate romanticism: Dale, *Maker and Craftsman,* p. 17.

page 184   "going on silent retreats, making auricular confession": Ralph C. Wood,
"Dorothy Sayers's Workshop," *Books & Culture* 3, no. 4 (1997): 31.

page 184   "keep a stiff upper lip, never cry in public": Dale, *Maker and Craftsman,* p. 17.

page 185   By fifteen, Sayers had her sights set on Oxford University: Ibid., pp. 22-23.

page 185   "tall and plain and lanky, with a long neck": Ibid., p. 24.

page 185   she also started in a lower grade: Ibid., p. 25.

page 185   "indelicate, and only to be mentioned in periphrastic whispers": Sayers, *Cat 'o Mary,* quoted in Reynolds, *Dorothy L. Sayers,* p. 38.

page 185   "At the name of Jesus, every voice goes plummy": Reynolds cites an article in the *Guardian* titled "Divine Comedy," in which, according to Reynolds, "[Sayers] had wittily put the case for the realistic, natural production and acting of religious plays." Ibid., p. 301.

page 186   "It was stimulating to be told": Dale, *Maker and Craftsman,* p. 38.

page 186   There were also bright spots in her time at Godolphin: Ibid., p. 30.

page 186   haunting Oxford's ancient Bodleian Library: Ibid., p. 38.

page 186   "any language that appeared after Latin and Greek": Ibid., p. 32.

page 186   she did so with distinction on the "battlefield": Adds Dale, "She went on the rest of her life operating in men's fields of work and proving herself their equal." Ibid., p. 43.

page 186   She also found at Oxford, at last, kindred spirits: Ibid., pp. 36-37.

page 186   With some of these friends Sayers formed a sort of Inklings group: Ibid., pp. 41-43.

page 187   The fairyland towers of Oxford could not protect those within: Ibid., p. 47.

page 187   Out from the medieval city and into the modern world: Ibid., p. 53.

page 187   "dismayed by a rector's daughter who spent hours reading novels": Ibid., p. 46.

page 187   During her off hours the social scene in Oxford was bleak: Ibid., pp. 54-55.

page 188   "The life expectancy of a young officer in the army was two weeks": Ibid., pp. 55-56.

page 188   "Christ is mocked daily by ecclesiastical wrangling": Reynolds, *Dorothy L. Sayers,* p. 81.

page 188   "When she heard the good news": Dale, *Maker and Craftsman,* pp. 60-61.

page 189   "Even before World War I": Ibid., p. 63.

page 189   "the whole agency became frantic": Ibid., p. 65.

page 189   A number of her Oxford friends were near enough to her: Ibid., pp. 67-69.

page 189   "a slim, rabbity fellow with a monocle": Ibid., p. 56.

page 189   The moral world of her Wimsey books was recognizably Christian: Ibid., p. 70.

page 190   "his bubbling cheerfulness": Reynolds, *Dorothy L. Sayers,* p. 175.

page 190   Before her husband came a pair of ill-fated relationships: Dale, *Maker and Craftsman*, p. 156.

page 191   "an adherent of the philosophy of free love": Reynolds, *Dorothy L. Sayers*, p. 109.

page 191   "rather a defeatist sort of person": Ibid., p. 114.

page 191   "they were sufficiently attracted to each other": Ibid., p. 119.

page 192   "Society in general still had heavy penalties": Dale, *Maker and Craftsman*, p. 73.

page 192   As an Anglo-Catholic she initially: Reynolds, *Dorothy L. Sayers*, pp. 141-42.

page 192-93   "for the most part she probably kept the habit": Dale, *Maker and Craftsman*, p. 103.

page 193   He was an accomplished storyteller: Reynolds, *Dorothy L. Sayers*, p. 154.

page 193   In the early years of her marriage: Dale, *Maker and Craftsman*, p. 123.

page 194   "He bitterly resented being pointed out": Reynolds, *Dorothy L. Sayers*, p. 243.

page 194   "her real vocation and full emotional fulfillment": Ibid., p. 249.

page 195   "a recognizable, living example of the modern, creative independent woman": Barbara Reynolds, "The Importance of Being Dorothy L. Sayers," online at <http://www.taylor.edu/academics/supportservices/cslewis/colloquium/2004/reynolds.shtml>.

page 195   Reynolds still hears many women respond to *Gaudy Night:* Telephone interview in 2005 with Barbara Reynolds by author for article, "Dorothy Sayers: The Dogma Is the Drama," *Christian History & Biography* 88 (Fall 2005): 45-48.

page 195   Sayers accepted, and she wrote for the 1937 festival: Dale, *Maker and Craftsman*, pp. 106-8.

page 196   "Official Christianity . . . has been having": Sayers, cited in ibid., p. 108.

page 196   "What Do We Believe?": These and others have recently been collected in Dorothy L. Sayers, *Letters to a Diminished Church: Passionate Arguments for the Relevance of Christian Doctrine* (Nashville: Word Publishing Group, 2004). Sadly, the meticulous Sayers has been betrayed, as the anthology is marred by atrocious failures in copyediting.

page 196   "in a nightmare of muddle": Reynolds, *Dorothy L. Sayers*, p. 333.

page 196   By mid-August of 1939: Dale, *Maker and Craftsman*, p. 114.

page 197   No longer capable of making or understanding a coherent argument: Some of these arguments were repeated in Sayers's essay "The Lost

Tools of Learning," which has been used today as the foundation for a movement of "classical schools" in America.

page 198   "I feel very strongly that the prohibition against representing": Reynolds, *Dorothy L. Sayers,* p. 300.

page 198   "Nobody cares nowadays": Ibid., p. 326.

page 199   "behave like common soldiers hanging a common criminal": Ibid.

page 199   "whether the Ministry was going to revise the plays": Dale, *Maker and Craftsman,* p. 127.

page 199   "Rapturous letters poured in from listeners of all ages": Reynolds, *Dorothy L. Sayers,* p. 327.

page 199   "writes with his eye on the spiritual box-office": Mary Brian Durkin, "Dorothy L. Sayers: A Christian Humanist for Today," *Christian Century,* November 14, 1979, pp. 1114-19.

page 200   "I bolted my meals, neglected my sleep": Dale, *Maker and Craftsman,* p. 131.

page 200   "What Dante had to say about people": Ibid., pp. 132-33.

page 201   On December 17, 1957, Dorothy L. Sayers: Ibid., pp. 152-53.

page 201   two biographical books: Reynolds, *Dorothy L. Sayers;* and Reynolds, *The Passionate Intellect: Dorothy L. Sayers' Encounter with Dante* (Kent, Ohio: Kent State University Press, 1989).

page 201   Bishops, dignitaries and many friends attended: Dale, *Maker and Craftsman,* pp. 153-54.

Conclusion

page 202   "Many readers . . . find it so distasteful": Geoffrey F. Nuttall, *The Faith of Dante* (London: SPCK, 1969), pp. 20-21.

page 203   "Hell is the state in which the will remains fixed eternally": Dorothy Sayers, "The Divine Poet and the Angelic Doctor," *Further Papers on Dante* (London: Methuen, 1957), p. 47.

page 203   "pulsates with a passionate energy": Sayers, "The Divine Poet," p. 49.

page 203   Dante is the ninth most written-about person: At the turn of the twenty-first century the Library of Congress listed 2,878 books on Dante, the ninth-largest number on any one person. See Raymond A. Schroth, S.J., *Dante to Dead Man Walking: One Reader's Journey Through the Christian Classics* (Chicago: Loyola Press, 2001), p. 33.

page 205   their "gestures, facial expressions, and other 'outward looks'": Dominic M. McIver Lopes, "Mimesis and Moral Vision: The Moral Content of Pictures," *Soundings* 83, no. 1 (2000): 197; "outward looks" is quoted from *Purgatorio* 28.44-45, trans. Mark Musa (Harmondsworth, U.K.: Penguin, 1985).

page 205   "Compared with the martyrological literature": R. A. Markus, *Gregory the Great and His World* (New York: Cambridge University Press, 1997), pp. 62, 66.

page 206   Sayers came to call his *Comedy* "the drama of the soul's choice": Robert Hollander, "Dante: A Party of One," *First Things* 92 (April 1999): 48.

page 206   "that good and evil exist": Barbara Reynolds, "Dante, Poet of Joy," *Theology* 97, no. 778 (1994): 266.

page 206   "*The Divine Comedy* is precisely the drama of the soul's choice": Dorothy L. Sayers, introduction to *The Comedy of Dante Alighieri the Florentine—Cantica I: Hell (L'inferno),* trans. Dorothy L. Sayers (Harmondsworth, U.K.: Penguin Books, 1980), p. 11.